THE GILDED STAGE

THE GILDED STAGE
The Years of the Great International Actresses

By Henry Knepler

WILLIAM MORROW & COMPANY, INC.
NEW YORK 1968

To the Memory of / MY PARENTS

AUTHOR'S NOTE

THIS book has been longer in the making than I care to remember and many people have talked with me about it and helped me to develop it.

Napier Wilt, above all, contributed his wide knowledge of the theater and the drama both in discussion and in a critical reading of the manuscript itself. Marvin Felheim and William W. McCollum were of great help as readers of work in progress, and Mollie Cohen, Elizabeth Hayes, James Schroeter and Howard Vincent gave me advice and information.

My debt to libraries and museums, and to librarians and curators is extensive. To the Harvard Theatre Collection, the University of Chicago Libraries, the British Museum, the Victoria and Albert Museum, the New York Public Library, especially its theater collection, the Ringling Museum of Art, the Library of Illinois Institute of Technology, the Chicago Historical Society, and the Art Institute of Chicago I am particularly indebted. Stanley E. Gwynn, Paul Myers, Fred Oxtoby, Mrs. Paul M. Rhymer and Miss Helen D. Willard gave me time and expert advice and facilitated the use of the collections for which they are responsible.

Mrs. Charlotte Polk suffered my handwriting with patience and good humor and produced a typescript from it.

It seems customary to mention one's wife last in these acknowledgments. Mine was my most outspoken and most detailed critic, and therefore the most helpful.

H.K.
Chicago
February, 1968

CONTENTS

ILLUSTRATIONS

PROLOGUE / Terrific and Fatal Rito

On THURSDAY, May 10, 1849, at eleven in the morning, Caleb S. Woodhull, who had been sworn in as Mayor of New York the day before, held a conference in his office. Present were the Chief of Police, the Sheriff, the Recorder, and Major General Sandford, commanding the military forces of the County. Also present were Messrs. Niblo and Hackett, the proprietors of the Astor Place Opera House on Eighth Street near Broadway. The meeting was the result of widespread apprehension that the performance that evening of *Macbeth*, with William Charles Macready in the title role, would lead to serious rioting. The proprietors refused to cancel the performance, and so the Mayor instructed the others to take the necessary precautions against disorder. However, the events which followed exceeded his expectations.

At six o'clock the Chief of Police placed thirteen platoons of police officers in the Opera House. Meanwhile General Sandford prepared his troops further downtown: eight companies of infantry, two troops and two companies of cavalry, and two cannons. Most of these were hastily mustered units of the National Guard.

Messrs. Niblo and Hackett had taken their own precautions to ensure that a full house would witness the events of the evening: the rush of buyers had been great that day, and they had sold more tickets than there were seats. Any twinges of concern they might have felt about that turned out to be unnecessary. By 7:15 Astor Place between Broadway and the Bowery was packed solid with people, and the crush was such that the police

I

had to bar the doors before the house was filled. When Macready came on stage he was greeted with hisses and groans. The pro-Macready portion of the audience, not to be left out, began to cheer him, spurring the opposition on to yet greater efforts. Together they drowned out the performance, and toward the end of Act I the Chief of Police and his men proceeded to arrest some of the rioters. The windows of the Opera House had been boarded up in the afternoon, but a member of the audience managed to wedge his head through to let the crowds in Astor Place know about the fate of their patriotic friends in the theater. Thereupon the attack began; the crowd outside laid siege to the Opera House. Paving stones were dug up and sent crashing through boards and windows into the auditorium. Crews organized to batter down the doors. Under attack inside and out, the police were driven back and suffered a large number of casualties. Mayor Woodhull's personal precautions had been more successful than those of the police; he could not be found at the crucial time to make a decision. After considerable hesitation, General Sandford was therefore informed of events and asked to quell the riot with his troops. His poorly trained cavalry was quickly routed by the yelling crowds, because the horses fled from the sticks and stones, but at first it seemed that his infantry would succeed in clearing the streets. It did not. There were casualties, the rifles were snatched from the soldiers, their lines were broken. Finally the order to shoot came. By midnight it was all over: thirty-one dead, more than a hundred injured. The "terrific and fatal riot," as a contemporary pamphlet called it, has been the worst theater riot in American history.

Earlier in the day handbills had been widely distributed in New York which asked "Workingmen—Shall Americans or English Rule this City?" and invited all to "express their opinion this night at the English Aristocratic Opera House." The handbills were the work of the "American Committee" headed by E. Z. C. Judson, better known as the man who, twenty years later, made W. F. Cody into Buffalo Bill. This bit of know-nothing xenophobia was one of the final items in a long war between the actors William Macready and Edwin Forrest. Macready was probably the most famous English actor of his day. Forrest was the first great native American actor; in his actions, in his very existence he was a declaration of independence from the English who had dominated the theatrical life of America since colonial days. He did much to foster native drama, and was the first American actor to achieve a considerable success in England. His acquaintance with Macready went back to 1826, when Forrest performed at the Bowery Theatre in New York, and Macready at the Park Theatre. The Bowery was one of the theaters of the "masses," the common people, and the Park one of the "classes," or the upper-class clientele. Essentially both actors remained true to their respective social levels.

In spite of these differences they got along well for some time. Their mutual hostility was a gradual development, aided, cherished, and even created by the press, and by friends and managers. Critics and audiences were not satisfied to compare the two; they had to be set against each other; they were forced to compete. Combat was what the public wanted: the theater was as much a spectator sport as an artistic undertaking. Whether willing or not, actors and actresses were forced into the roles of gladiators. Macready and Forrest were urged on until they themselves became emotionally embroiled.

The first public display had been a hiss. During a performance of *Hamlet* at the Theatre Royal in Edinburgh in 1846, Forrest, seated in a box, hissed a bit of Macready's stage business. Forrest later said that he thought that bit of action, which involved the waving of a handkerchief, in very bad taste, and simply expressed his disapproval as one expert to another. Macready never forgave it, and remembered it when he embarked on another American tour in 1848, at a time when Forrest was also touring the country. Much of the fall and winter season in New York, Philadelphia and other eastern and midwestern cities was played to the accompaniment of open letters and recriminations which delighted the press and presumably also the theater managers and the public. At each stop, the exchanges became more acrimonious.

On May 7, 1849, the people of New York had the choice of three different performances of *Macbeth:* Forrest was performing at the Broadway Theatre, Macready was scheduled to open his farewell season that day at the Astor Place Opera House, and Hamblin, a less famous actor trying to profit from the competition, was given the same play at the Bowery Theatre. All performances were well attended, the Astor Place was oversold as usual, and Macready was booed, hissed and pelted with overripe fruit sufficiently to turn the play into a dumb show. Macready was a brave man, but by the time the third act had been reached and the box-holders had started to throw their chairs at the audience in the pit, he canceled the performance.

Macready decided to leave for England at once. He had had enough. On the next day, however, he received a letter signed by forty-seven prominent citizens who asked him to continue to act, and promised him their support. Washington Irving and Herman Melville were among the signers. The result was a further public series of charges and counter charges between Forrest's and Macready's representatives; and finally the performance of May 10, which resulted in the riot.

Theater riots were sufficiently frequent in the eighteenth and nineteenth centuries for Charles Kemble to have written in his journal in 1791: "Whenever there is danger of a riot always act an Opera, for Musick drowns the Noise of Opposition." The theater was a passionate concern of a large number of people, a concern which transcended the simple desire to be entertained. The stage had, or was felt to have, a pervasive intellectual and moral impact. It was further, in keeping with the social norms of the time, an arena for combat. Without exaggeration it was what Étienne called it—"the expression of society." As that it was made to serve the causes of social reform and the purposes of the vast new middle class which had resulted from the industrial revolution. The theater therefore reflected the gilded age which it served: its hypocrisies and its moral doubts; its revolutionary fervor and its complacency; its competitiveness, in transition from caste society to mass man; its new nationalism and its even newer internationalism.

The image of the age emerges with a special clarity when its reflection is cast by four particular actresses. They were the first truly international stage actresses—and the last, for the genre disappeared with them. The film presents a different kind of impact. Only Rachel Félix, Adelaide Ristori, Sarah Bernhardt and Eleonora Duse are true international actresses. They are the only ones who managed to transcend the limitations of language and national culture; who for an extended period of time, a decade at least, traveled to perform in the entire world, civilized and not so civilized; and who performed to international acclaim in languages which most of their audiences did not understand.

The age of the international actresses lasted from the middle of the 1840's when Rachel began to go to London from Paris, to the death of Bernhardt and Duse in 1923 and 1924. In these eighty years those four women exercised an unrivaled dominion and provided the standard against which other actresses were measured. Rachel (1821–1858) and Ristori (1822–1905) formed the first generation, Bernhardt (1844–1923) and Duse (1858–1924) the second. Two, Rachel and Bernhardt, were French of Jewish origin; the other two were Italians, both of them children of traveling actor families in Venetia. These correspondences are not simply accidental, but part cause of their rise to the top. America was their promised land, and two of them ended their careers here, though by accident rather than design. They are interesting beyond the usual sequence of biographical progression and anecdotage—another first night, another triumph, and so on, for decade after decade. Their lives are expressions, often heightened and clarified, of their time and hold up a mirror to it which can explain much about an age to which the mid-twentieth century is at times an unwilling heir. All four were at the top of their profession in their respective generations and countries; they acted against each other and were constantly compared. Each generation had one climactic encounter on the bloodiest of artistic battlefields, Paris. Ristori challenged Rachel there in 1855, and Duse performed against Bernhardt in 1897.

Matching the astuteness of Daniel Drew and the predatoriness of Commodore Vanderbilt, they battled like railroad magnates for the control of the stage. The survival of the fittest, in the manner in which the gilded age chose to interpret Darwin, was the rule of their lives and, too, the subject of many of their plays.

Their success was not the result of any one particular style of acting, some sort of melodramatic grand manner. On the contrary, they were strong individuals and their capabilities and ways differed fundamentally. They all used their obviously superior artistry, and their cool intelligence, to retain, reject and modify the traditions from which they came. They were aided by the fact that French was the language of culture generally and Italian the language of opera, both of them more euphonious to foreign ears than German or English, both in vogue as cultural assets with the middle class, even if one only pretended to know them.

The age of the international actresses was also the age of Queen Victoria when the concern about morality, which meant sexual morality only, was as pervasive as the swarms of prostitutes in the streets of London, Paris or Vienna. In spite of all the international acclaim, these actresses still managed to scandalize the middle-class society that made up their audience, through their lives or their plays or both. Much of their repertoire concentrated on one of the prime fascinations of the nineteenth-century middle class: "the fallen woman." All four women came from cultural backgrounds with which Londoners, Muscovites and Bostonians could associate a large degree of pleasant iniquity far from home.

Their extraordinary fame was made possible by an audience ready and eager to exalt them. Their international status was a result of the development of a new mass audience, an audience that wanted to aggrandize the already great. They were generally more famous and acclaimed in foreign countries than in their own. They came like fairy princesses from afar, in their private Pullman cars, after long and perilous voyages on board ship, to bestow—in person—on Lima, Peru, or Melbourne, Australia, or Milwaukee, Wisconsin, membership in the inner circle of great world culture.

In the end the airplane began to destroy distance and the celluloid strip made the presence of their successors a daily synthetic occurrence. The coming of the film marks the end of their era, though the social changes in the decade before World War I had already made Bernhardt and Duse into living anachronisms, for their peers were not actors and directors, but kings and queens, and they disappeared from the scene with them.

CHAPTER 1 / The Peddler's Daughter

THE sense of change that the American and French Revolutions spread through Europe had not died after the defeat of Napoleon in 1815, in spite of all the repressive efforts of the Holy Alliance. The Industrial Revolution, spreading gradually east from England across the continent and west to North America, ended any hope of holding to the *status quo*.

People were on the move everywhere, as if the movement of Napoleon's armies between Madrid and Moscow had set the pattern for the civilian population. People moved no longer merely to escape outright persecution, or to search for adventure, but simply to better themselves according to the economic principles which were spreading with the Industrial Revolution. Hunger or discrimination were no longer something God-sent to be endured, but something to be escaped.

The movement across the Atlantic was not the only one. Within Europe people were on the move from farms and villages to the new industrial centers, nothing more at first than huge, ugly villages surrounding the new manor house of the nineteenth century: the factory.

Industry attracted the peasant lad to new settlements nearby, but the really ambitious would finally be drawn to the great centers of commerce and industry, of a burgeoning bureaucracy, and of rapidly spreading culture and pseudo-culture. London, Paris, and the other major capitals became the prime magnets of the movement, causing them to spread far into the countryside.

For the Jews of Western Europe the changes brought about

by the French Revolution had been more tangible than for the rest of the population. In 1790 the Rights of Man had been extended to them, and the ghettos abolished in France. The restrictions under which they had suffered since the Middle Ages disappeared wherever the French army went in its conquests across Europe, and, except for Russia, the walls of the ghetto did not rise again after Napoleon had been swept away. In France the brothers of the guillotined Louis XVI returned to the throne after the defeat of the Emperor, and tried to restore the ways of the eighteenth century. They failed, and the last Bourbon king, Charles XI, was deposed by the July revolution in 1830. His successor, Louis Philippe, Duke of Orleans, was expected to usher in a new era and a bright future.

Some months after the revolution, a Jewish peddler named Jacob Félix brought his wife and growing family to Paris from Lyon, where they had been living for a few years, and settled them temporarily in a cheap hotel opposite the morgue. He had achieved the aim of the many who felt drawn to the metropolis for the prospect of advancement which it held out to them.

Jacob Félix came from Metz in Lorraine, and must have been born shortly after the emancipation of the Jews. His early history is not well recorded; he was largely itinerant until 1830. He and his wife Esther moved slowly across Germany, Switzerland and France in the second and third decades of the nineteenth century. They moved on foot, trundling a cart on which they carried their belongings and the goods they had for sale. They sold old clothes which Esther had repaired, and whatever else the traffic would bear. German rather than French was their native language, and Jacob Félix gave lessons in that language when the family settled first in Lyon and later in Paris. Whatever early education his children received, they received from him and in that language.

The second of these children became the greatest actress of her time and perhaps of all time. The truth is remarkable enough; it need not be embellished by asserting that Jacob Félix was merely an ignorant peddler. A contemporary reports that as a young man he studied to become a rabbi, a pursuit presumably broken off for economic reasons. But even without that background, which gave him a degree of superiority within his own environment, it is not hard to show that the Jews of the Rhineland and the adjacent territories were neither backward nor unintelligent. Few people adapted themselves with more celerity and enterprise to their emancipation.

Jacob and Esther Félix had their first child near Frankfurt-am-Main. The second child was born on February 28, 1821, in the quaintly named town of Mumpf in the German-speaking part of Switzerland. Esther Félix was alone at that time; her husband had followed his obscure business somewhere else. The place of birth was Room 13 of the Golden Sun Inn, and the child was named Elisa or Elizabeth. The name of the innkeeper and midwife are known, but there is no official record of the birth. At any rate, a few days later the family was on its way again, cart, dog, children and all, trading for their meager livelihood. The future Rachel—she took that name at the start of her acting career—was in a bundle placed on the cart.

From that stage she graduated very early into the hands of her sister Sarah, or Sophie, two years older than Rachel, with whom a fierce though misplaced loyalty united her for the rest of her life. With Sarah she started her first artistic undertaking, singing in the streets of the towns in which their parents sold their wares, in order to earn pocket money. Of the children who survived infancy, the third, a son named Raphael, was born in Mâcon; a fourth child was born in Lyon in 1829 and named Rachel, which was later changed to Rebecca when her older sister assumed her stage name. And two more sisters were born in Paris.

In Lyon the girls sang in cafés rather than in the street, and they continued that practice in Paris. Naturally there are many anecdotes about Rachel's early childhood, and though most of them seem fictitious, it is hard to say so with certainty. Rachel and her family were conscious of the value of publicity, and the humbleness of her background added to the romance of her great career. Rachel is likely to have invented some of her past herself. One of the anecdotes tells of a dignified gentleman who stopped in astonishment to hear Rachel's performance in the Place Royale in Paris and gave the little girl a large gold coin for her remarkable talents. Victor Hugo, of whom that story is told, may have enjoyed it, but its likelihood is impaired by the fact that he was a revolutionary still in his twenties at the time, not a dignified gentleman with gold coins.

Jacob Félix was a proper *pater familias* who brooked no contradiction, even when his children became rich and famous. He was also a realist who saw to it that the family stayed close together and that all members contributed to its support. This, too, was never to change. The whole Félix clan dealt with adversity in the same matter-of-fact way in which they dealt with their dazzling good fortune later on. Their heads were not easily turned; but they also never managed to rid themselves of the feeling that poverty remained just around the corner. Jacob Félix was a hard taskmaster and a rapacious man, but he also had the great vision of his era. Paris was his ultimate aim, like that of so many men of his time, and part of the reason seems to have been concerned with the training of his children. He hoped for talents in Sarah and Rachel that would lift them out of their present station in life.

In 1832 Rachel, together with Sarah, was apprenticed to Étienne Choron, the Director of the Institut Royal de la Musique Religieuse, who endured the willful and wayward girl for several months before deciding that her voice was not promising enough. He recommended Rachel to his friend Pagnon Saint-Aulaire, a former actor at the Comédie Française. In his school Rachel found what she wanted. She threw herself into mastering the classic French drama, Saint-Aulaire's main subject of teaching, with the fierce energy and single-minded attention which never left her again. Somehow she managed to transcend her background and the general artistic mediocrity surrounding her, and began to suggest that intensity and high seriousness which was to awe audiences later on.

She could be found almost daily working at M. Saint-Aulaire's establishment in the Rue de Lancry, dressed in a short calico frock with the usual long pantaloons underneath, coarse shoes, her black hair parted in the middle and two braids hanging down on her shoulders. She looked small, wiry, neat, clean, precise, dignified, modest and slightly starved.

In April of 1835 Saint-Aulaire took over the Salle Molière to enable his pupils to perform on a stage. The system of choosing actors for the parts was simple. The plays were selected and lists of characters hung up. Any pupil could choose any part, it seems, but the larger the part the more he had to pay, anywhere from one to ten francs. Rachel would not have had many parts under such a system if Saint-Aulaire had not thought well of her and given her good roles. She was perfectly indiscriminate and undertook everything she could get. The writer Villemot tells the story that a friend of his, a lover of amateur theatricals, once took him to the Salle Molière where he saw, upon entering, a "meagre, black, scraggy, poverty-stricken little girl" to whom his friend offered two sous and the choice of getting either a small cake or a bag of fried potatoes. The girl chose the fried potatoes—she would!—with Villemot adding another two sous to the project. When the girl brought the potatoes and offered some to her benefactors, it "was the only time," wrote Villemot, "I ever partook of a meal with Mademoiselle Rachel."

Somehow she was admitted to the Conservatoire of the Comédie Française in 1836. She was to study under Samson, Provost and Michelot, and to receive a small stipend that was evidently not paid. Samson did not occupy himself much with her development at that time; Michelot said that her voice was good and she had a talent for tragedy, but that her figure was unsuited to it. Provost said that her figure might enable her to be in comedy, but that her voice was not good enough.

She left within a short time and applied for help once more to Saint-Aulaire, who obtained for her an audition at one of the smaller popular theaters, the Gymnase, where she was launched in a reasonably good role, at an annual salary of 3,000 francs. Her debut was on July 24, 1837, in a standard melodrama, *La*

Vendéenne by Paul Duport, fashioned after Sir Walter Scott's novel *The Heart of Midlothian*. To make her new start Elisa Félix adopted a stage name which she seems to have chosen from a currently successful opera, Halévy's *La Juive*. Thereafter she was to be, simply, Rachel.

La Vendéenne established with certainty that melodrama was not her field, but it brought her a few good notices in the press. The most important of these, because it came from the most important critic, was Jules Janin's review in the *Journal des Débats* of May 1, 1837. He found that Rachel was not a child prodigy, thank God, in spite of her fifteen years, but an actress who could intuitively understand the role she was to play. He saw no overdrawn gestures, no exaggeration, no cries, no straining, no coquetry.

After a few months at the Gymnase she applied to the Comédie Française for a place in the company. When she received no reply, she went to Samson, and his real interest in her dated from that time. He obtained a contract for her, at 4,000 francs this time. Poirson, the manager of the Gymnase, kindly released her from her contract; and as the spring of 1838 wore on, Rachel waited for her first role, and waited.

Finally, on June 10, with the theatrical season about over, she went to see the director, Védel, to remind him of her existence. He at once offered her a debut as Camille in Corneille's *Horace* for June 12.

That Rachel should start out in a major role instead of serving her apprenticeship in minor ones was common practice at the Théâtre Français and elsewhere in Paris. It was a rather cruel but effective means of determining talent—or, perhaps, not so much talent as gladiatorial fortitude. New actors or actresses would have a short series of debuts in main roles and attempt to establish themselves in the favor of the public and the critics. If they did not succeed—and usually they did not—then they would start at the bottom or simply disappear. It was therefore a test not only of acting ability, but of strength of mind and purpose. Anyone who was not bold enough to face a nineteenth-century audience, notably a Parisian audience, at the start of his career had small hope of success in the theater.

It took courage. A nineteenth-century audience did not applaud politely and as a matter of course, whether it was really satisfied or not. The favorites might have to dodge bouquets of flowers and metal crowns thrown to them, or at them, even during the performance. On the other hand, that audience could hiss and boo, or envelop actors with a really glacial chill. Or it would simply ignore the play. The auditorium was not darkened during the performance as it was to be toward the end of the century when gaslight began to be replaced by electricity. The customers could therefore read the newspaper, talk, laugh, or visit friends in other parts of the house, completely disregarding the actors going through their roles.

Rachel's great opportunity on June 12 was a hazardous proposition on other grounds as well. It is not promising to begin one's debuts at the outset of the dead season; and to begin with a standard work of Corneille was practically the kiss of death. Corneille and Racine, in 1838, were as dead as the season. Their classical tragedies were *passé*, finished, a lost cause, performed at the state-supported theaters as traditional historical necessities before very empty houses.

The 1830's in France had witnessed the triumph of the romantic drama over the classical. On February 15, 1830, amidst pandemonium in the Comédie Française, Victor Hugo's drama *Hernani* provided the first full-fledged, direct challenge to tradition, a challenge which had been building up slowly for several decades. The two-hundred-year reign of the classical tragedy was pronounced finished: Hugo, Vigny, Gautier and all the other young romantic poets, outlandishly dressed in colorful garments, bearded intellectual revolutionaries in a clean-shaven age, crowded into the Comédie to give tragedy, so they thought, its *coup de grâce*.

The classic French tragedy that *Hernani* seemed to obliterate had been played out as a living tradition for nearly a century. Its impact is hard to grasp for an English-speaking audience, whose basic tradition is Shakespearean. W. T. Arnold said: "The wit of man never devised a more extraordinary *tour de force* than the French classical tragedy." It has been played in the English-speaking countries by Rachel, Sarah Bernhardt and a few others, mostly to the stupefaction of audiences who came to see it. Essentially it is the classical Greek drama made a little more subtle and much more polite. It follows Aristotle or, better to say, the Renaissance followers of Aristotle, and adheres to the Three Unities of time, place and action. The plot unrolls itself in one day, and in one place, which means that only the climactic, final moments of the particular story are presented, and the rest must be told to the audience at second hand. To readers or viewers accustomed to Shakespeare, with his large variety of scenes, the French classical method will not seem overly inventive. Its principle is to associate with the main characters of the action, a Phaedra, for example, or a Hyppolitus or an Andromache, a character known as the confidant, the person to whom matters are told or confided for the sake of providing the possibility of dialogue. The plays contain only the most necessary main characters and their confidants; the reason for this economy is the third of these Three Unities, that of action: subplots are not tolerated, there are no deviations, all must bear directly on the main issue of the plot. Battles, deaths, or violence of any sort must never be shown on stage, only reported. All this is done in rhymed verse, in lines of twelve syllables, which must rhyme in very precisely alternating couplets, which must not run on beyond that two-line unit, which must break in the middle of each line, and which must on no account whatever call any conceivable spade by that very direct rustic designation, and must moreover do so, or rather avoid doing so, in a large number of carefully linked, sonorous circumlocutory phrases.

The whole system of the French classical tragedy seems therefore like a magnificent game, in which the player-dramatist attempts to outwit, in five acts, the most magnificently restrictive set of rules ever devised. The result is surprising once one enters into the spirit of it. The simplicity of plot and idea, the fact that the dramatist is independent of questions of locale and time, freed of various characters such as innkeepers or schoolmasters or rogues or harlots, gives him scope to develop his main characters in all their subtlety. The subtlety emerges not only in what is said, but even more in what is not said. The restraint of the system leads to extremely detailed portraits of character and hidden emotions in the hands of the masters—and to unutterable boredom in the hands of the lesser practitioners.

The political and cultural explosion of 1830 seemed to put an end to the tradition of the classical tragedy, replacing it with the blood, thunder and variety of action and characters that Schiller and the young Goethe had introduced to the European continent. Corneille and Racine became the backwater of the theatrical stream.

Therefore, as Dr. Véron reports, he was one of the five people who seated themselves on the main floor of the Comédie that June 12, for Corneille's *Horace*. Dr. Véron was lying, as usual. There were seventeen paying customers in the orchestra section, not five. It would be pleasant to report that those seventeen, and the few others in the gallery, felt that they were present at a historic occasion. They did not. After an unnoticed *Horace* came Rachel's second debut, in another play of Corneille's, *Cinna*; then Racine's *Andromaque*, later one of Rachel's most successful plays; then Voltaire's *Tancrède* and Racine's *Iphigénie*. All shared the same distinction: nobody noticed them, or her. So June ground on into July, into August—nothing. Védel reports that he fought a serious battle on Rachel's behalf. By August 16, Rachel had had ten debut performances, more than are usually accorded a newcomer; success had not struck, and the actress who usually had Rachel's roles wanted to make use of her right to recover them; it was better to act, even in front of an empty house, than not to act at all. All seemed lost. Védel resisted, however, vigorously, and for the moment saved the day for Rachel and classical tragedy. Receipts were rising slowly, from a low of 303 francs, 10 centimes on June 23, to 715 francs on August 16; not enough, however, to justify Rachel. There

had been hardly any reviews. Hippolyte Rolle had acknowledged her talent in passing in the *National*. Frédéric Soulié, in
the *Journal des Débats*, the most influential review, had dismissed
all the new young recruits of the summer with contempt. He
was, however, himself only a summer replacement, and the
ranking critic of Paris, Jules Janin, was returning at the end of
August from a summer in Italy. Three men claim the honor of
having persuaded him to see the young actress at the Comédie.
He recorded later that he first saw her in *Horace* on August 18.
If that is true, then he took his time for his revelation, because
his first article on Rachel in the *Débats* did not appear until
September 10. On September 11 the receipts at the Théâtre
Français were up to 1,300 francs.

"Be advised," he wrote to his public on September 10, "that
at the moment I am speaking to you there exists at the Théâtre
Français itself, I repeat, at the *Théâtre Français*, an unheralded
victory, one of those happy triumphs of which a nation like ours
is rightly proud." The triumph was that of a return to honest
feelings, brave language and chaste love, an escape from unmen-
tionable violences and endless barbarisms, by which he of course
meant the romantic drama. He expressed the joy that the nation
would now be able to return to the masterpieces which had been
left unrecognized for so long, meaning, of course, the classical
tragedies:

> Now at last we have the most stunning and marvellous young
> girl whom the present generation has seen on the stage. That
> child (learn her name!) is Mlle. Rachel. It is about a year since
> she had her debut at the Gymnase, and I, almost alone, I said
> then that there was a serious, natural, great talent, a limitless
> future; then nobody would believe me; I was told that I exag-
> gerated. All alone I could not uphold that little girl at that little
> theater. A few days after her debut, the child disappeared from
> the Gymnase, and I alone, perhaps, gave it some thought when
> suddenly she reappeared at the Théâtre Français in the inde-
> structible tragedies of Corneille, Racine and Voltaire. This time
> the child is listened to, encouraged, applauded, admired. . . .

A strange thing: a young, ignorant, artless girl, fallen among
the ancient tragedies. She resuscitates them, blowing vigorously
on these venerable embers. Yes, this is admirable! And please
note well that this girl is small and rather ugly; [she has] a
narrow chest, a vulgar air and a trivial way of speaking. . . . Let
her grow, this little girl who is bringing a revolution without
knowing it . . .

It is true that Janin had a slight vested interest in Rachel, as
he himself explained: he had seen her first. He also had an interest in reviving tragedy, in supporting the old versus the new.
The main supporter of the new romantic drama among the
critics, Théophile Gautier, did not review Rachel's performances once throughout the summer and early fall. His first com-
ment was the merest offhand reference to her on November 4.
Yet, though Janin had a number of reasons for supporting
Rachel, that alone would not have been enough to bring forth
these praises. He was a cautious man. But he had a specific talent,
one that gave him his pre-eminence as a critic: he had the ability
to recognize the as yet unformed wishes of his public.

That he recognized the rightness of the moment he showed
in his next *feuilleton* on September 24, when he said, "Luckily
the new tragic actress arrives in a good time, at a propitious and
favorable hour, when she is going to find the Parisian public
quite ready to receive her well, her and the revolution which she
brings . . . just at the moment when the people themselves are
about to give [the signal], not too soon, not too late. . . . If she
had come into the time of *Hernani* or *Marion Delorme* . . .
bringing us her gods and her altars, it would have been hard
[for the public] to follow her, and she would perhaps have been
left in the street, in spite of her genius."

That was the signal. For the enemies of the Romantics, Rachel
became the club with which to beat the revolution that had
brought King Louis Philippe his throne in 1830, and that he and
his government were now hard at work to disavow and counter-
act.

In 1829 and 1830, the new romantic drama had served as the

symbol of the overthrow of the old order. But once the revolution had taken place, the people who came to power were not the ones likely to encourage the realization of its aims. The theory was freedom. The reality was the passing of power from a defunct aristocracy to a functioning bourgeoisie. This bourgeoisie, once it had arrived at the status of being the governing body, was inclined to become as much like the old governing body as possible. It was, in most respects, as conservative as the regime it replaced, and the people in charge were soon as interested in suppressing the liberal opposition as their predecessors. The reaction was not long in coming: In 1832 the first, unsuccessful republican uprising of Louis Philippe's reign took place in Paris while, at the same time, the conservative supporters of the Bourbon monarchy rose in the Vendée. In April, 1834, came "the massacre of innocents" at 12 Rue Transnonain. In 1835–1836 the Peers of France officiated at the great trials of republicans, and the laws of September 9, 1835, made by the Thiers government, re-established censorship. The *juste milieu* of Louis Philippe, the happy medium acidly satirized by Daumier and Gavarni, was to create a somnolescent France where industry and commerce would enrich a contented industrial ruling class. Vigny, one of the romantic playwrights, called it a "society based on gold," and George Sand has scathing words to say about its greed. That greed extended to the King, who was capable of extracting a king's ransom from the French treasury when he found that he owned a piece of real estate needed for the building of a new canal.

The theater depended on the ruling classes, and they were not long for the romantic, and therefore liberal side. Arsène Houssaye, looking back upon that period late in the century, placed the cause for the decline of the new movement accurately: The romantic revolution preceded the bourgeois one, only to find itself engulfed by the bourgeoisie, and done to death by it. The romantics were not men of the *juste milieu*. They had profited by the five-year lapse of censorship to raise moral and political issues which antagonized the government and its supporters.

Their efforts were directed initially "pour épater le bourgeois" (to dazzle the bourgeois), but the bourgeois refused to be dazzled. The more he refused, the more they tried. In the end, instead of trying to dazzle him, they began to bait him: Hugo produced blameless courtesans and a Lucrezia Borgia ennobled by mother love. Dumas outdid him in orgies of blood and horror in *La Tour de Nèsle* and *Richard Darlington*. "Heroic Bandits! Sublime galley slaves! Courtesans purer than virgins!" Pontmartin described these plays which went overboard to turn established order and morality upside down. The greatest actors of the day, Frédéric Lemaître and Marie Dorval, lent them their talents.

By the second half of the decade a change was beginning to be apparent. The excesses of the new drama, its frightful middle ages of murder and treason, its poisonings, stabbings, ambushes, imprecations and assassinations were becoming tiresome to the public. In January, 1838, *Hernani* was revived at the Comédie Française. It now seemed mild compared to the more recent romantic plays. Gautier, in reviewing it, recalled the battle of 1830 in which he had been a prominent participant. A tone of regret and nostalgia pervades the review: "The revival of *Hernani* has not caused the least murmur; everyone listened to it with the most religious attention and applauded with admirable discernment; not a single beautiful verse, not a single heroic movement have gone uncomprehended; the public has given way to the poet and followed him complacently in his flights of phantasy." No better description of a ruling class could be given. Complacency reflects the assurance of power. The new drama had been smothered, but that left the stage even emptier than before, now that both the old and the new seemed dead.

Rachel therefore came at the right moment. The old drama, in contrast to the new, had an aura of respectability. And the way Rachel acted was so entirely new and impressive that it quickly became not merely respectable but exciting to go and see her.

In the fall of 1838 the reviews, all but those of a few partisans

"Her most magnificent creation was neither Hermione or Phèdre nor Thisbé. It was that *chef d'oeuvre*, worthy of Balzac and Gavarni, the Parisienne Rachel."

One of her first social supports was the eminent Jewish lawyer and philanthropist Adolphe Crémieux. At his house she learned table manners, culture, and at least some spelling, though her letters remained rather quaint in that respect through her life. Crémieux, however, soon ceased to be her main help. Within months she had been presented in the great salons of the aristocracy. She was received by the Duchesse de Noailles in the Faubourg Saint-Germain, by the Comtesse Duchâtel, the wife of the Minister of the Interior, and by that pillar of the defunct Bourbon monarchy and the Catholic church, Madame Recamier, at the Abbaye-aux-bois. There she met Châteaubriand, now past seventy, and gained his enthusiastic admiration. On his arm, the young girl, all in white, unadorned except by youth, was gliding into high society. She carried her great, cool intelligence with her. She was careful, she listened, she did not ask questions but merely spoke when spoken to, she did not start new topics of conversation. And she used everything she found. The Duc de Noailles answered "questionnaires" she wrote out, and furthered her general education. Her sometimes exquisite letters were drafted by Crémieux, who spent many hours in that service. Another eminent lawyer, Berryer, helped her with her elocution. The Marquis de Custine advised her on her reading, and Dr. Véron at times served functions which one can only describe as those of a public relations counsel.

Dr. Véron also had other functions in her life. That he was her lover is certain, but it is not certain if he was the first. He may have been preceded by a certain Charles-Maurice, a small-time journalist who in 1850 wrote a book called *La Vérité Rachel*, possibly the most scurrilous, anti-Semitic attack ever made on her in print. The explanation given for his enmity was the usual one: he was a disappointed lover. It was the same that Sainte-Beuve gave for Janin's review of *Bajazet*, the same given in hundreds of cases involving Rachel and any other major actress. It betrays a one-track mind, but the preoccupation was not with Venus, the goddess of love. The real consecration was to Diana, the goddess of the hunt.

The hunt for wealth and power which had led the French bourgeoisie to demolish the aristocracy did not confine itself to politics and finance. Like all totally absorbing pursuits, it pervaded most aspects of life; the trophies of victory were not only mansions and ministries, but lovers. Parisian society appears as a vast array of the proverbial Redskins—not the noble savages of Châteaubriand's novels, but the ones whose main occupation, according to story, was the amassing of scalps. Scalp collecting was done with considerably less finesse and considerably more abandon than at Versailles in the preceding century. A victim's head was not touched as such but his or her colors were worn in public, so to speak, and later the considerably discolored linen was washed in public also. A new lover, male or female, was a triumph, especially if the scalp had been wrested from another major collector. Dr. Véron was one of the greatest collectors and therefore himself also a prize item. Piquancy was added by the fact that he was physically a very unlikely specimen. Barbey d'Aurevilly simply called him "the leper of Paris." Ponsard, later one of Rachel's lovers, described him a little more precisely as "gross, ugly and scrofulous." The scrofula, together with the absence of a neck, were hidden by an enormous cravat, often caricatured by Daumier. He had made his money with patent medicines, and parlayed his way into the directorship of the Opéra, a central location for the amassing of scalps. By the time Rachel was added to the collection he had become the editor of the *Constitutionnel*, one of the most influential newspapers of Paris.

Rachel's biographer James Agate calls him the pillmaker and suggests that his conquest of Rachel was made possible only by those first disastrous weeks at the Comédie. He contradicts those who say that the liaison began in the fall of 1838, and believes that Véron could not have obtained Rachel the moment she had begun to be successful. This attributes Victorian attitudes to her which she did not have. To the young girl such an important conqueror of women would be an enticement as such. Though she was ashamed later on of having been one of Véron's many successes, in 1838 she may well have relished it. He was also of course eminently useful as an influential editor, a loud publicist of her greatness, and a rich and open-handed man. Many were to follow him, several were soon concurrent with him, but the liaison endured for some time. When she finally rejected him as her lover, he had his revenge: He gave a large dinner and as a special dessert he treated the assembled guests to readings from Rachel's more intimate letters.

After that the pose of the young lady in white was no longer possible, but for the first year or more of her career she managed it to perfection. The world of great Parisian society was open to her, because she symbolized artistic respectability.

The enthusiasm with which Rachel, the Jewish peddler's daughter, was received was increased by the fact that she was such an unusual object of affection, and that one could be so excellently broadminded about her.

Anti-Semitism had not yet spread. Sarah Bernhardt had to contend with it a generation later, but Rachel remained relatively untouched. Rather, her faith contributed to the romance of Rachel in the early part of her career. The Baron de La-mothe-Langon wrote a book about her, which, with twentieth-century speed, he managed to publish in 1838, within three months of her success. (It should be noted, however, that of its two hundred and nineteen pages the first one hundred and sixty do not deal with Rachel, but with the history of the Comédie Française.) In it the baron, untouched by knowledge of the subject, spins a marvelous, romantic tale of Rachel's Jewish background. According to him, her spiritual life began on her eighth day when she was taken to a synagogue, and there was circumcised.

In certain influential circles, Rachel was made welcome, actually, because she was Jewish, not in spite of it. She was a favorite among the Jews, of course, who were rising in the economic and cultural spheres of Paris. Besides that, she was the darling of the large anticlerical element of the bourgeoisie. The Bourbon regime had been strongly and conservatively Catholic, and all revolutions, including the one that brought Louis Philippe to the throne, had anticlerical aspects. But the aristocratic right wing, or portions of it, welcomed her as well. She had, after all, revived the classical theater which in the minds of the aristocracy was closely associated with the *ancien régime* to whose passing they were not reconciled. Moreover, actors and actresses were for the first time made welcome by society on almost equal terms, merely because they were charming, interesting, and, above all, because one could be sure that the equality was not real. While the old aristocratic society was being inundated by the captains of industry—the new society—social recognition bestowed upon performing artists was of use to the upper orders: the aristocracy could receive them with pleasure; for one, they were kings and queens on stage, and much better behaved than the *nouveaux riches* of the iron mills; and second, if one had to extend the limit of those who were to be "recognized," one might as well extend it beyond the new industrial rich to people who were at least interesting.

It did not take Rachel long to find out that much of the old society was boring. At times she was not able to disguise her sarcasm. When the Cabinet minister Merlé said to her sententiously, "Mademoiselle, you have saved the French language," she replied, "How surprising; and I never even learned it." The episode is also told of a countess in the Faubourg Saint-Germain who graciously took Rachel on a promenade in her carriage. When Rachel was taking her leave of the countess afterwards, she curtsied deeply, down to her knees, and said: "Oh madame, a proof of such esteem is more precious to me than my talent." But when she felt herself unobserved a moment later in the anteroom, she made so obscene a gesture that it sent the countess' young daughter, who happened to see it, crying to her mother's lap. To some very good friends she said that at

times, after these forays into society, "J'ai besoin de m'encanail-
ler." (I have got to be a bitch sometimes.)

Only once, early in her career, did Rachel lose her poise for
a moment. King Louis Philippe, with his Queen and the King
and Queen of Belgium, came to see her in *Cinna*. When he said
to her afterwards: "Mademoiselle, you are bringing on a rebirth
of the best days of French tragedy," she could only blush and
stammer. Louis Philippe did not care about the theater, but he
could see the advantages of Rachel's renaissance. He went several times and overcame his natural miserliness sufficiently to
send her a gift of 1,000 francs, the first and almost the only gift
of his reign to an actor or actress.

Rachel's shyness soon disappeared, and with it her reluctance
to deal with the royal family. Dr. Véron's successor as her main
lover was the Duc de Joinville, a son of Louis Philippe. Before
his arrival on the scene she had been suspected of an affair with
Musset. Rightly, it seems, though in general she was suspected
as a matter of course of affairs with everyone she was ever seen
with, from her teacher Samson to the Emperor Napoleon III.
Musset, if he was her lover, must have been concurrent with
Dr. Véron. At any rate, she was taken not only with his handsome appearance but also with the appeal of having one of the
foremost poets of the age as her lover. Another practical aspect
was involved: from Musset she wanted the great modern poetic
drama; it was never completed, however, and the two finally
parted unamicably.

To the poet Musset Rachel was, of course, a social equal. The
days were past when actors and actresses were social and moral
outcasts whom the Church denied proper burial. But Rachel's
relationships with the Duc de Joinville and, later, the Prince
Napoleon also did not bear even the faintest resemblance to the
old status of the actress as backstairs mistress. There were noble-
men in the Faubourg Saint-Germain who offered their affections
and, when that had no effect, even their hands in marriage.
Rachel's motives in her choice of lovers were not merely mer-
cenary or utilitarian. She seems to have desired some thrill of

greatness—not necessarily sex, for one cannot be sure how much real interest Rachel had in that—not love so much as adventure, the excitement of being part of history: Orleans history, Bonaparte history, intellectual and cultural history. That was scalp-collecting on the highest level.

CHAPTER 2 / Panther of the Stage

Edmund Kean, like the other stars of the theater, used to tour for one-week or one-night stands with local stock companies. He once arrived in an English provincial town on the day of his performance and went to his hotel. The manager of the local company came, not without trepidation, to ask when it would please the great man to rehearse.

"Rehearse? I'm not going to rehearse. I'm going to sleep."

"But sir—the company—have you any instructions for them?"

"Instructions!" Kean roared. "Tell 'em to keep a long arm's length away from me and do their damned worst."

The point about Kean at that moment was not that he was drunk but that he was a star, with all that the term implied in the nineteenth century. Every theatrical era has had its stars, but their positions have not been the same from age to age or country to country. In the twentieth century, carefully rehearsed, integrated performances are the rule in which the stars—usually several stars in one play or film—perform the central roles. The nineteenth century, the gilded age of competition, had a different attitude. The star was the centerpiece of the whole system, and the "star system," as it was called, dominated the theatrical arrangement until the eighteen-nineties.

The term "star system" implied more than the size of a role or the emphasis on it. It implied that everything in the performance was completely subordinated to the star and to his wishes. The main purpose of the performance was to exhibit the star and to have everything and everyone contribute to make that exhibition as stark and extensive as possible. All other actors and actresses were subordinated. *Punch* once reported of Helen Faucit, Macready's leading lady before she became a star herself: "Mr. Macready thought Miss Helen Faucit had a very handsome back for, when on stage with her, he always managed that the audience should see it and little else." Scenes that did not include the star were reduced or eliminated, as for example in Adelaide Ristori's performance of that famous play by William Shakespeare, *Lady Macbeth*, which ended within a few minutes of the sleepwalking scene.

With the play cut to fit the star, and the rest of the cast completely subordinated, rehearsals became much less important. Kean's refusal to rehearse with a provincial company was not exceptional, for even in the great centers the stars paid little attention to the preparation of the play. Macready acknowledged that it was customary for the leading London actors to do no more than to read or repeat the words of their role in rehearsal, and to mark their exits and entrances. Some stars did not participate in rehearsals at all. Otis Skinner reports that in his youth he once played Seyton in *Macbeth*, in which Mme. Fanny Janauschek was the star. Her stage manager stood in for her at all rehearsals, and Skinner was petrified at the prospect of meeting the formidable Madame on stage during the performance for the first time in his life. If there was any direction at all for the performance, it was given by the star, and he was interested only in his part. Clifton Tayleure once played a small part in Shakespeare's *Richard III*, with the elder Booth in the title role. Tayleure entered on the wrong side of the stage; upset at his mistake he went after the performance to apologize humbly to the great actor. Booth answered kindly: "Young man, it makes no difference to me; only come on; I'll find you."

One could reasonably expect that such attitudes produced complete chaos on stage, but they did not, for several reasons. Plays were, first of all, performed in repertory: all theaters would do a different play every night, or at least be ready to perform anywhere from ten to thirty or more plays in the course of a season. The long-term play was very rare, and there were no companies specifically collected to perform one play only, as there were to be in the twentieth century.

A company would therefore have a large number of plays in its repertoire and be ready to provide a mantle of *Macbeth* for Macready or an envelope called *Hamlet* for Kean. At times, of course, it would have a week's notice to prepare some new play, because that was what Forrest had decided to do, and then the prompter would be a very important man that night. Even then the situation was not necessarily hopeless. The members of a company, acting with each other day after day in a wide variety of plays, were generally experienced and in tune with each other. They were, moreover, not expected to give individualistic performances, but merely to surround the star with their generalized action.

The star stood out not only because his role was central but because his acting differed very often not only in quality, but in kind from that of the rest of the company. Average acting in the eighteenth and nineteenth century resembled opera, or even the classical ballet, more than it resembles mid-twentieth century acting. Gestures and movements were standardized: hand to heart—love or trust; arms raised—imprecation; arms stretched forward—supplication; and so on. Acting was volatile: there was much falling on one's knees and much rolling on the ground in agony. The minor practitioners of the art did not need much beyond a knowledge of the lines; they suited to them the standard gestures they had learned, as long as these did not interfere with or distract the audience from the gestures of the star. Even for the star the quality and volume of the voice, and the commanding sweep of the gesture brought on the applause; he did not need to present a completely thought out, idiosyncratic character. The star's acting therefore resembled the performance of a prima donna in opera rather than the central character of a play; he or she played for "points"—for those stunning bits of vocal exertion or stage business that brought applause. Playing for "points" was the accepted mode of acting; great stars often became known for a particularly stunning effect at a climactic moment.

The audience abetted the system. It rarely came to see the play; it came to see the performance. Performances were compared as they still are in opera and ballet, where several stars perform the same role, and as they cannot be when the single, long-run play is the rule. The nineteenth-century audience had a keen sense of its own power as it watched for good and bad performances, and it could be generous as well as cruel. It was quick to be offended, and could be merciless. Jules Claretie found that out as a boy when he was taken to see *Marie Tudor* in Limoges, with the old, played-out Mlle. George. At one point she went down on her knees and then realized that she could not get up again. All his life Claretie carried in his mind the memory of the old actress stranded on stage, her eyes rolling wildly and tears streaming down her face, while the audience roared with laughter.

On the other hand, a well-placed act of audacity could sometimes put a novice on the road to stardom. A new talent could be set to combat old talent, and audiences and managers were watching for that opportunity at all times. The undirected, unrehearsed performance was a pit of hell for the unwary, and a great opportunity for the few who combined talent with daring.

The Comédie Française, the oldest acting company in existence in Europe, predated the star system, and was not geared to it. It had its great actors and actresses from the beginning—Molière was the first—but until Rachel's time their power was circumscribed. Before 1789 the names of the actors were not even listed on the posted announcements of the performances. After that they were listed in order of seniority, so that even the famous Marie Dorval, during her brief stay at the Comédie in 1835, was listed last because she was the latest arrival.

The Comédie was not administered by a director, but was collectively in the hands of its actor members, the *sociétaires*, over whom an administrator appointed by the government exercised an ill-defined, tenuous authority. The whole arrangement

was regulated according to the *Décret de Moscou*, the tablets
of commandment which the Emperor Napoleon had drafted in
Moscow in 1812, to pass the time while he was waiting for the
Russian Czar to surrender. The surrender did not come, the
French army disintegrated on the return journey, but the *Décret
de Moscou* remained the law of the Comédie for a century.

The *Décret* was a good bureaucratic arrangement. It provided
for twenty-four shares in the company; there could be more
than twenty-four members, as shares could be subdivided into
halves, quarters and even eighths. The *sociétaires* were to have
twenty-year contracts and a pension upon retirement. Besides
their shares they had rights to benefits, performances whose income from raised prices of admission went to them; and they
also received certain *feu*, literally "fires" or money for candles,
money which came to them usually as additional sums per performance.

The government by committee extended to the directing of
plays, such as it was. The *régisseur* or director, whose main object is the interpretation of roles today, then looked after everything on and off stage except interpretation. The actors agreed
on that among themselves. In succeeding performances of the
same work the Comédie employed the services of a *semainier*,
usually an experienced actor, but only to remind the actors of
their previous agreement and to keep the performances more
or less in line with it.

The collective arrangements for the government of the Comédie also extended to the auditorium, and applied first of all to
the "claque," the group of spectators employed to initiate and
stimulate applause. Claques were the rule in the theaters, as they
still are in opera houses. They were universally hated and feared,
and often received payments to applaud and counter-payments
not to applaud. At the Comédie the chief claqueur attended
the final rehearsals of a new play in order to plan his effects. It
is typical of the encrustation of custom that the effusions of
the claque were regulated, too: a *sociétaire* or member of the
Théâtre Français had the right to a salvo upon coming on stage;

the salvo was longer if he was a member of the Reading Committee (the committee of *sociétaires* that judged new plays) or
one of the two *semainiers;* at his exit he was to receive a similar
salvo. The rest of the claque's work would be to start the applause for the major speeches and the climactic "points." Without the help of the claque a newcomer had little hope of success.

The chief of the claque had to do his job well, hire the right
kind of people, often women as well who were then to laugh or
cry loudly according to requirements. According to Dr. Véron,
ten claqueurs were enough for an established play; at openings
or other special occasions, more were needed.

When Rachel for the first time stepped onto the stage of the
Comédie on June 12, 1838, she was aware that she was entering
a competition. As the debut had been agreed on just two days
before, rehearsals were obviously not contemplated—the Comédie Française was not going to go to the trouble and expense
of special preparation for a routine event of that sort. Rachel
would have to find her way through the production as best she
could, perhaps with a hint or gentle push from a kindly fellow
actor or protector, and with the chance of being tripped up or
ridiculed by some other participant for reasons she would never
know.

The play through which Rachel had to find, or fight, her way
that evening, *Horace* by Corneille, remained one of her favorites,
and the role of Camille gradually became one of her finest performances. *Horace* is a fairly typical tragedy in the classical
French style, with its basic plot taken from Roman mythology,
and its close adherence to the Three Unities of time, place and
action. Its male heroes are uniformly heroic, but its two female
protagonists contrast strongly: Sabine is yielding, indecisive,
weak, anguished; Camille is logical, decisive, strong, powerful.
Camille is also the more plausible portrayal of human reaction
and feeling in that improbable plot.

The conflict of *Horace* hinges on the dilemma between love
and honor common to many of Corneille's plays. Alba and
Rome, the two neighboring cities, are at war, a war that is

fratricidal and may, if protracted, lead to the undoing of both. A proposal is made that three men from each side fight for the victory of their city, and that the winners lead the others into honorable subjection. The Horatii and Curiatii are among the noblest of noble Romans and Albans respectively; they are chosen to fight. Horace, the oldest of his clan, is married to Sabine, whose brother Curiace, in turn, is to marry Horace's sister, Camille. So the two families are linked, and victory for either side must inevitably bring misfortune to both. Sabine is torn between her sense of family honor and loyalty to her husband; Camille, on the other hand, is infuriated by the whole impossible proposition. When her brother Horace returns in the end, the only survivor of all six combatants and therefore the victor for Rome, Camille receives him with imprecations, not congratulations. He is so infuriated by her lack of a proper sense of honor that he kills her. That killing, at the end of the fourth act, is done according to the rule that violence or death must not be shown on stage. Therefore, when Horace draws his sword, Camille runs off, an action which seems out of character for such an intrepid woman. Camille is mortally wounded off stage, comes on stage once more to utter her final cry, and then has to leave the stage once more to die. (On tour in several foreign countries Rachel, as Camille, died on stage, in violation of Corneille's instructions but in keeping with the expectations of the audience.)

For Camille, the high point of the play is the moment in Act IV where Horace returns alone and she receives the news of the others' death in a fury of despair rather than in sorrowful pride. Jules Janin in his book, *Rachel et la Tragédie*, recorded the astonishment of her fellow actors on that June 12, 1838, when she reached the climactic moment: instead of crying out in all directions in the accepted manner, of hurling shouts of vengeance and anger, arms flung high, Rachel gave the speech in a low voice and "growled in the manner of a tiger whose prey was being taken away." Varenne, a member of the Français, confirms this: "Instead of the classic elevation of the voice and those loud outbursts of grief which carry away the audience and force applause, Mademoiselle Rachel, either through fatigue, calculation, or disdain of received traditions, uttered those words hoarsely, and with concentrated feelings, so that the public, which expected something different, did not applaud."

Calculation and disdain of received traditions—to a man like Varenne the traditions were sacred and their breach a crime. But tradition as such did not have much meaning for Rachel. She was one generation removed from the ghetto and had no particular veneration for the new-old world in which she now participated. The Comédie Française did not awe her. The hostility which her act of audacity might arouse mattered as little; she belonged to a people to whom exposure to hostility was an everyday experience.

The traditional mode of acting tragedy in France was to declaim it, more or less. The emphasis was placed on its qualities as poetry, and at times in the past the declamation must have verged on a melodious chant: Mlle. Clairon and Mlle. Champmeslé in the eighteenth century chanted. Others, such as Adrienne Lecouvreur, the first great tragic actress, and Talma, Rachel's most famous predecessor in the nineteenth century, used a more dramatic mode of rendering the lines. All of them, however, had a certain intonation associated with their training at the Conservatoire, and with the tradition of the Théâtre Français itself. The acting, too, was heavily influenced by tradition. Certain lines of speeches were associated with definite intonation and gesture; the audience watched for them, and watchfully compared their rendering by one or the other actor.

Rachel used her great, cool intelligence to select from the traditions those aspects that she wanted, leaving aside all that she considered inappropriate. Her kind of speech—clean, clipped, impassioned—was the exact contrary of the ample periods and elegant circumlocutions of classical tragedy itself. She rejected the notion that certain feelings "naturally" and inevitably associated themselves with certain tones of voice and movements of the body. She rejected the generalized expressions of emotion

current until her time among all but the very exceptional classical actors like the great Talma. The economy of her movements
and use of voice were her chief assets. The old mode of declamation was swirling, grimacing and chanting around her, but she
held back and never cried out until passion could really be shown
to have reached the breaking point. The greatest effect, the most
stunning impression she made was caused by that skillful holding
back of her anger, fury, sarcasm or remorse; then, when the dam
broke and her feelings burst forth with fearful violence, the
effect electrified—a favorite term—and stunned the audience.
This basic plan of long restraint and ultimate outburst moved
G. H. Lewes to call her "the panther of the stage."

Many objections were raised to her way of acting, of course.
"Rachel reads," the old actress Mlle. George wrote, "she does
not act. She articulates well and distinctly, but that is all."

Mlle. George did not see the point: Rachel did act, but she
did not declaim. Gautier saw it clearly: The public, he said, is
no longer concerned with the drawn-out, musical rendering of
the classical line of poetry. Its rhythm is no longer interesting
to the audience which wants and admires above all "the actors
who give it the allure and the sound of prose. It is in this way
that Mlle. Rachel makes her great impression." In other words,
she injected something akin to realistic speech into the classical
tragedy. This was not a lyrical but a dramatic rendering, in
keeping with the new dramatic and melodramatic plays of Hugo,
Vigny and the boulevard theaters.

In part her innovations came from the boulevard theaters, and
in particular its greatest stars, Frédéric Lemaître and Marie Dorval, who acted in the romantic dramas. Their strength lay, in
part, in their ability to use more economical means of gesture
and voice to achieve the stunning effects that were the necessary
requirement in the romantic plays. They did not have to scream
and roll on the ground as much as their colleagues in order to
electrify their audiences. More important, they managed to convey meaning in ways that seemed stunningly true to life. They
did not only select from the existing concepts of how a particu-

lar emotion should be expressed on stage. They looked inward
and used their intelligence not only to calculate effects, but to
observe human nature. They transcended stage effect to create
character.

Rachel followed them. As she was unawed by the prescrip-
tions of tradition she could take a look at the characters she
portrayed and see not only what novel dramatic effects could
be achieved, but what the characters were. Human psychology
was developing as a subject of study in her time; Rachel used
her own psychological insight, and moreover felt free to do so
and to let it lead her where it may. She could go beyond an
understanding of theatrical effectiveness, of the moment played
with stunning naturalness, the stage business superbly carried
out. She could create a character and make her actions, bearing,
demeanor, costume and everything else form a unified, planned,
harmonious whole.

Rachel's appeal lay in her ability to apply her new methods
to the old tragedies. With infinite talent and tact, she enabled
her respectable audience to eat its cake and have it: it could have
the elevating, heroic, distant tragedies of the great age of Louis
XIV instead of the upsetting plays of Hugo and Dumas. And it
could have them newly created in a manner befitting the new
age.

The novelty of Rachel's power was enhanced by her physical
appearance. Here she triumphantly converted a liability into a
spectacular asset. "Small, ugly, narrow-chested" had been Janin's
description of the little girl at the Gymnase. Samson quite dis-
passionately explained later that "the smallness of her features
and the fact that her eyes were set too close together gave her
an undecided expression and she was declared plain. In later
years, however, people said that she was beautiful. Neither state-
ment was true, or let me say that both were true according to
the day, the hour and the expression she *willed* her features to
assume." At any rate, he stressed, she was not at all like the
actresses of her day, "with a muscular neck and with enormous
physical charms drowned in purple."

The last point is particularly important. The ideal of beauty of her age, at least on stage, was still that of the faded Mlle. George, the former mistress of Napoleon: full blown, florid, heavy, with very ample charms. Rachel was its complete antithesis.

She accented what beauty she possessed—lustrous brown hair, a fine, delicate, slightly aquiline nose, a charming, small, rather round mouth, white, newly regulated teeth, a long patrician neck. But posture, bearing, demeanor above all were the important assets which she added to her complement. In an age which endorsed plumpness, the slender, even lean Rachel could have felt defeated at the outset. But she managed to capitalize on that supposed disability by means of movement and especially by her sudden displays of strength and force. The heroines of Brunhild proportions could be expected to develop massive force in their voices and bearing. The same massive force breaking suddenly from so frail a person as Rachel aroused the fascinated enthusiasm of a whole generation of playgoers. They never ceased to remark on the tremendous outbursts of which she was capable.

No role better exemplifies her gradual process toward perfection than *Phèdre*, which she performed for the first time on January 21, 1843. It became her greatest success as well as her greatest achievement. Racine's play is generally considered the most important of the whole classical repertoire; Phèdre herself, the title role, is the touchstone in the career of a French tragedienne. It showed Rachel's professional attitude that she did not attempt that part until she had been at the Comédie for more than four and one half years. She rehearsed it meticulously with Samson, scene by scene, line by line. "I have studied my sobs in Act IV," she wrote him on one occasion.

Phèdre had hardly been presented in the preceding twenty years. After the death of Mlle. Duchesnois there was no point in it. One had to be an old playgoer to remember any of its glory. Rachel created a new Phèdre from the first moment of her entrance: Even Gautier, the opponent of tragedy, said that "upon her first step from the wings her success was no longer in doubt." With her arms hanging lifelessly to her side, her dragging feet, her bent body, sunken head, and deathly pale face, she had the sinister and fateful air of a victim offered up for some horrible expiation. Phèdre's passion and fate is to love Hippolyte, who does not return that love and who is, moreover, her own husband's son. She is filled with shame, torn by moral conflicts regarding her husband and her unconquerable love, and finally undone by her inability to find peace. The play opens when her internal conflict has brought her to the breaking point. Phèdre is near death, and less occurs in five acts in the sense of positive action than in a Chekhov play. But Phèdre's anguished conflict is one of the finest single sustained characterizations in literature.

Rachel wore a severely simple gown, which fell around her in carefully arranged folds. There was no overt glamor in it, and no anachronism. The immediate success of her appearance was the first measure of her triumph. The full measure of her triumph, however, was that a critic like Gautier simply declined to review Rachel's performance line by line, verse by verse. That was the real victory of her style—the critic felt he needed to forget the encrustations of the past, the rendering of a hundred familiar verses, lines known to every schoolboy in all their traditional means. He could see only Rachel-Phèdre, the whole character created by her because "she has given us Phèdre without a moment's cessation of the illusion." She had done so, he added, in spite of the abominable setting provided by the Comédie, "these frightful office chairs with doilies on their backs, the tunic of Hippolyte whose color is somewhere between apricot and pumpkin, and the dining-room curtains which clothe [Phèdre's confidante] Oenone. . . . Her success was immense. Recalled after the fourth act Mlle. Rachel had the good taste not to appear, for fear that she would destroy the illusion in showing herself with her normal face. Thunders of applause rewarded her for this restraint at curtain time." (The curtain was not lowered between acts.)

Not only the French were ecstatic. G. H. Lewes, who saw her Phèdre in its later, most perfect state, simply said: "Whoever saw Rachel play Phèdre may be pardoned if he doubts whether he will ever see such acting again." Another English critic said of it: "To this hour it stands out in solitary splendour, for the attempts of Ristori and of Sarah Bernhardt in the part are unworthy to be named in the same breath." And Hans Christian Andersen, during a visit to Paris, wrote in his diary: "Dear God, I thank you for having given me the mercy of living to this evening. This evening, I shall see Mlle. Rachel in *Phèdre*."

Rachel as Phèdre was the pinnacle, the final, indisputable restoration of classical tragedy, a triumph which no one could deny, not even the spokesmen of the romantics. Gautier had repeatedly complained that no new (romantic) drama had been given at the Comédie since Dumas' *Caligula* in 1838, shortly before Rachel's first triumphs. Now at last, a few weeks after her *Phèdre*, on March 7, 1843, a new play by the foremost romantic poet was given its first night at the Comédie: Victor Hugo's *Les Burgraves*. It turned out to be not a counter-move, but a *coup de grâce:* Its immediate failure persuaded Victor Hugo to leave the drama forever.

The greatest poet of the age might resent her bitterly. Daumier might draw a whole series of caricatures of classic heroes and heroines, including in them hints of Rachel and her unusual facial features. It did not matter. She was the queen of the *Juste Milieu.* As the Duc de Dondeauville said to her: "You understand society as you understand the theater. You are equally perfect on the one stage as on the other."

CHAPTER 3 / Tout ou Rien

As an artistic achievement Rachel's Phèdre was the high point of her career. At twenty-two she was now the equal of the greatest actresses Paris had known, from Adrienne Lecouvreur to Duchesnois and Mars. In the remaining twelve years of her career Rachel achieved a status that transcended that of any of her predecessors.

That she became an international actress—in fact *the* international actress—was not due to the superiority of her talent over all others, past and present, however great her talent was. She achieved that rank because the world was ready to give it to her, because she was part of the new order of the nineteenth century.

The new industrial society believed in absolutes. The fit were intended to survive and the unfit to perish even before Darwin supplied the scientific framework as well as the catch-phrases for these beliefs. Napoleon had fought his way to the top. The traditional social restraints were shunted aside as men and women followed his example. To reach the top became the aim in any field: a really ambitious man would want to corner the market—the word cornering, with its connotation of fighting, is notable—corner it in railroads, or in oil, or in gold. With that idea of absolute eminence another new idea spread through Western industrial society: a new internationalism for the age of nationalism. What had simply been a proud show of progress at the Crystal Palace in 1851 became a new rule and standard: World's Fairs, as the central showplaces of Western commerce and industry, could provide international crowns for the best, from watches to whiskeys. If you could not corner the market

43

in mousetraps, at least you could strive to have your mousetrap acclaimed the best anywhere.

Politics and economics had their repercussions in other aspects of culture; the tycoons had their imitators in the arts. Paganini was the first recognized international champion of the violin, Fanny Elssler of the dance, Jenny Lind, in the next generation, was the world's foremost singer, Liszt the foremost pianist. The same idea of absolute eminence spread further: local boxing bouts became national, then international; soon there were world champions in running, jumping and other sports and, in the end, the natural culmination of that development, the first modern Olympic games of 1894.

Rachel's magnificent silver service and letterhead bore her motto: *tout ou rien*. All or nothing—the same desire for the absolute that led Gould to an attempt to corner the gold market led Rachel to her artistic conquests of Russia and America.

It was not a conscious enterprise at first. Money was the original driving force. Rachel's tours to the provincial cities of France were obviously not artistic undertakings, and different from the worlds conquered beyond the borders of her country. The provinces were not new conquests, they were in bondage to the capital and mere sources of revenue. In Paris she played no more than twice a week; in the provinces she played every day, with a constant eye on the box office. She endured the backbreaking labor of constant, difficult travel, stage coaches, poor hotels, wretched food and general inconvenience, broken only by the cheers of the crowd. In a letter to Janin from Bordeaux on August 4, 1841, she reports both that she was serenaded by 10,000 people and that the income from the tour is the sole matter of interest to her. "What a trip! What fatigue!! But what loot!!!" she wrote to Dr. Véron in 1849, from such a tour.

There is Mlle. Rachel once more on tour through the provinces [her colleague Edmond Got wrote in his Journal in 1850], and for three months, I am told, like last year, when she acted ninety-one times in ninety days, while it is so hard, when she is in Paris, to get two regular performances per week out of her.

What preparations and what terrible fatigue that ought to be, though! To go out with a company made up in part by her family, in part by minor hired actors of the Comédie, whom she thereby turns from their normal careers; to pack them all with the baggage like sardines into a carriage at their expense, where she sleeps across the seats, not without admitting to it— so they say—some male member of the band; to unpack, and then to repack the costumes at each stop . . . and no letup! At times there are two performances per day, ten leagues apart.

Got was telling a lie about the male member, but otherwise he was right.

The tours abroad were quite another matter. There, apart from money, new crowns could be won, and conquests had meaning. London was a natural first stop. The artistic exchange between the major western European centers had died down in the century before Rachel. In the sixteenth and seventeenth centuries some English companies had traveled to the continent, mostly to Germany; and the Italian companies of the *commedia dell' arte* had made France their second home. But in the eighteenth century these movements had virtually disappeared. David Garrick, on his European journey, was honored and feasted in Paris as befitting one of the foremost actors of his day, but he did not perform. English companies had briefly performed in Paris in the 1820's, and Mlle. Mars had played in London in 1832.

It was therefore still an unusual step when, in May of 1841, the Comédie sent a troupe to London, with Rachel as star. The *Times* of May 10 reviewed the first offering, *Andromaque* by Racine, with Rachel as Hermione. In spite of difficulties with the French classical drama—not the linguistic difficulties, to which no one admitted, but the difficulties with that alien form of tragedy—the *Times* reported that Rachel succeeded in "electrifying" the audience. The *Athenaeum* in its next issue (May 15) reviewed the performance and praised her highly, in spite of her very poor supporting cast. Her passion is marveled at and her power to awe: "Few who saw her went away without those deeper chords being touched which belong to Terror rather than Grief." Others might provoke tears; Rachel evoked the true effect of tragedy.

Within weeks London was at her feet as much as Paris had ever been. Macready gave a dinner for her, but that formal attention by a fellow artist was eclipsed by the rush of high society. Lord Normanby dined her and took her to the races at Epsom. Lords Palmerston, Clarendon, and Lovelace entertained her lavishly. The Duke of Wellington called on her. A chapter in Disraeli's *Tancred* records the strong impression Rachel made on him.

On June 3 she performed before Queen Victoria at Marlborough House. Victoria herself wrote down some of the guests: "Aunt Gloucester, the Cambridges, George and Augusta [Cambridge], Ld. Melbourne, Duke of Wellington, Duke and Ds. of Sutherland, D. of Devonshire, Archbp. of Canterbury." From that day Victoria was a firm convert to the art of Rachel. She attended the performance of *Mary Stuart* on June 21, and of *Bajazet* on July 2. Finally she invited Rachel to perform at Windsor Castle, entertained her there like a visiting foreign dignitary, and presented her with a bracelet inscribed "Victoria Reine à Mlle. Rachel." The Duchess of Kent, noticing a shiver in the twenty-year-old guest—excitement more likely than cold —put her own cashmere shawl around her shoulders, which soon after found its resting place on the more ample shoulders of Mama Félix. The income from each evening was several times that of a Paris performance, and at her benefit, *Marie Stuart* on June 14, she received thirty thousand francs, apart from ten bouquets and two crowns.

When, on October 9, 1841, Rachel returned from her tour of England she made her first reappearance at the Théâtre Français as Camille in *Horace*, her original starting role. "The public," Gautier reports, "behaved somewhat coldly toward her at first —absence is always dangerous, for human nature is made of forgetfulness." As on later occasions, the public was won back and before the end of the evening it was at her feet again. But a

residue of that resentment remained. Paris did not like to be
shown that a world worth having existed outside its limits. And
that resentment, increased by longer tours—tours to farther
places, Italy, Holland, Germany, Austria, even Russia—that resentment was eventually to overwhelm her.

Rachel's fight to reach the top could not be confined to the
theater. Even if she had wanted to do so—and there is no reason
to assume that she did—the general climate of competition would
have made it very difficult to avoid the scalp hunt. One had to
rise or be defeated, and victory over a rival seemed more important than the man, or woman, acquired as a result of the war.

Rachel was rarely the one from whom a man was taken. Mlle.
Nathalie of the Comédie seems to have taken the dramatist Émile
Augier from her; but it went the other way more often, and no
one was better at twisting the knife in the wound than Rachel.
Old Mlle. Mars, writing a chatty letter to a friend in the '40's,
could not contain herself about a long, involved war between
Rachel and her older colleague Anaïs Aubert:

> I should hold back what I am going to tell you, and wait for the
> fireworks, but my tongue and hand cannot contain themselves
> any longer. I am fearful that I may move your feelings too
> much and that you may be too upset at the despair of our poor
> little Anaïs, who has just been abandoned by her faithless lover
> and replaced by Mlle. Rachel. A complete break. When one is
> a female rake like Anaïs, it is unpleasant and surprising to find
> someone who is more accomplished. Well, that is exactly what
> has just happened to her. In that piece of treachery there are a
> few charming details: the victorious lady went to see her victim
> to amuse herself and to acquaint her with the happiness of two
> well-joined hearts.

When Anaïs found out about the new liaison she made her
former lover a great scene; but he in turn defeated her counter-
offensive by freely admitting the whole charge and accounting
for it by his intention to get married; not to Rachel, of course;
he merely said that his affair with Anaïs was too well known to
permit his marriage; therefore, a new mistress was called for.

The intrigue did not end there, however; tales kept being carried back and forth, some of them by the "betrayer" himself, who saw both women for a time. Anaïs eventually managed to console herself with Thiers, the future prime minister.

The man involved in this transfer of affections was most likely Count Alexander Colonna-Walewski, who played a central role in Rachel's lovelife. His mother had been the Polish countess Walewska, his father the Emperor Napoleon. Though illegitimate, he was socially near the top of Paris society in the July monarchy. He was rich, in his thirties, and had a fairly distinguished career as soldier and diplomat before he met Rachel.

The meeting was a paradox in itself, and symptomatic of Rachel's Paris. Anaïs herself introduced Walewski and Rachel, partly because Rachel wanted to see if the Count was really as charming as her friend Anaïs said, and partly because Anaïs wanted to keep her hold on Walewski by showing off Rachel to him. She had underestimated his charm or overestimated Rachel's friendship. At any rate, the affair began in 1842 and, unexpectedly, lasted for more than three years. Rachel seems to have been quite reasonably faithful in this period at the height of her artistic success. He installed her in an elegant house in the Rue Trudon, which she kept for most of her life, and in which she also invested large sums of her own money. It was a showplace, overdecorated even for its day, and in particular it sported a bedroom with a bed that more nearly resembled a triumphal chariot. Rachel rarely used it. She preferred a smaller, simpler, more secluded bedroom behind it.

Count Walewski was the father of her first child, Alexandre Antoine Colonna-Walewski, whom he officially recognized as his son; Alexandre, born at Marly-le-Roi on November 3, 1844, was the chief object of his mother's devotion, and became a government servant; he died as French consul in Turin in 1898.

Walewski set out to cultivate Rachel's mind as well. He gave her books of history, politics and literature to read, and the impressive library in the Rue Trudon was mainly due to his influence. He gave her lessons of various kinds and, to judge by his notes and letters to her, let her know how lucky she was to have him. That idea, so often reiterated, may have been somewhat trying to the greatest actress of her time. Towards the end of their relationship the Count seems to have been sufficiently plagued by her infidelities. There had been three reconciliations since the preceding November when, on March 12, 1846, the final break came. The cause of the break was, of course, another man—who, one does not know. Two likely candidates are young Jules Samson, the son of her teacher, and the editor Émile de Girardin who, so Arsène Houssaye said, "is the husband of all women except his wife, to whom he is a friend." On March 11 there seems to have been a violent scene, and on the following day the Count departed for Turin, leaving behind a note: "I am leaving this moment. When you receive this letter I shall be far away. I have forgotten *everything* that happened yesterday. It is enough to tell you that I have spoken about it to *nobody, nobody.* If, as I hope, you regret the words that escaped you, write to me and I shall reply at once." He then gave his forwarding address and concluded: "I leave without rancor and wish you the best, in spite of all. Would that your son will be your good angel; kiss him for me. Adieu, Rachel."

On March 20, one week after the break, Walewski wrote to his half brother from Turin. In his letter he said that he wanted to change his life and therefore looked for a woman to marry. He asked his brother if he could find him a young woman, not over thirty, with a pleasant disposition and at least 300,000 francs. As it turned out, he did not need help. When he stopped off in Florence on his way to Rome, he met Marianne Ricci, who conformed to his specifications. They were married on June 3, 1846, and it luckily fell to Anaïs Aubert to inform Rachel.

When Walewski left Rachel, their son was nineteen months old. After a year Walewski wanted to look to his upbringing himself, and after some delays, he did obtain the boy. That brought forth the lioness in his former mistress: "What have *you* suffered for that child to dare to tear him from me without pity? . . . Am I then a monster? . . . If you give me back my child, I shall live for him *alone*. I shall know how to tame my own nature in order to be worthy of him always. My heart will not open itself to anyone but him. My whole life will be too brief to prove to him my tenderness, my love, my devotion . . ."

Rachel loved Alexandre sincerely, but she promised more than she could fulfill. Walewski returned the boy to her after that letter, though he did not finally cede his rights to him until 1852. Alexandre does not seem to have been harmed by the continued association with his mercurial mother. She was always good to him, and looked after him. Rachel also loved her second child, Gabriel Victor Félix, born on January 26, 1848, at Neuilly-sur-Seine, eighteen months after the break with Walewski. Gabriel's father did not recognize him, as Walewski had done for his son; he was in every sense a decline from the father of her first child. Arthur Bertrand was a worthless, reckless character, an unstable man; and while his predecessor had been a son of Napoleon, he was merely the son of one of the Emperor's marshals.

By the time of Gabriel's birth the Second Republic had replaced the July Monarchy and the Second Empire was on the horizon. Some biographers assert that its Emperor, Napoleon III, had been Rachel's lover in England in 1846, and possibly even after his return to France in 1848. That is uncertain, but it was well known that his cousin Prince Napoleon, "Plon-Plon," the son of King Jerome of Westphalia, held that position for some time, and, like so many others, remained her faithful friend until death. In 1848, an active year in France, Lockroy, the administrator of the Comédie, also held Plon-Plon's rank, as did two others, if we are to believe hints in a letter from Rachel to her sister Sarah.

Rachel was a scalp collector by nature rather than design. Her incessant seeking for money was also not simply a matter of greed. She herself said in a letter: "These tours do me a lot of good. Movement and excitement drive away the bad thoughts. They silence the bad inclinations." She went on restlessly, heedlessly, greedily, going from man to man, country to country, forgetting promises, ignoring commitments. She was driven, as Sarah Bernhardt was to be a generation later, by something for which artistic and economic causes cannot account.

Phèdre had been the top. She could deepen her hold on that role, but artistically nothing remained to be added. What she did add, at the Comédie, was inferior. Between Phèdre in January of 1843 and the February revolution in 1848, she tried twelve new roles, classical and contemporary. None were successful. In the classical repertoire she had exhausted the suitable roles. The contemporary plays were worse.

Several critics said that Rachel, after her triumphs, could have turned to the writers of genius of her day, but instead she turned to the second-rate ones, "the little bastards of Corneille." It is very doubtful that she could have done otherwise, even if she had wanted to.

She had succeeded precisely because she did not act in the murky cloak and dagger stories of the romantics; in avoiding Vigny and Hugo she showed judgment rather than lack of it. By the late 1840's Vigny had in any case withdrawn from the theater; Hugo was deeply enmeshed in politics; Dumas, as the director of a theater, turned out potboilers in a matter of days, which did not prevent him from resenting deeply that Rachel did not act in them.

Rachel's years after *Phèdre* were demoralizing for the Comédie. Her fellow actor Got wrote in his diary in 1846:

> What is going to happen to the Comédie Française? For the last two years, no great successes, and for the future, few hopes; all the famous authors have left, the personnel is incomplete and insufficient, and, apart from a few talented people, there is with the exception of Mlle. Rachel no actor who makes an impact at the box office. The administration is feeble and discouraged, the entire press is running wild and the public taste is deadened.

The stagnation was largely due to Rachel herself. Her tremendous success had been artistic only in part; she owed much

of it to political and cultural forces, to a bourgeoisie which, far
from wanting to be dazzled by the romantics, wanted to dazzle
itself by imitating the aristocracy, by being its reflection.

In the late 1840's the bourgeois July Monarchy was running
out of steam, and so did Rachel's hold on the public. She was
politically uninterested, but her associations inclined her toward
the conservatives. Count Duchâtel had once taken her to see the
Prime Minister, Guizot, give a speech in Parliament, and she
had been enthused by the performance. "I would like to act
tragedy with that man," she is reported to have said. Guizot
came close—he killed the July Monarchy; but his monarch did
not have the makings of a tragic hero.

> If the monarchy of Louis Philippe had been prolonged in a
> sweet bourgeois drowsiness [writes Lucas-Dubreton]; if M.
> Guizot, that unrecognized tragedian, had not directly led
> royalty to its ruin through his conservative, protestant intran-
> sigence, then the torrent which had carried Rachel along would
> in all probability have slowed down to lose itself in the sand.
> Fortunately, the democratic revolution of 1848 freed the lion-
> ess of the Théâtre Français to find other means to conquer the
> public; she had to assume a new guise, and adapt herself.

The revolution of February 22–24, 1848, seems accidental,
unpremeditated. Guizot was removed too late to appease the
aroused opposition, and the King of the *juste milieu* left for
England with no more noise, and no less readiness, than a man
setting out on a business trip. This time it seemed to be a real
revolution, and the result a real republic; there was no Lafayette
any more to make the people, hesitating on the brink of further
disorder, accept an Orléans in place of a Bourbon.

The adherents of the July Monarchy and what it had stood
for were afraid. Dr. Véron, no republican, gave 10,000 francs
for the wounded of the revolution. The Republic made a number of far-reaching social reforms in the winter and spring of
1848 that could well scare the middle class. In June the forces
opposed to these reforms had some successes, and the consequent

uprising of the workers on June 23–26 was bloodily suppressed by General Cavaignac. After that the ruling classes were ruling again, and the danger was over. On December 10, a plebiscite elected Prince Louis Napoleon President of the Republic. A Bonaparte dictatorship was replacing an Orléans one.

The Comédie had closed during the days of the revolution in February, and reopened on the 27th with two innocuous comedies. Patriotic airs were played at intermissions, and Brindeau, in the uniform of the National Guard, sang the *Marseillaise* at the end. There was no charge for admission, but boxes were provided to receive donations. Nine hundred francs were the result of that collection. Better than on the very worst days, but the outlook was dim.

On March 6, 1848, one week after the Comédie had reopened as the Théâtre de la République, Rachel returned to the stage in the role which she so often chose as her "rentrée," Camille in *Horace*. At the end of it, that former mistress of one of the Orléans princes came forward, on demand, and gave a rendering of the *Marseillaise*. It was an emotional occasion, and she made her rendition worthy of it. She acted and chanted at the same time, brandishing the tricolor; the last stanza she performed kneeling down, the flag pressed to her heart. The success was enormous, and she performed the anthem two or three times a week for several months, on those evenings on which she did not appear in a play. It was a help for the Comédie, fallen on hard times. The promise of a performance of the *Marseillaise* was enough to take some of the curse off those evenings on which Rachel did not perform. Her service in these critical months was forgotten in later years, when she absented herself more and more from the Français. But that was only to be expected.

In 1848 and 1849 Rachel's role at the Comédie—not on stage, but behind the scenes—was curiously analogous to the political developments. Her relations with François Buloz, the last administrator of the Comédie under the July Monarchy, had worsened throughout 1847. Rachel was fighting to have him removed. Finally the Commission of the Royal Theatres was called in to mediate in the war; on February 21, it found for Buloz and against Rachel. Buloz's joy was short-lived, however. Three days later the July Monarchy was dead, and soon after he was replaced by Lockroy, who was more tractable; in fact his relations to Rachel transcended his official position so much that he eventually had to resign. One week after his resignation, on October 18, Rachel resigned from the Français and stopped her performances. The threat of a damage suit forced her to return, because, according to the *Décret de Moscou*, a *sociétaire* who wished to resign had to give one year's notice.

Even before the Revolution Rachel had advocated that a strong director should replace the government by committee, with the administrator as an ill-defined head. Lockroy had been a failure, but in Arsène Houssaye she finally found the man for it. Houssaye, a general man of letters and gossip about town, hard hit by the upheavals and uncertainties of Paris in 1848, records in his *Confessions* that Rachel asked him point blank that year if he would like to be director of the Comédie. Later on, when he went to thank the Prince-President Louis Napoleon for the appointment, he received the reply, "Don't thank me, thank Mlle. Rachel. She was given a list of ten men of letters to choose from, and she chose you, I don't know why." When he asked Rachel, she said: "[I chose you] because I knew you less well than the others."

Napoleon III, like his uncle, wanted the theater to be a brilliant cultural enhancement of his reign even before he assumed the imperial title officially. The Republic had lifted censorship in 1848, and Napoleon looked to Hugo and Dumas, the great romantics, to become his Corneille and Racine. Houssaye was to promote the endeavor. He restored their plays to the repertoire, and, among other things, engineered an encounter between Rachel and Victor Hugo in his office in 1849. Their effusive conversation resulted in her promise to play all his major roles.

In 1850, Rachel made the first attempt. The only plays by Dumas and Hugo in which she ever performed were given for the first time in February and May of that year. Neither of them were conspicuous successes, and she turned from the romantics back to the little bastards of Corneille.

The task was made easier by official action. Censorship, abolished by the Revolution, was re-established by the Prince-President on July 30, 1850. The romantic poet-playwrights turned more and more against the new regime; the break came when the Prince-President became Emperor. Victor Hugo spent most of the Second Empire in uncomfortable exile in the Channel Islands. By then, of course, the *Marseillaise* had long disappeared from Rachel's repertoire. With complete impartiality, on October 22, 1852, a few weeks before the proclamation of the Second Empire, she performed on a gala occasion at the Comédie an ode by Houssaye: "L'Empire, c'est la paix," the text based on a speech which the Prince-President had given at Bordeaux, and which was the prelude to the re-establishment of the Empire. The new Emperor sent her a magnificent bracelet as a reward.

Rachel had given her year's notice in October, 1848, and kept her promise. She resigned from the Comédie when her time was up, in October, 1849. By then Houssaye was taking over, and Rachel *sociétaire* was immediately replaced by Rachel *pensionnaire* at an annual salary of 42,000 francs with six months' leave. On December 1 she returned as *Phèdre*, with her brother Raphael as Hippolyte.

Rachel's new contract merely legalized an existing situation. Her leaves from the Comédie, by one means or another, had been extensive; she had pleaded illness or pregnancy, and she had threatened to be obstructive in various ways. As early as 1844 she had been absent five months; the following year it was four, in 1846 it was five again, and in 1847 nearly seven months. When she was present she performed twice a week. On tour, she performed every day. It is no surprise that her enemies accused her of turning the Comédie into a paid vacation.

Mlle. George exemplified that attitude. Rachel, she said, made fools of all the actors at the Comédie, "She makes a new contract, provides for benefits, special pay, leaves, mountains of

gold. When it is all signed, she says: Oh, by the way, I forgot
to tell you, I am four and a half months pregnant, I won't be
able to act for five months. She does well. If I had managed
things that way, I would not be kicking the bucket like a dog
now."

The dissenting voices of Paris were mute on Rachel's tours.
The mark of the international actress was that she was always
much more renowned and adulated abroad than at home. In
Paris Rachel was the main attraction, even the salvation of the
Comédie, the mistress of famous men, the greatest success in the
theater of her age. Elsewhere she was the fairy princess—the
fairy princess from Paris at that—who came, touched the Emperor, the King, and even the lowly *nouveau riche*, with her
magic wand of great Parisian heritage and supreme classical culture, and, floating on across the map, left them all somehow
enriched and more civilized.

The earlier tours had pointed to what was to come. No other
foreign actress had ever received so much acclamation. Even in
Victorian England her reputation and appeal increased with each
visit. Tours of the Low Countries, almost as frequent as the
English visits, were equally successful, except for the revolutionary year 1848. ("The Republic is costing me dearly," she wrote
from Liège on June 12.)

Rachel went to Belgium for the first time in 1842 and to both
Belgium and the Netherlands in 1846, receiving the obligatory
bracelet from the Queen in the Hague. "Repetition of my reception in England: everything the same, even the bracelet, which
is quite handsome and not exactly unroyal." Writing to Mme.
de Girardin from London on July 14, 1846, she well shows why
the foreign tours attract her: "In Amsterdam [I had] the reward of the most religious silence (maybe the most flattering
effect), then stupendous financial receipts and finally enthusiasm, that is, stamping of feet, cries, bouquets and crowns thrown
to me; nothing was lacking."

The Dutch King had exacted a promise from her to return

in 1847, which she fulfilled, earning 52,000 francs in a two-week tour, more than her annual basic salary at home.

At one point, in the Low Countries, Rachel managed her itinerary in a way that foreshadowed later days with different modes of transportation. She was about to leave Amsterdam to go to Liège in Belgium, when the Queen of the Netherlands let her know that she would like to see her in the Hague. What was Rachel to do about her next, closely spaced commitments? She planned and devised the following: She left Amsterdam at 10 A.M. At 1 P.M. she was in the Hague, rested, had a meal at 5 P.M., and appeared at the palace (with Raphael) at 6. The party ended at 10 P.M. and by 1 A.M. she was on the road to Liège, by coach, to perform there on the following evening.

In Brussels a young English governess saw her and was both fascinated and repelled. Charlotte Brontë later in *Vilette* left a lengthy description of that evening, the evening when the young governess was taken to see Vashti, the greatest star of all:

> The theater was full—crammed to its roof. Royal and noble were there. Palace and hotel had emptied their inmates into those tiers so thronged and so hushed. Deeply did I feel myself privileged in having a place before that stage. I longed to see a being of whose powers I had heard reports which made me conceive peculiar anticipations. I wondered if she would justify her renown. With strange curiosity, with feelings severe and austere, yet of riveted interest, I waited. . . .
>
> For a while,—a long while—I thought it was only a woman, though a unique woman, who moved in might and grace before this multitude. By-and-by I recognized my mistake. Behold! I found upon her something neither of woman nor of man: in each of her eyes sat the devil. These evil forces bore her through the tragedy, kept up her feeble strength—for she is but a frail creature; and as the action rose and the stir deepened, how wildly they shook her with the passions of the pit! They wrote HELL on her straight haughty brow. They turned her voice to the note of torment. They writhed her regal face to a demoniac mask. Hate and murder and madness incarnate she stood.

It was a marvellous sight, a mighty revelation.

It was a spectacle low, horrible, immoral.

The strong magnetism of genius drew my heart out of its wonted orbit; the sunflower turned from the south to a fierce light, not solar—a rushing, red, cometary light—hot on vision and to sensation. I had seen acting before, but never anything like this—never anything which astonished Hope and hushed Desire; which outstripped Impulse and paled Conception; which, instead of merely irritating imagination with the thought of what might be done, at the same time fevering the nerves because it was not done, disclosed power like a deep, swollen winter river, thundering in cataract, and bearing the soul, like a leaf, on the steep and steely sweep of its descent.

Another literary figure of Victorian England also felt Rachel's spell. Matthew Arnold saw her in August of 1847 and promptly followed her to Paris, where he attended every one of her performances for two months. His criticism of her was penetrating; he clearly saw the high degree of intellectual power that lay behind her acting. Many years later his niece Mrs. Humphry Ward returned from Paris full of her new-found enthusiasm for Sarah Bernhardt. He listened to her effusions indulgently and said in the end: "But my dear child, you see—you never saw Rachel."

Rachel had five seasons in England, including one of two months during the great exposition of 1851, and a last brief stay on her way to the United States. During the tour of 1846 Prince Louis Napoleon, just escaped from the French fortress of Ham, was her companion and may have traveled with her to Edinburgh. That was shortly before the beginning of his liaison with Miss Howard, who was very rich and helped to finance the restoration of the Empire.

It is asserted that Queen Victoria and her court withdrew their attention once the details of Rachel's private life had become known in the 1840's. The contrary is true. In 1846 Victoria requested and attended a performance of *Phèdre*, and in

1855, during Rachel's last brief stay, a performance took place under the Queen's patronage.

The tours of the forties amounted to little compared to those of the fifties, which ranged to Rome, Moscow and New York, the longest and most highly acclaimed tours that had ever been undertaken by an actor or actress. The spirit of the century demanded that these first voyages be extended again and again, and that the stars could not rest until Ristori had been to Sydney or Bernhardt to Constantinople or Duse to Montevideo.

One reason for the international career of Rachel and her successors is obvious: the steam engine. Ristori would hardly have traveled to Australia on Captain Bligh's *Bounty*. Some of the initial impetus lies therefore in the exuberance aroused by early rail and steamship travel, which for the first time began to tie together the world in a net of scheduled arrivals and departures. Reasonably dependable and frequent sailing schedules may account in part for making the international status of these actresses possible, but they do not account for the desire of millions to see them, to view them in plays whose language they could not understand. The competitive drive spurred on the artist to greater and greater exertions; the audience was drawn by a different idea, but one that also arose from the desire for competition.

The idea of continual progress—ever forward, ever upward— had taken hold of that part of the world that consciously considered itself civilized. Men and women who could see themselves reaching for the absolute, could naturally see the prospect of the millennium. Progress and universal betterment had found its first conscious international manifestation at the Great Exposition at the Crystal Palace in London in 1851, the first world's fair. The inventions of man, the new scientific, technological, medical and other discoveries, the great industrial development were expected inevitably and steadily to lead man onward towards one great universal civilization. This belief, this optimistic internationalism, found its ready echoes in the upper middle class, which was steadily increasing in wealth, power and numbers. It is this class that endorsed Rachel, that provided the audience and the adulation all over the world. The clever and understanding Emile de Girardin developed this idea to Paul de Saint-Victor in a letter on June 15, 1855, suggesting that he write a *feuilleton* about it:

> That Mlle. Rachel, in having gone to Russia in the past year, and in leaving for the United States this year, contributes instinctively, and perhaps without suspecting it herself, to the fulfillment of true progress. Unknowingly she creates universality, unity, that is to say, civilization. A great artist no longer belongs to his native country; he belongs to the civilized universe. . . .

She was thus a major manifestation of the great progress of the civilized world, in which that world so strongly believed. And to see her, to applaud her, was to be enlightened, progressive, and at the same time to be at the ancient fountainheads of civilization, to be one with the classical heritage, and to be in a class with Queen Victoria and the Emperor Napoleon and the Czar of all the Russias. One could not be in better company. In fact, one could not afford not to be in such company. If one did not know French, one could pretend to know it. If one was bored by Racine, one could hide it before others with applause and before oneself with rationalizations about progress and culture. To see Rachel was undoubtedly a great experience; many sensitive observers attest to that. But the less sensitive could find consolation in elevating thoughts for an evening spent uncomfortably, and at great expense.

The men and women below the level of kings and emperors who formed the mainstay of her international support, also believed in certain aims in life, which Guizot's instruction to the French, "Enrich yourselves," indicated in part. The nineteenth century was the age of absolutist theories in economics, in politics, and in human behavior. The checks and balances, the moderation and search for the possible, of the Age of Enlightenment were replaced by ruthless directness and the search for the abso-

lute. The French Revolution had turned in that direction. Napoleon had shown, dangerously, how large and tall was the room
at the top. If there was room at the top, the top had to be
reached. That is why the ranks of the international actresses
tolerated only one French and one Italian in each generation,
and why even these two had somehow to meet in decisive combat across the barriers of language and dramatic heritage.

Charlotte Brontë saw the result: "Rachel's acting thrilled me
with horror. That tremendous force with which she expresses
the very worst passions in their strongest essence forms an exhibition as exciting as the bull fights of Spain and the gladiatorial
combats of old Rome, and (it seems to me) not one whit more
moral." Her simile provides an additional facet for an understanding of Rachel's international success. Her immense talent and understanding not only carried the French classical drama to the
rest of Europe, but it did so in a way that was comprehensible
to those to whom the subtleties—or even the language—of that
drama were unknown. She managed to make her repertoire international through her acting by using non-classical as well as
classical means. She did, in the new, non-classical manner, *jouer
le mot*, that is, she carried through the phrase with the appropriate gesture. When she referred to Hippolyte's *tête charmante*
in *Phèdre*, she would actually touch his head. Or she would do
the psychological correct thing, as when she stretched out her
arms to Hippolyte in passion at the end of a long speech, then
tightened her fists in suppression of her feelings and finally
lowered them in a gesture of despair, all movements flowing
smoothly from her intonation and connected with each other in
a natural manner. G. H. Lewes characterizes the over-all effect:

In the second act, where she declares her passion, Rachel was
transcendent. There was a *subtle* indication of *diseased* passion,
of its fiery, but unhealthy—irresistible yet odious—character, in
the febrile energy with which she portrayed it. It was terrible
in its vehemence and abandonment; eloquent in its horror; fierce
and rapid, as if the thoughts were crowding upon her brain in

tumult, and varied with such amazing compass of tones, that when she left the scene our nerves were quivering with excitement almost unsupportable.

Yet, as Salvini said, "When she was silent, she seemed almost more eloquent than when she spoke." This was the other aspect, the classical. She could be febrile, but she could also be calm, in control; she could provide a glimpse of the seemingly ordered, self-assured civilization of the past much in the manner of David's historical paintings. She could stand still, and even sit through major scenes and yet control the action and the audience. "Rachel elicited reverence by her tragic dignity," Houssaye wrote. "Even when she smiled it always seemed that she had descended from a bas-relief of Cleomenes, if not Phidias."

Gautier summarized the effect carefully in one term, after a performance of *Athalie:* "Mlle. Rachel possesses that one superior endowment which makes a great tragedienne: authority. When one sees her, one understands her power; in her bearing, her gesture, her glance one recognizes a queen."

An English critic said almost the same, characterizing the appropriateness of this woman to an age that formed the transition from that of the nobility to that of the common man; an age in which kings and emperors still counted as more than relics or curios, and for the last time could exalt the lower orders. George Henry Lewes said: "She was a born empress, her grace, her *distinction*, her simple dignity, the ineffable majesty of her attitudes and gestures, crowned as they are by that small but singularly intellectual head, make her the most queenly woman now seen anywhere."

She had come from far away, intellectually and physically, and part of her success was due precisely to the fact that she could keep her intellectual distance. She could keep her distance as that empress, that statue, unawed by the traditions of the Comédie, of Racinian tragedy. But the fact that she could do so, coolly and intelligently, meant also that she would not give to that proud tradition, in that proudest of cities, the homage and fealty which had been exacted from all her predecessors. "Her fault," says Janin, "was that roving life, that vagabond existence across the borders which she liked, which amused her and which killed her. She did not love Paris as it should be loved, with that violent exalted and exclusive love, a love which knows no other." The fact that she could create a new image also meant that she would not surrender to the domination of the tradition. Paris could not have it both ways, but Paris did not know that, and resented it. The rest of the world, to which she came from Paris, was easier to conquer, and to these conquests she turned almost exclusively in the last five years of her career.

In the summer and fall of 1850 she toured the southern German capitals, and the major cities of the Austrian Empire, Budapest, Prague, Trieste, etc., ending up in Vienna in September and October. "My success in Austria surpasses all the others I have ever had," she wrote. The Emperor himself was one of the few crowned heads who did not come to see her or invite her to act before him, but she was a guest at one of his palaces. In 1851 she toured Italy, and in Rome, chaperoned by dukes and marquesses, stole two oranges from the Papal gardens. In 1852 she revisited Germany, where the King of Prussia proved less unbending than the Austrian Emperor. She performed at Sans-Souci Palace in Potsdam on July 8, 1852, during her second stay in Berlin. She described the whole event fairly sarcastically in a letter to her family, including the sumptuous dinner served to her and her actors before the performance. The Empress of Russia, who was a guest of the King and Queen, declared herself too overwhelmed to applaud. The Czar himself arrived a few days later, and on July 14 Rachel performed *Phèdre* in Potsdam. Before that event the King of Prussia had sent her 20,000 francs ("a really royal gift") and now, after it, the Czar sent Count Orloff to bring her "two magnificent opals surrounded by diamonds" which she immediately evaluated at 10,000 francs. More, even: The Royal Opera House, Berlin, was put at her disposal free of charge for six performances; all the income of that week was therefore hers. And—she almost forgot to set it down in that

long letter—the "men of letters of Berlin" gave her a small statue
of Shakespeare by a famous sculptor whose name she does not
know. "I am told that this little masterpiece has an exorbitant
moral value; it does not look like it." She concludes the letter:
"You may boast that I have written you at such length. But I
am not proud, even though [it is true that] never before have
so many emperors, kings, princes and princesses spoken to one
and the same person as they have to your tragedienne on her
tour of inspection of royalty."

She is proud, her head does spin, but the tone of her observations here as elsewhere indicates that she never lost control of
herself, and always managed to keep the distance which enabled
her to impress and awe even the people who were used to impress and awe those with whom they came into contact. She
knew her effect and her power. She wrote from Berlin: "I
assure you that one needs a strong head to resist such things; all
the flatteries I am told, all the incense I breathe, make complete
the life of an ambitious artist. Neither Talma nor Mars, my great
predecessors in public favor, ever received anything like it."

On her last European tour, on the way to St. Petersburg,
Rachel, with her manager-brother Raphael and her troupe,
stopped in Warsaw, and was appalled at what she found there.
She wrote to her mother:

> As far as the town is concerned, it is nothing to look at. The
> sidewalks are shameful; the people are dirty and the best hotel
> lacks in comfort. What am I saying? It lacks in everything,
> even necessities. I just looked over the menu to set up our din-
> ner, and I nearly fell over backward at the prices. A miserable
> breaded cutlet 4 francs, soup 3 francs, a roll 24 centimes, and
> as for the wine, one must not even think about it: a mediocre
> one is 14 francs per bottle and an acceptable one, that is, one
> which has a more or less deceptive label, costs more than 20
> francs. I am convinced that if the six of us have dinner this eve-
> ning, Raphael will not have enough money left to take us to
> Petersburg. So here is what I think I ought to do: I am going to
> pretend to be violently indisposed, and so put my companions

into a state of anxiety great enough that not one would dare to ask for dinner; in order not to be mistaken in that expectation, I shall ask them all to remain close to me, around my bed. At one o'clock in the morning, when the cook of the hotel will be asleep, I shall permit my company to do the same, and tomorrow before daybreak we shall flee from a country to which I have not come to leave money behind.

Warsaw was the first stop of Rachel's climactic tour, and her successes in St. Petersburg and Moscow surpassed anything that had ever happened to her. "Yesterday," she wrote home, "I was treated like a monarch. Not like a pasteboard monarch in a tragedy with a crown of gilt cardboard, but like a real sovereign, the true, minted article." After her benefit performance in St. Petersburg, she wrote, "the Empress gave me some splendid earrings, and various subscribers combined to offer me a marvellous bracelet of diamonds and rubies. Box office receipts were more than 20,000 francs. Of these I gave 15,000 to the poor and to the theater." Her generosity could be as great as her avarice. To Rebecca she wrote, "A very highly placed personage has offered me 200,000 francs per annum, *i.e.*, for the six winter months, for an engagement of five years' duration." The Minister Count Adelbert came three times to persuade her to sign the agreement. She did not sign, but gave her promise to return the following winter. That promise she did not keep—she may have wanted to, but on February 6, 1854, France and Russia severed diplomatic relations. The start of the Crimean War did not, however, prevent Rachel from finishing her tour. On February 23, 1854, she wrote to Rebecca from Moscow: "Moscow will soon be taken. The Moscovites are returning, with usurious interest, what they took from us in 1812." In spite of the war she performed daily at 1 P.M. to finish her engagement, which netted her 300,000 francs (and 100,000 for Raphael), including a daily average of nearly 12,000 francs in Moscow. At the end of her last performance, *Adrienne Lecouvreur*, she had twenty-two curtain calls.

The height, however, had come one evening in St. Petersburg. Rachel wrote home to her sister Sarah:

Well, the other day I was invited to a great banquet given in my honor at the Imperial Palace. That's it, just for the daughter of Father and Mother Félix . . . ! When I arrived at the palace the tall footmen with their lace and powdered wigs received and escorted me, just like at home: one took my pelisse, one preceded and announced me, and there I was in a gilded salon where everybody rushed towards me. A Grand Duke, a brother of the Czar, came himself to offer me his arm to conduct me to the banquet table; the table was immense, on a raised platform, but the company was small: only about thirty people were dining; but what a choice of diners! The imperial family, grand-dukes, little dukes, and arch-dukes, all sorts of dukes of all calibers, and all that tralala of princes and princesses paying curious and rapt attention, devouring me with their eyes, all ears for my smallest movements, my words, smiles, in other words, not letting go of me with their eyes for a single moment. Well, don't think that I was embarrassed. Not at all. I acted quite normal, at least during the meal, which incidentally was very good. But everyone seemed more occupied with me than with the food being served. Finally the toasts in my honor got under way: and thereupon began a rather extraordinary show. The young archdukes left their places in order to get a better view of me, and mounted their chairs and even put their feet on the table—I was going to say into their dishes. This did not seem to shock anyone, because even the princes of that country still have something of the savage in them. They shouted deafening bravos and asked me to say something. To give a speech from a tragedy in reply seemed a weird thing to do. But I am not undone by such a small matter. I rose and, pushing back my chair, I assumed the most tragic pose of my repertoire and embarked upon the great scene from *Phèdre*. There was utter silence; one could have heard a fly, if there was one in that country. They all listened to me religiously, leaning towards me, limiting themselves to admiring gestures and suppressed murmurs. Then, when I had finished, there was a new outburst of cries, bravos, clinking glasses and renewed toasts to the point that I was completely dumbfounded for a time. But then I became excited myself, and flushed by the scent of wines and flowers and by all that enthusiasm which could not but flatter my small pride, I rose once more and intoned or rather declaimed with great fervor the Russian national anthem. That brought on not enthusiasm, but delirium: they pressed around me, pressed my hand, thanked me; I was the greatest tragedienne of the world, past and future —all that for a full quarter of an hour. But even the best things have to come to an end, and the hour of retreat was striking. I managed it with the same sovereign dignity as at my arrival, being led back to the great staircase by the same grandduke who had led me in, very gallant, very ceremonious. Then the great powdered footmen arrived, one of whom carried my pelisse; I put it on and was escorted to my carriage which was surrounded by more footmen who carried torches to light my departure . . .

CHAPTER 4 / Battle at the Summit

Rachel returned from Russia in the early spring of 1854. It had been her greatest triumph as an international actress. At home, the Emperor Napoleon III, his minister Fould, his director of the Comédie, Houssaye, would deny her nothing. Abroad, St. Petersburg and Moscow, Vienna and Berlin, Munich and Rome had been at her feet, completing the circle of her earlier conquests, of London, Brussels, Amsterdam, and the major cities of France. No actor or actress in history had ever reached such heights.

To reach them, however, Rachel had to prove herself the fittest to survive—at the expense of many others. Rivals for the great were constantly sought by management as well as audience, to tempt jaded appetites and attract new spectators to the gladiatorial combats on stage, some of which were artificially produced. One such straw man (or woman) seems to have been a girl named Maxime, touted to rival Rachel at one point in the early 1840's. "Maxime was not without energy and talent," as Janin reports, and the amateur spectators thought that she and Rachel would revive the happy days in which the clash between the beauty of Mlle. George and the talent of Mlle. Duchesnois had provided such excellent sport. But Rachel did not need to play the game. She bided her time. One evening she was Mary Stuart in Lebrun's adaptation of Schiller's play, and Maxime acted her rival, Queen Elizabeth. The audience, aware of Maxime's position as the challenger, drove her on with excessive applause. Rachel held back, acting calmly and competently until the climactic third act, which provides the only encounter

of the two queens in the play. The beginning brought a hur-
ricane of applause for Maxime; Rachel, her head lowered, acted,
as befitted the captive Scots Queen come to beg her freedom of
her "sister." Elizabeth, disdainful and overbearing, is to drive
Mary slowly beyond the limits of her endurance so that, in the
end, she bursts out with all her queenly pride and power. And
Rachel did. By the end of the scene Maxime was pale, confused,
exhausted; Rachel literally acted her off the stage and out of the
profession. When Rachel, in the end, turned full face to the
audience for her line of triumph and moral victory, "j'enforce le
poignard au sein de ma rivale!" no one doubted that she had
really driven the dagger home in her rival's breast. The combat
was over and Maxime ended up as a hotel manager.

Really serious rivalries are not produced in this way. The
rivalries between equals, such as that of Mlle. George and Mlle.
Duchesnois, or that of Mlle. Clairon and Mlle. Dumesnil in the
preceding century, were long-drawn-out affairs. For Rachel
there simply was no worthy rival in France; she towered above
her colleagues, male and female, and was naturally resented by
the other members of the Comédie Française. Her absences, her
control of the management, her enormous financial success, all
made her enemies as well.

Eventually a reversal had to come; so much plotting by her,
against her, so much straining after success and gain could not
continue. As in a well-made play by Scribe, the woman who was
the villain in so many people's books had to get her deserts.

When Rachel returned from Russia in Spring 1854, her public
at home had two reasons to resent her: except for an Imperial
command performance, she had not acted in Paris for a whole
year; and she had continued to act and triumph in Moscow even
after the outbreak of war between France and Russia.

Rachel returned exhausted to find the one human being she
had consistently loved, her younger sister Rebecca, near death.
Rachel rushed to Pau in the south of France where Rebecca was
dying of consumption, rushed back to fulfill some obligations,
and was not present during her sister's final hours. She was un-

nerved by overwork, by Rebecca's death, by thoughts of her own precarious health, her hectic concern for the future of her two children. Her best friends, Janin among them, could not help her. Her increasingly nervous state deepened gratuitous enmities, none more unnecessary than that of her old teacher Samson. After Rebecca's death, Samson had at first declined Michel Lévy's request to speak at her funeral. He was tired of the Félix family. But at the side of her grave he was moved, either by genuine feeling or by a sense of propriety, to give a short speech, talking about Rebecca in the name of her colleagues at the Comédie, and omitting Rachel's name entirely. Shortly thereafter Rachel refused to act with him in *Lady Tartuffe*, "with a man who had calumniated her sister Rebecca at her grave." That was the final break between teacher and pupil. Only after her death Samson expressed his sorrow, and his desire to speak at her funeral. That time M. Félix, the father, had the final revenge. He forbade it.

Then there was the affair of Legouvé's *Medée*, whose beginning had antedated Rachel's departure for Russia. Originally she had demanded a new play from Legouvé, who had, with Scribe, written her last major success, *Adrienne Lecouvreur*. At the first reading of *Medée* before the Reading Committee of the Comédie she showed her displeasure and managed to have it turned down. Later she accepted the role, though with great misgivings. Rehearsals started on September 2, 1853, but were broken off and not resumed. When Legouvé received a note from Rachel informing him of her impending tour of Russia, he tried to see her. First he was told that she was not home, then that she was ill, but he finally managed to catch her during a performance of *Polyeucte*. He asked her point blank if she would, yes or no, resume the rehearsals, got an equally abrupt "no" as an answer, and the war was on. Even now Rachel fluctuated. On October 5, Rachel's secretary wrote to Legouvé that she would play *Medée* in May after her return. Rachel, in turn, wrote to him from Warsaw on March 17, 1854, that she would not play it because she would (again) resign from the Comédie, an action she did not carry out. On April 9, she decided to do *Medée* after all, to oblige Legouvé. Rebecca died on June 10, and Rachel in her emotional stress again refused to act in the play. Two things are clear: that no one, even a man less proud than Legouvé, would have put up with all these changes, and that Rachel, usually calm and self-controlled in matters of repertoire and acting, was losing her nerve more and more.

Medée was never performed at the Comédie, but that was not the end of its history. Rachel seemed to add insult to injury with the two new plays she did perform in that time, her last new creations. The first, *Rosemonde*, a long one-act by Latour-Saint-Ybars, added insult because it was a poor, very violent play; it presented two poisonings and one murder, all in less than an hour. At the end Rachel had to drink her death potion from a cup made of the skull of her father, as punishment for her adultery. (The violent nature of the plot of *Medée* had been Rachel's main excuse for rejecting it.) The second play of that final period was *La Czarine* by Scribe, a poor, hastily contrived work intended for a triumphant return to Russia that never took place.

As 1855 continued, an ailing, tense, unhappy Rachel was feverishly planning tours and successes, further absences from Paris where she felt less and less happy in her work and her life. America was beginning to appear as the final aim, the crowning achievement, financial and otherwise. But Nemesis was waiting in the wings.

Schiller's *Maria Stuart* contains as its climactic scene a meeting between the two rival queens, Elizabeth of England and her prisoner, Mary of Scotland. In that meeting Mary is the moral victor, but Elizabeth the actual one; she signs Mary's death warrant soon after. Schiller's meeting is unhistorical; the two queens never met in reality. The rival queens of the stage did meet: Rachel and Ristori confronted each other in 1855, Bernhardt and Duse in 1897. These were the battles at the summit, one for each generation, and both in Paris. For Rachel it was the last gladiatorial experience, and it was not a victory.

Adelaide Ristori was only a year younger than Rachel, but when their paths crossed Rachel was about to embark on her last tour. For Ristori the encounter meant the beginning of her international career. The two never met except to observe each other's performances, and that only twice. Ristori wisely declined to act in French, though the Emperor Napoleon III asked her to stay in Paris when Rachel left for America, and Rachel never returned to the stage after that journey.

Rachel and Ristori present the most vivid contrast. The one was small, spare, almost thin, the other, more in tune with the ideal of beauty of the time, was tall and well, even amply proportioned. She had a finely formed head, luxuriant brown hair, an open intelligent brow, and a slender, elegant neck. She had a Roman nose, slightly aquiline, and a voice of unusual range over which she had perfect control.

In their background the two actresses could not have been more different either. Rachel was an outsider to the world in which she moved, particularly the tradition of the French theater. Ristori, on the other hand, was a child of a theatrical family in Venetia, the center of the Italian acting tradition, the country of the *commedia dell' arte*, of Goldoni and Gozzi.

Adelaide Ristori was born on January 29, 1822, at Cividale in the northwest of Venetia; her father Antonio Ristori and her mother Maddalena Pomatelli were both members of Caviechi's wandering troupe of actors. At the age of three months she served as a stage property for the first time in a farce called *The New Year's Gift*; at four she was a regular member of the company; at ten she had small speaking parts, and at fifteen she ventured as far as Francesca da Rimini. All that was not unusual for her time and background. Her father, aware of her talent and appeal, was wise enough not to strain her. Instead of letting her play major roles with a minor company, he procured her an engagement as an ingenue with one of the foremost companies of Italy—the Royal Sardinian. The company was based in Turin, the capital of the Kingdom of Sardinia, for part of the year. For the rest it traveled from city to city, like most of the numerous other theatrical organizations of Italy. At little more than eighteen years of age Ristori became herself the *diva assoluta* of the company and by 1840 she was well on the way to becoming the foremost actress of Italy.

Ristori's very long life, in spite of her extraordinary professional successes, was not very unusual. She was quite unlike Rachel in that respect as well. She had no love affairs, and led as quiet, well-organized and moral an existence as the position of the world's foremost actress—she was that undoubtedly from about 1855 to 1875—would permit. Only one story related to her private life stands out. It compensates, however, for the absence of spice or spite in the rest of it.

In 1846 she was playing in Rome at the Teatro Capranica, which was owned by a noble family, that of the Marchese Capranica del Grillo. The Marchese's young son, Giuliano, fell in love with the famous actress, then twenty-four years old, and wanted to marry her. His father of course forbade him to marry so far beneath his rank and arranged that Giuliano should be forbidden to leave the Papal States, then one of the several independent countries of the Italian peninsula. He knew that Ristori would soon have to go to Florence in Tuscany, a small neighboring country, for some performances. But she arranged to interrupt her stay in Florence, hurry secretly to the port city of Leghorn, and sail to Civita Vecchia, a port in Papal territory. There the two lovers met clandestinely. The Marquese heard of this meeting and at once contrived to spoil the brief *tête-à-tête* by having his son sent on an official mission to Cesena, at the other end of the Papal States. But he had not counted on the persistence of his son and the endurance of the actress. Across the Apennine mountain range, on the wretched Papal roads, the two made the journey together by coach and on horseback, as far as they could go, before she had to return to Florence. On the evening before their final parting, they arrived at a small village; there they entered the church and in the presence of Adelaide's father and several witnesses, they swore eternal fealty to each other, like the lovers in Manzoni's novel *I Promessi Sposi*.

In the province of Romagna, where they were at that point, such an action constituted a legal bond of marriage. The two had to separate the next morning, but Giuliano, in disguise and with a false passport, soon managed to leave the Papal States and join his bride in Florence, surprising her there in the evening as she was coming off stage at the theater. By now several others, including Giuliano's mother, were taking his side, a reconciliation with the old Marchese was arranged, and the marriage was properly celebrated in 1847. Before leaving the Marchese Giuliano—he will not function in this narrative again—one report ought to be added to bring this story down from the clouds: During Ristori's stay in Paris in 1855, she once dined with a large company at the house of the composer Halévy. Delacroix, who was present, reported in his diary on June 17: "Ristori is a large woman with a cold expression: one would never think that she has her kind of talent. Her little husband looks as if he were her oldest son. He is a marquis or a Roman prince."

One condition of the reconciliation in 1847 had been that Ristori promised to withdraw from the stage, but that did not last. In 1848 the plight of a former friend, a theatrical manager imprisoned for debt, moved her to appear in a benefit performance. She was frenetically received by the audience. More important to her, perhaps, her father-in-law saw her, and as a consequence finally received her fully into his family. From that time onwards she acted again, to have perhaps the most extensive career of any actor or actress until her time.

Italy in the 1840's and 1850's was, in Lamartine's phrase, the Land of the Dead. More obviously, it was a deeply divided country. After the defeat of Napoleon, the Congress of Vienna had restored the old petty states of the eighteenth century which the French Revolution had eliminated. Austria dominated the north and center, and the Papal States separated them from the Bourbon Kingdom of the Two Sicilies in the southern third of the country. Only Piedmont and Savoy in the northwest, united with the Island of Sardinia into the kingdom of that name, en-

joyed a certain amount of independence as a buffer state between the Austrian Empire and France.

The granddukes, dukes and princes intrigued against each
other, against unification, against anything that might lead to
change. Stendhal portrayed them in *La Chartreuse de Parme*.
The *risorgimento*, the movement for the unification of a country
that had not been one nation since antiquity, expressed itself in
abortive revolts and revolutions. The movements were hampered
not only by Austrian arms and by dissension among the revolutionaries, but by the deeply entrenched sectionalism of the peninsula which often led one city or "country" to stand idly by
while its neighbor was being crushed. The Carbonari, a society
of masonic inclinations, organized into secret cells and beset with
elaborate rituals, led a rebellion in Naples in 1829 and in the
Papal States in 1830–1831, both without success. In that 1831
rebellion in the Romagna, the northernmost Papal province, one
of the Carbonari who fought for Italian freedom was Prince
Louis Napoleon, the twenty-three-year-old nephew of the dead
Emperor. When the neighboring Duke of Modena, who had at
first collaborated with the uprising, betrayed it, the affair collapsed and the prince barely escaped imprisonment and death.
He did not forget the experience.

In the 1830's and 1840's all the revolts were local; none were
nationwide or even coordinated. In the year of revolutions,
1848, most of Italy rose for the first time, but the rebellions
were still uncoordinated and failed everywhere.

Repression was better organized after 1849. Only the King of
Sardinia, Victor Emanuel, could remain relatively liberal, protected by his powerful neighbor France, whose Prince-President
was the former Carbonaro Louis Napoleon. For the rest of the
peninsula the next ten years until the coming of unification and
independence in 1859–1860 were harder than ever. The rulers,
native and foreign, used every means available to stamp out national resistance: hangings, floggings, large-scale imprisonments.
Censorship was rampant, and Ristori's memoirs contain a number of examples of the workings of the official mind in the Aus-

trian provinces and particularly in the Papal States. New plays
were virtually impossible, and the old were heavily censored.

What remained of Italian art was being wrecked much more
than the public morals or national feelings: Verdi, the greatest
Italian operatic composer, had to suffer the particular suspicions
of the ruling powers because his name was used as a battle cry
of the nationalist movement; it comprises the first letters of Vittorio Emanuele Re d'Italia, referring to the King of Sardinia,
who was a rallying point for unification. Ristori herself was a
similar rallying point for patriotic fervor because she was the
foremost actress of Italy. Her pre-eminent position was due in
turn not only to her talent; but to the fact that any *one* person,
idea, or object that was common to all of Italy did through its
very existence contribute to the desired sense of national unity.

In 1852 the King of Sardinia, Victor Emanuel, appointed
Count Camillo Cavour as his prime minister. Cavour realized
that Italy could not achieve unification and independence
through her efforts alone. She needed allies. The most obvious
possible ally was her neighbor France, whose Prince-President,
now the Emperor Napoleon III, was bound emotionally at least
to support the unification of Italy. Cavour's task was to link that
emotional support to the realistic aims and policies of Sardinia.

Cavour's first tangible action in this design was Sardinia's par-
ticipation in the Crimean War. In spite of Austrian protests,
Sardinia joined Britain and France in the war against Russia
which started in 1854. The Sardinian contingent was large for
a small country, more than 15,000 men, and well publicized;
Great Britain and France were obliged to feel a sense of gratitude. More important, Sardinia had drawn attention to herself
and broken the isolation of Italy as a backwater dependency of
Austria. It was up to Cavour to use whatever means he had to
keep alive that interest in his small country, and to gain the
notice of public opinion in France, especially in Paris.

As a member of the Turin aristocracy, Cavour spoke French
better than Italian. He was aware of the importance of cultural
elements in cementing political ties, especially in the case of a

country like France. French culture had spread across the world; French actors and actresses, Rachel above all, had carried the theatrical life of France through all of civilized Europe. Italians could reflect that Italy had not always been a backwater. Her art, her music, her theater had led Europe in times past. For two centuries the actors of the *commedia dell' arte* had enjoyed an unrivaled reputation throughtout Central and Western Europe. Moreover, it was 1855, and the eyes of the world were on Paris as seldom before. It was the year of the second international exposition, carrying on the tradition of the new age of progress which Queen Victoria and her Prince Consort had inaugurated at the Crystal Palace four years before.

Why should Sardinia not try to draw attention to herself, and to Italy, on that occasion? Ristori reports in her memoirs that, by 1855, she was ready to retire from the stage because she felt so constrained in her activities by the various governments of the peninsula. Then, she says, "like a flash of lightning, the bold project of an artistic tour of France sprang from the bottom of my heart. . . . My object was to vindicate abroad the true artistic genius of the Italian stage, and to show that Italy is not only the 'Land of the Dead.' "

The patriotic project for which Ristori takes credit fitted perfectly with the designs of Count Cavour, her friend and a frequent visitor to the green room at Ristori's performances. On a later occasion, in 1861, he was to write to her: "Do use that authority of yours for the benefit of your country, and I will not only applaud in you the first actress of Europe, but also the most efficacious cooperator of our diplomatic negotiations." In 1855, however, Ristori was the first actress of Italy, not of Europe. Fiorentino, an Italian and a critic of importance in Paris, saw the situation correctly: "Whatever happens in Italy stays in Italy, whatever happens in Germany does not penetrate beyond Germany; but if you are known in Paris, you will instantly be known everywhere." Paris took its eminence for granted and rather resented that Rachel thought other places worthy of conquest. Ristori, on the other hand, came with the fervent best wishes of her countrymen, hoping to help them, and to rise to further glory at the same time. Like any challenger, she had less to lose than her opponent.

In April of 1855 the Sardinian contingent left for the war in the Crimea. In May the Royal Sardinian Company went from Turin to Paris.

On May 15, 1855, the French Emperor, with Queen Victoria as his guest, opened the International Exposition. Among its material and cultural manifestations of progress it contained the first major inter-European exposition of contemporary art. It also was planned to present two foreign theatrical companies, one English and the other Italian, performing on alternate nights at the Salle Ventadour. The English company failed immediately and the Italians helped financially to enable it to return home. Once that was done the Italians had the theater to themselves, and the undivided attention of whatever public they might attract. Initially that did not amount to very much; the French, secure in their cultural omnipotence, were unlikely to look too carefully at a company doing inferior plays in a foreign language. The Royal Sardinian Company opened its season on May 22, with Silvio Pellico's *Francesca da Rimini*, in which Ristori and her leading man, Ernesto Rossi, played the main roles. In spite of the general interest in the new gallant little ally Sardinia, most of the early paying customers at the Salle Ventadour seem to have been Italians; Paris contained a large number of political exiles from the various European revolutions. The opening on May 22 therefore turned into a patriotic event that left the French portion of the audience aside. An ode to Italy was performed, also written by Pellico, who had at one time been a political prisoner in Austria.

The acting company was very small, partly because the casts of Italian plays are smaller than those of the French. Alfieri's tragedies, for example, do not, in contrast to Racine's, contain those male and female confidants that are used as sounding boards by the main characters. The smallness of cast accentuated the fact that the Salle Ventadour, or Théâtre Italien, was too large for them, and more suited to Italian opera, which was its usual fare. They seemed lost on that large stage, in that large city.

Then came the change and, like a well-made play, the change was brought about by the same man who prided himself on having "created" Rachel: Jules Janin, the most influential critic in Paris. In September 1838 he had come, seen Rachel, and made possible her conquest of Paris. In 1855, he came, saw Ristori, and published a panegyric on May 27, which sent the French audience in masses to the Salle Ventadour: "In the third act, at a moment when we did not expect more than a *succès d'estime*, the whole theater came alive with a start, amazed at the miracle. Everyone listened, looked, shed tears, admired. I have rarely seen public enthusiasm manifest itself more unexpectedly and suddenly." The wall between the audience and the actress, erected by the unfamiliar style and language, suddenly fell; suddenly all was understood, every silence, every word, gesture, glance. At one moment she was a foreigner whom the well-brought-up public listened to out of a sense of politeness; and then, in one scene, the great love scene between Paolo and Francesca, she suddenly was a great artist followed by everyone.

That was not all. Janin not only "created" Ristori with his considerable eloquence; he also created the combat between her and Rachel, right away, in this first, enthusiastic review. "La Ristori! We cannot compare her here to anyone. What good, indeed, would be a comparison impossible to make. We possessed of late an incomparable tragic actress. Italy has one, and that is why one must not compare the one with the other," whereupon he immediately compares them at length and in great detail. The comparison is subtle, and in many ways just. Its considerable eloquence works against Rachel. The phrase, "we possessed of late an incomparable tragic actress" is the key to his attitude. The scent of blood drew audiences in large numbers to see the challenger.

Why did Janin do it? One must say at once that his excellent taste had in fact led him to an impressive actress. Ristori, as her

later career was to show, aroused the enthusiasm of two generations of playgoers all over the world. But that does not account
for the immediate enthusiasm he displayed, and his immediate
detailed comparison which pitted Ristori against Rachel as the
challenger for the championship. It also does not account for
the role he played in the maneuvers of May and June, 1855, in
which he succeeded in keeping the two actresses apart and in
pouring oil on the fire, constantly pretending that it was water.

He is not likely to have been annoyed with Rachel; no cause
for it is known. True, Janin was terribly vain and had to be
flattered and cajoled, even by Rachel. She had taken his measure
as an antagonist as early as 1838, in the case of *Bajazet;* she had
evidently never forgotten it, and had remained his admiring
friend. Only a few months before, after Rebecca's death, he had
written her a charming and friendly letter, exhorting her to return to work, reminding her how much she meant both to her
children and her art, and telling her that she was the great hope
of the serious drama.

If it was not pique, only one possibility remains: Janin was as
consummate an artist in his field as Rachel in hers. The key to
his personality may be in a remark the Goncourt brothers report
of him: "Do you know why I have lasted twenty years? Because
I have changed my opinion every two weeks." Every two weeks,
when his article in the *Journal des Débats* appeared, eagerly
awaited or feared, he would not necessarily change his mind,
but he would play off his very canny and accurate estimation
of the public temper against his critical judgment. If Ristori had
been a mediocrity, he would surely have said nothing and bided
his time. But she was good, and could therefore be used to open
a valve that would release the pent-up feelings of a public eager
to see Rachel challenged at last after more than sixteen years of
absolute pre-eminence, a public antagonized by her public and
private behavior, and above all by her evident disregard of the
hub of the universe, Paris. It is this last, perhaps, that weighed
most heavily. The public resented her long travels abroad, her
manifest unwillingness to give more performances at the Comé-

die than were absolutely necessary, and above all, her impending departure for America. The public wanted to be cajoled and flattered; she did not obey. Now, led by the infallible Janin, it was to have its revenge.

On Janin's signal, all the resentment burst forth. Dumas *père*, whom Rachel had slighted both as a playwright and a lover, was the first; his first remark was the more cutting because it seemed so quiet: "Last night I was at the performance of *Francesca da Rimini* at the Salle Ventadour. I looked around the theater, but did not see Rachel. I beg her to go and see how the death scene is performed." Emboldened by the general outcry which was developing, he wrote a short time later: "Don't bother us with the mortal terrors of Mlle. Rachel's departure. What does it matter if Mlle. Rachel goes or if Mlle. Rachel stays, if one sells or does not sell her leaves of absence! Like Ingres at the International Exposition, she has the hall all to herself—the hall of the dead; may she rest there." Again, pique was not the only cause for his action. As an admirer of Italy and Italian culture, an extensive traveler in that country, and a writer of travel books, he had a better knowledge of Italian drama and acting than most, a clearer appreciation of Ristori, and a vested interest in propagating Italy. He was very interested in opera, the usual fare of the Salle Ventadour, and a friend of many of the singers. His paper *Le Mousquetaire* had published articles about Ristori before her arrival.

Dr. Véron, whose anger was long past, recognized what was being done: "Let us admit that we are all harnessed to the triumphal chariot of Ristori only to crush poor Rachel." In the quiet of their private journals, some observers expressed their doubts. Edmond Got wrote of Ristori's opening night, May 22, 1855: "A talented artist, who seems to compose her roles with intelligence and a sure hand, but angular and almost always overemphatic." Delacroix wrote some weeks later: "Went to see *Myrrha* with my cousin. That Ristori is really very talented; but how tedious these plays are!"

Rachel's repertoire consisted of the main plays of the French classical period, and a few contemporary plays, the majority of which were in the classical tradition; the only play not originally French, Schiller's *Maria Stuart*, had been thoroughly reworked in the French tradition by Lebrun. Ristori, on the other hand, had no native dramatic tradition of similar scope and excellence to give her a repertoire. The serious Italian drama was not as important, and its tradition not nearly as ingrained in the theater as the French. This was due in part to the importance of opera, the dominance of music over the spoken word, and in part to the general cultural stagnation of eighteenth- and nineteenth-century Italy. Metastasio, one of the most important dramatic talents of eighteenth-century Italy, wrote opera libretti in preference to plays, and, like many of his talented countrymen, spent much of his time away from home. Count Vittorio Alfieri, Italy's main writer of classical tragedies, who lived in the second half of the eighteenth century, looked for his examples to the French rather than to the Greco-Roman or Renaissance traditions of his own country.

Apart from Alfieri Italian serious drama was slim indeed. Niccolini's and Manzoni's patriotic historical plays on the romantic pattern had little appeal outside Italy. Ristori had to go outside her own country to find most of her plays, and part of her international appeal, like that of Duse later on, was based on her international repertoire.

Throughout the world Ristori was to be known as a great tragic and dramatic actress; in Italy her fame rested as much, or more, on her performance in eighteenth-century comedies, in particular the works of Goldoni. Like Ristori, Goldoni was a Venetian, and wrote most of his comedies for Venetian acting companies. In 1762 he went to Paris where he remained for the last twenty years of his life, and where he wrote his later plays in French. His comedies were attempts to blend the style of Molière with that of the older Italian Comedy. The Goldoni tradition and the Italian Comedy, or *commedia dell' arte*, form the native background of Ristori's acting.

The *commedia dell' arte* is not a fully composed or written play. Its basis is a scenario, or plot outline, on which the actors improvise the actual dialogue; it is fast and funny and contains a lot of physical activity and stage business with or without speeches. Its roots go back to the *atellanae*, the pantomimes of ancient Rome. Rome, the most polyglot city of antiquity, needed entertainment without words for the lower classes who spoke various languages. Renaissance Italy also was divided linguistically as well as politically; the only drama that could have wide popular appeal throughout the peninsula had to be one that relied on the visual element more than the verbal and that used easily understood stock characters like Harlequin and Columbine who survive as types until today. Those aspects also made it particularly suitable for export. The *commedia dell' arte* spread throughout Europe as far as England and Russia. Its beginnings were in the sixteenth century, and its heyday in the seventeenth around the time of Molière; after that it became too fixed in its ways. Goldoni transformed it from an impromptu system relying on stock situations and characters into fully written comedy whose characters, though based on the old stock types, display considerable degrees of individuality.

The great and enduring appeal of the *commedia dell' arte* rested in the accomplishments of acting companies, some of whom became famous throughout Europe. A system wherein the dialogue is generally arranged but not written down needs a group of actors very much attuned to each other; it does not allow a star system. It needs a small group of men and women, quick witted, intelligent, ready to switch from one joke to another, to insert new jokes or pantomimes whenever the audience became restless. The actors of the Italian comedy had to be finely attuned to each other and to their audiences.

Venice provided the best training ground for them for two centuries, until the time of Goldoni. Life in Venice itself had its theatrical qualities. The city with its canals, its black gondolas, its great naval establishments, its elaborate government ritual, and its wide economic and colonial connections was a fitting backdrop for a kind of life that sought out display rather than quiet living. As Venetian power declined through the seventeenth and eighteenth centuries the display became more pompous, as if the oligarchy wanted to assure itself of its continued vitality. Some of the most magnificent displays came in the last years before Napoleon put a sudden end to the Republic in 1799, such as in the reception for the Emperor Joseph II in 1769, and for Pope Pius VI in 1782, upon his return from Vienna.

The same passion for display pervaded the lives of the ordinary people. Travelers remarked on the great skill of the *ciarlatani*, the drug sellers of Venice from whom the term charlatan is derived. Thomas Coryat in his *Crudities* gives a description of them: ". . . they would tell their tales with such admirable volubility and plausible grace, even extempore, and seasoned with that singular variety of elegant jests and witty conceits, that they did often strike great admiration into strangers that never heard them before." Ben Jonson has his Volpone impersonate such a seller of drugs. They also served as characters in Italian plays and operas such as Dulcamare in Donizetti's *L'Elisir d'Amore*. Their impromptu displays of wit and verbal skill were related to the vivacious, skillful acting of the *commedia dell' arte*.

Theaters everywhere were much more lively places in the eighteenth and nineteenth centuries than they are in the twentieth, but the consistent rowdiness of Venice, more even than that of the other Italian cities, was known and feared. The Venice of Ristori's youth was no longer the Venice of Goldoni and his great enemy, Count Carlo Gozzi; it had sunk to the level of an Austrian provincial capital, a part of the Land of the Dead, but the audience was not dead. Ristori repeatedly remarked what great pleasure and satisfaction it was to her to be greeted, not with applause, but with a very flattering silence, upon her entry on the stage.

When Hamlet exhorts the players to hold, as it were, a mirror up to nature, the nature he had in mind would most likely not seem natural in the twentieth century. The concept of naturalness, of natural acting, differs from age to age. The realistic drama of the twentieth century demands a semblance of subdued everyday behavior: The common man mumbles and gropes his way through a series of believable situations. In the typical nineteenth-century play, the characters, hardly ever common, meet up against situations most men and women mercifully never encounter in their lives: conscious choices of life and death; wild irrepressible urges leading to disaster. The reactions required of the actor may be natural—but it is the naturalness of man under extreme stress, in the throes of agony. That realm of nature was Ristori's. She was at her best in "conflicts of the impassioned heart and amidst the amorous physical passions. She could express, in absolute perfection, the fury of a woman scorned. Her manifestations of ferocity, the wild anguish of remorse, and the delirium of desolation were tremendous . . ." Her "colored naturalness," as she called it, led her to heighten these effects as much as she could. "Who has not felt his blood run cold" one English critic asked regarding her Medea, "at the hissing tones of concentrated rage, as she moves across the stage with the stealthy, sidling gait of a hyena . . . ?"

For many critics, especially the French, that naturalism of the climactic moment went too far. Delacroix recorded in his journal in 1856 that "Madame Ristori in *Pia* last year rendered the agony of man in a very true but very repulsive manner." Others found that in *Mirra,* for example, she presented the spectacle of a woman possessed, and that the play was full of her shrieks, convulsions, spasms, terror, and her transports of agony or joy.

Here lay her great contrast to Rachel. Rachel had rejected Legouvé's *Medée* largely because of the amount of physical action it would have involved: "I see," she wrote, "that the part is full of rapid and violent movements; I have to rush to my children, I have to lift them up, to carry them off the stage, to contend for them with the people. This external vivacity is not my style. Whatever may be expressed by physiognomy, by attitude, by sober and measured gesture—that I can command; but where broad and energetic pantomime begins, there my talent of execution ends."

Ristori's enemies criticized her for her excessive physical activity, her outbursts, her search for stunning effects. Rachel's enemies in 1855, on the other hand, called her an animated statue, a Greek sculpture; the fire of her eye, the modulation of her voice, the majesty and grace of her movements, and her great tragic outbursts, though impressive, were all too much regulated by her profound intelligence; they were, in other words, too conscious and too accomplished. They found that her women were goddesses and demons, not humans, and that passion and emotion were absent except as a general representation of passion and emotion. To these critics Ristori represented nature, human life, motion and emotion, in contrast to academic art.

In this latter view Ristori herself concurred, not unnaturally:

> We were following two totally opposite ways [she wrote]; we had two different manners of expression. She could inflame an audience with her outbursts, though academic, so beautiful was her diction, so stately her acting. In the most passionate situations, her expressions, her poses, everything was regulated by the rules of the traditional French school; nevertheless the power of her voice, the fascination of her looks, were such that one had to admire and applaud her.
>
> We Italians, in playing tragedy, do not admit that in culminating points of passion, the body should remain in repose; and in fact, when one is struck either with a sudden grief or joy, is it not a natural instinct to carry one's hands to the head? Well then, in the Italian school, we maintain that one of the principal objects in reciting is to portray life and reality, what nature shows us.

The Paris critics who came to judge Rachel with severity during Ristori's stay forgot several things: They forgot what her repertoire contained, and what parts, in contrast, Ristori acted. Camille, Phèdre, Hermione, the basic characters of Rachel's repertoire, were not ordinary anguished or joyful humans; they had not been intended as such, and they could not be acted as such. They forgot that Rachel had been the one who had introduced a hitherto unheard-of naturalness into these characters,

The Astor Place Riot; from a contemporary lithograph

Rachel as Hermione in *Andromaque*, about 1839-1840

Rachel as Roxane in *Bajazet*, about 1839-1840

Count Alexandre Colonna-
Walewski

Rachel as Phèdre, from a helio-
graph

Ristori as Lucrezia Borgia, with Enordo Majeroni as the Duke of Ferrara

The Marchese Capranica del Grillo and his family

Ristori as Lady Macbeth in the 1870's

Ristori as Marie Antoinette in Giacometti's play, about 1875

Ristori as Queen Elizabeth in Giacometti's play, probably during her last American tour, 1884-1885

and had transformed Racine's and Corneille's tragedies from lyrical poems, chanted musically, to dramatic masterpieces. She alone had known how to do that, how far to go in the transformation without doing violence to these poetic plays.

In one respect the critics were not unjust. The Rachel of 1855 was not the Rachel of fifteen years before. Though of the same age as Ristori, her stage life was behind her, while Ristori's was only at its beginning. Rachel had made great innovations in her first few years, and then carried them to an admiring world. Over the years they had coarsened and become, at times, almost routine, a superb routine, but a routine nevertheless. Now, in 1855, Rachel was exhausted both physically and emotionally. By the time Ristori appeared on the scene, the contest between them was no longer equal.

Rachel's season at the Comédie Française had ended before Ristori's arrival. She was ill, and involved in the hectic preparation for her American tour. It is unlikely that she paid any attention to the Italians at the Salle Ventadour until Janin's paean to the new star had been published. Thereafter the maneuvers by her friends and enemies, including Janin and Dumas, heightened the combat. In the end, when she could not ignore the situation any longer, Rachel took action, but by then it was too late.

Ristori, on her part, pretended to an ingenuousness that seems very artificial. Paris, it was true, was the cultural capital of the world and Rachel its most eminent actress, but Ristori, at thirty-three the leading actress of Italy, was not a young ingenue coming to a big city for the first time. The picture she painted in her autobiography thirty years later, of sitting in the Café Véron on the evening of her arrival, frightened by the crowd, the spectacle and the babble of foreign voices, is a little too neat to be true. (And why the Café Véron, that name of all names?)

Before beginning her performances, Ristori presented a letter of introduction to Jules Janin and requested him to arrange a meeting between her and Rachel. Ristori intended to write to her and ask for permission to visit her in the country. Janin

persuaded her not to do so; Rachel would in any case be in town
soon, he said; and besides, as Ristori tells it:

> With a nervous and impressionable character like that of
> Madame Rachel, such a step from me might have caused the
> opposite of my desired purpose. Writing her without the for-
> mality of an introduction, was almost dealing with her as an
> equal, and she had good reason to consider herself in an excep-
> tionally privileged position. It was like trying to teach her a
> lesson in manners, what the laws of hospitality would have sug-
> gested to the mistress of the house to do for a stranger, who was
> about to cross her threshold.

One wonders what Janin had in mind. He may have wanted
to spare Rachel a visit from a stranger; he knew how nervous
and preoccupied she was. He may have wanted to save Ristori
the embarrassment of being refused admittance, as many had
been. But in the light of his reception accorded to the Italian
actress in the *Journal des Débats* one cannot help thinking that
he saw at least the possibility of a major challenge and wanted
to prevent premature fraternization. The passage is also interesting with regard to Ristori herself, who recorded it much later.
It reveals the ambivalence of the challenger who feels herself
to be in the position of an inferior, and at the same time con-
siders herself an equal. In any case, Ristori said, "I allowed myself to be convinced by those arguments though they seemed to
be rather subtle and puerile, and later in my life, I repented my
docility."

Ristori records sarcastically that most critics initially displayed
great timidity in praising her, which she attributes to the awe
in which Rachel was held. Here she was wrong on two counts:
First, the critics were quite friendly, though not overly interested; and second Rachel, in spite of her eminence, had no such
dictatorial powers over the press. Ristori also insinuates the idea
that national rivalry played its part in the supposedly unfavor-
able reviews. Once more her memory was at fault: the critics,
secure in their knowledge of French superiority over the Italians,

never injected nationalism into their reviews. Ristori creates the idea of a great, collective, antagonistic force in the reader's mind, mostly to emphasize the change which came later, and to increase the size of her victory.

Some of the devotees of Rachel timidly granted that I had facility in tragedy and agreed that I possessed, to a greater extent than Rachel, flexibility of voice, but claimed that I lacked the necessary vigor to interpret properly violent passions. They affirmed that I lacked plastic classicism of movements in my poses, the carriage of a goddess, which the great Rachel possessed as she crossed the stage wrapped in the *peplum*.

I might have bowed my head under those judgments and acknowledged that nature had denied me those gifts, which the sympathy, indulgence and loving interest of my countrymen had recognized in me, but a verdict, so quickly pronounced, was somewhat suspicious. To mention energy, strength, and violence in connection with the sweet and pathetic character of Francesca [Francesca da Rimini, her first role in Paris], was nonsense. It revealed their deliberate intentions of opposing me at any cost and of prejudicing the public at once, without giving time to reflect or compare, or even the chance to express literally its own opinion. That verdict might have excited my pride, rather than have awakened in me the honest sentiment of modesty, but pride was not indeed my failing. Those precocious criticisms vexed me, because they showed me that my appearance upon the French stage was, by some people, ill-interpreted.

Whenever I had a chance, I told both my most intimate friends and most severe critics, that I never had the presumption to come to Paris for the purpose of competing with their own sublime actress. My object was more modest and more generous. I only wished to show that in Italy also, dramatic art . . . was still alive and considered a passionate and superior cult.

Ristori therefore went about telling everyone that she had not come to challenge Rachel's eminence, no, not at all, and hinted that the enmity of the unreasoning press was causing her great concern. In the earlier reviews of the Italian company in

1855, some of the critics noted deficiencies in Ristori's acting, by which in their slightly myopic way they meant differences from the French manner, especially that of Rachel. When Janin eventually made his comparison in the *Journal des Débats* he noted the differences as differences, not as deficiencies.

The initial hesitation of the critics was also due to the foreign language and style. Got recorded on July 15:

> How many Frenchmen know enough Italian, or English for that matter, to understand a play in these languages which have neither the same tactics nor the same rhythm as ours? It is funny at times to see [people in] the orchestra and the boxes follow a printed translation with great pains, and watch for the claque to applaud the great moments, pretending all the while that they understood.

After *Francesca*, Ristori performed two Goldoni plays on May 26, without attracting much notice. Then, on the 27th came Janin's panegyric, and on the 28th the first performance of Alfieri's *Mirra*, a tragedy in the classical style and with a subject closely resembling that of *Phèdre*. Mirra is about to be married to Pereus, and the play presents her desperate struggle against her incestuous love for her father, King Cinrias. On the point of marriage she refuses to obey and declares that the furies have taken hold of her; Prince Pereus kills himself off stage, and the desperate parents try to find out why she constantly refuses to marry. In the end she half confesses herself to her father, and stabs herself. Her own death, unlike that of Camille in *Horace*, takes place on stage.

With *Mirra*, Ristori for the first time invited direct comparison with Rachel. *Mirra* was not in a class with *Phèdre*, but the similarity of the plot and the classical form indicated a possible challenge. The reception which Ristori received was out of all proportion to the event, no matter how good the performance may have been. (Ristori admitted that it had not been well rehearsed.) Those who wanted to exalt her at the expense of Rachel now came forward. To Ristori "the entire audience seemed delirious" at the end of the fourth act and the foyer was invaded by celebrated literary authorities. Janin, Legouvé, Scribe, Gautier were there, and Alexandre Dumas publicly kissed her hands and the hem of her cloak. A better list of literary men with grudges against Rachel could hardly be compiled. Edmond Got wrote: "The public has been carried away by Ristori, in obedience to the press, and with the evident intention of teasing Mlle. Rachel who, mad with resentment, goes to America in chase of the dollar."

Dumas wrote in *Le Mousquetaire* on May 31. "Oh! Rachel! Rachel! You who, after having reaped millions in Russia, are going to reap billions in America, come to see *Myrrha*, study it, try to join to the talent which you have, one-quarter of the talents of Mme. Ristori . . ."

Mirra also turned the tide financially. For the first two weeks the public had largely stayed away. Without the idea of a challenge the interest in the Italians had not been too great. When *Mirra* was repeated, the house was filled and remained so until the end of the Italian season in July.

On May 31, when Goldoni's *Il Burberino Benefico* had been scheduled, the news was brought to Ristori that Rachel had suddenly returned to Paris from her villa and would come to see her perform. Ristori felt a double embarrassment: The leading lady in the Goldoni play is overshadowed by the leading man; and Rachel had, unknown to the company, bought a box instead of making herself known, and permitting herself to be a guest. Now Ristori regretted not to have written and invited Rachel.

Rachel recorded no reaction. All one can say is that she came in the company of Prince Napoleon, that she stayed in the back of her box, unwilling to be stared at, and that she left during the ovations at the end of the third act. The audience hailed Ristori irrespective of the role she played, even in a minor comedy. Rachel evidently understood the meaning of the applause. Ernesto Rossi, Ristori's leading man, later told the story that Rachel fled from her box exclaiming, "Cette femme me fait mal" (That woman makes me sick).

Next Ristori undertook Maffei's *Maria Stuarda*, an adaptation of Schiller's *Maria Stuart*. There at last was the open challenge, and the comparison was possible with Lebrun's version of the same play, one of Rachel's most popular works of the modern repertoire. The comparison was made, and was found to be in favor of Ristori. From her point of view the choice was an excellent one. Lebrun's play was thirty-five years old, a watered-down accommodation of the classical proprieties of the day. It had been completely eclipsed by the work of the romantic poets in the 1830's until Rachel had resurrected it. Maffei's Italian version was no such compromise between the classical and the romantic. Schiller's Mary Stuart is a full-blown romantic heroine, beautiful, majestic, gentle except at one climactic moment, and much more sinned against than sinning, and Maffei preserves all her romantic traits. It fitted Ristori's talents perfectly, and was quite likely her favorite play, one of the three or four she performed most often during her entire career.

On June 6 Rachel somewhat precipitously took up the challenge thrown to her, more by her own compatriots than by the Italian actress. She reappeared on the stage of the Comédie Française in the role with which she traditionally began an engagement: Camille in *Horace*. It was not enough to regain her hold. In July she therefore once more, and for the last time in France, performed her greatest roles: *Horace*, *Andromaque*, *Polyeucte*, *Phèdre*, and, finally, *Marie Stuart*. Janin in his book *Rachel et La Tragédie* (in which Ristori's name is never mentioned) reports that she was coldly received at first but that, as always before, she managed to regain her hold on the public. These final performances had a feverish intensity, an almost supernatural quality which was reminiscent of her earliest years. The public returned to acknowledge her as the empress of the stage, it asked her not to leave.

Ristori saw Rachel's Camille on June 6, sitting in a box offered to her by Arsène Houssaye.

As soon as Rachel made her appearances on the stage, I understood the power of her fascination. She looked like a Roman statue! Her majestic carriage, her regal bearing, the fold of her mantle, everything was presented with admirable artistic skill. Perhaps the critics might have taken exception to the stiffness of the folds of her skirt, which were never disarranged. It is easy for me, as a woman, to comprehend the reasons for this. . . . Rachel was very thin and was using every method to conceal it.

Ristori, with the eyes of the audience upon her as much as upon the rival on stage, reports that she paid tribute "to her with my most frantic applause."

In her memoirs Ristori presents herself as a *grande dame* above the battle, but one must have his doubts. She speaks of the attacks against her, but her attacks on Rachel were not without resourcefulness. The two never did exchange words, but some sort of public reconciliation took place. Rachel took the initiative and used the good offices of Mme. Ode, the dressmaker of the Empress Eugénie. The negotiations between them were now conducted as between equals. Ristori refused to visit Rachel, and her suggestion that Rachel should call on her was naturally refused. But she accepted Rachel's offer of a box at the Comédie Française to see her in *Phèdre* on July 20. It was sent to her with a card saying, "To Madame Ristori from her fellow-tragedienne Rachel." Again she was in the public eye, again she applauded, and was very impressed. At the end she sent Rachel "a few lines upon one of my visiting cards." The two never came face to face again.

Dumas encouraged the status of equality conferred on the two actresses when he proposed, in *Le Mousquetaire* of June 20, that they should perform at a benefit at the Opéra, Rachel in *Phèdre* and Ristori in *Mirra,* casting lots who should come first. He added that Ristori was prepared to do it, so that it fell to Rachel to decline. She did not reply.

The battle seemed unending. Ristori announced her last performance in *Mary Stuart* for July 19. Rachel thereupon played it on July 21, and was praised even by Dumas. Ristori therefore performed it once more, on July 24. In the end even old Mlle. Georges got into the act, performing *Cinna* in the hope of sharing in the combat, but her time was long over.

Ristori's success had exceeded all bounds. Scribe sang her praise, Lamartine wrote a poem about her, Janin was in ecstasy, Legouvé offered her his *Medée*, Dumas cooked some of his incomparable macaroni for her in public. (Fifty years later she admitted that it had been so bad that only he could eat it.) The Emperor Napoleon sent her a magnificent bracelet and intimated that she might fall heir to Rachel's place at the Comédie. This she wisely declined, but obtained the promise of three annual seasons in Spring at the Salle Ventadour. At one stroke Ristori had opened the world to Italian acting. At thirty-three, she stood on the threshold of her international career.

Rachel, on the other hand, was at thirty-four close to the end. She had been an international star at twenty. Now, only one world remained for her to conquer: the new one across the Atlantic. On July 27 Rachel left Paris for London, to give what came to be her last week of European performances. After the experiences of the recent months they were a relief. The critics were as generous as ever, the public as enthusiastic. On August 11, 1855, with many doubts and misgivings, she departed from Europe with her father, brother, three sisters and company, to the sound of Auguste Vacquérie's parting remark: "May Rachel succeed in America; may she be crushed under an avalanche of dollars, and may she be at home over there. Let her have Racine, marry him, and may they produce many tragedies—but only in America."

CHAPTER 5 / A New World

O<small>N JUNE</small> 13, 1847, Rachel wrote to her sister Sarah: "I have just received magnificent offers to undertake the same voyage as Mlle. Fanny Elssler has made; and, to tell you frankly as well as confidentially, I am not far from a contract. My health is good at present but it does not leave me without anxiety. You know, my dear Sarah, that this weakness of which I complain more and more is very hard to cure."

That particular contract was never made, but the two connected points raised in this letter remained in Rachel's mind. She had before her the example of the ballerina Fanny Elssler and later, the singer Jenny Lind, both of whom had made large amounts of money in the United States; and she was troubled by her precarious health. Her concern was not so much for herself as for her children. Though she was fiercely attached to her family, she knew that she could trust them to strike their own hard bargains in matters of money. As her children were both illegitimate, she was not entitled to leave them all her money, and she knew that the Félix clan surrounding her would collect the maximum they could get from her inheritance, no matter what she made them promise to do. As she began to feel her health wane more and more, she worked harder and harder to assure her children's future. One must not, however, attribute her incessant and self-destructive struggle for money completely to altruistic motives; the struggle was part of her background, she had been brought up on it, and would most likely not have stopped in any case.

Her attitude toward money led her to one fateful mistake.

According to the *Gazette des Théâtres* of December 29, 1853,
Phineas T. Barnum, the man who had managed Jenny Lind's
tour of America in its first, fabulous stages, had come to France
that autumn to persuade Rachel to undertake a similar tour.
Rachel and Raphael refused. If they were to tour America at all,
they would do so on their own, and not share the profits with
on outsider.

Then came Rachel's overwhelming success in Russia in 1854
and the subsequent death of her sister Rebecca, which moved
her partly because it touched so closely upon a vision of her
own fate; these events finally enabled her father and brother to
persuade her to undertake the American tour. The contract between her and her brother as the manager or producer provided
a munificent reward—200 performances at a salary of 6000 francs
each, or 1,200,000 francs exclusive of benefits and personal expenses. Income in excess of 4,612,000 francs was to be split between her and Raphael. The Russian tour had exceeded their
highest expectations. There was every reason to believe that the
American tour would be even more lucrative. Rachel's million
needs to be compared with the 60,000 francs allotted to her
sisters Sarah and Lia, the 50,000 for Dinah, the fourth sister to
travel with the company, and the 6,000–30,000 for the rest of
the cast. The contract also provided for penalties for nonfulfill-
ment that were so extreme in Rachel's case that the idea cannot
be avoided that father and brother were aware of her bad state
of health and wanted to safeguard themselves against any losses.
She agreed to pay 5000 francs for every performance below the
stipulated total of 200, and pay other damages besides. For the
cast the contract provided for ludicrous regimentation, amount-
ing to a state of virtual serfdom; for example, no member of the
cast was permitted to leave the town in which the company
found itself, even during the summer recess, let alone on free
days, without Raphael's written permission. Raphael never really
enforced these strange provisions, forfeitures, and fines. They
stand rather as a sign of apprehension before this enormous un-

dertaking. For Rachel, scheduled to play every night of performance, it was gilded servitude.

Late in 1854 Raphael traveled to the United States to make the necessary arrangements for the tour. He landed in New York on October 20, and traveled to most of the cities where Rachel was scheduled to appear, as far as New Orleans and Havana. He returned to Paris in January, 1855, satisfied that he had taken all the necessary steps. In June he sent Gustave Naquet to New York to act as advance agent, and to arrange for publicity and ticket sales.

The undertaking itself began ominously. The departure from Liverpool was set for August 11, aboard the paddle wheeler *Pacific* commanded by Captain Ezra Nye. The ship belonged to the same Collins Line as the *Atlantic* which had carried Jenny Lind to America five years before, but there the comparison ends. When Jenny Lind left, tens of thousands had lined the docks and the Merseyside to cheer her and to wish her a good voyage and speedy return. They had sung and waved their hats for hours and had brought tears to Jenny's eyes. When Rachel left there was no one, no one at all. Partly because Rachel was not as great a concern of Liverpudlians as Jenny; mostly, however, because they did not know of the event. Raphael had made no arrangements to let them know and to arouse their interest. It was the first of his sins of omission.

An Atlantic crossing was no pleasure in 1855. The *Pacific* was one of the latest models in that traffic, but she was still far from comfortable. She measured a mere 306 by 50 feet, and even the best cabins, those that had two beds, two chairs and a washstand, were very cramped. There was, of course, no refrigeration; before the voyage was long under way, the butter was turning rancid, the vegetables were wilting, and the meat was rotting in spite of the ice.

The soberness of the voyage was compounded by the death of a passenger one day out of port, and by an unseasonable storm. Rachel did not have Jenny Lind's rugged health. She was seasick and dispirited, and kept to her stateroom. She emerged only for the final dinner on board, gave 500 francs for the crew but refused to entertain or be entertained. Shortly before landing, she wrote to her mother trying to reassure her; even so one can note the sense of ennui and general depression in her lines.

On August 22 the *Pacific* docked in New York. Rachel was relieved to have arrived. If she was shocked at her reception she did not say so. Again the inevitable comparison to Jenny Lind had to be made. The welcome Barnum had arranged for the singer resembled a royal visit rather than a publicity stunt. Thousands came, stood for hours, and watched; carriages, flags, bunting, all were there to enhance the occasion. Not only that, but Barnum had succeeded in working up interest in Jenny to a fever pitch, by carefully controlled releases to the press and by other means of public relations. M. Naquet, Raphael's agent, had done his duty, so he thought, but he could not measure up to Barnum's inventiveness. Moreover, he considered the circus man highly undignified and contented himself with quiet, gravely sedate announcements and modest advertisements. The citizens of New York could buy a biography of Rachel for a quarter, they could see portraits and statuettes in a number of places, they could obtain an engraving of her as Camille for three dollars, a photo as Phèdre for two, and could even, from a certain bakery, get a cake in the form of a statue of Camille, for twenty dollars. M. Naquet had labored diligently. But he was not an American, he did not know how to excite Barnum's compatriots—he most likely did not even know how signally he had failed. Neither Raphael nor Rachel seem to have realized how much could have been done in place of the little impromptu reception at the pier where the *Pacific* had docked. Sarah Bernhardt was never going to make the same mistake.

Actually, the potential interest in Rachel was as great as in Lind, and could have been worked to the same pitch with some local knowledge and some financial generosity. By late September, quite spontaneously, there was Pudding à la Rachel, Rachel's Little Neck Clams, Rachel hams, hairdos, cigars, nightcaps, a Rachel Polka, a Rachel Schottische, and more. These were followed by a biographical play by Boucicault, *The Life of an Actress*, which was given in September in Cincinnati and later performed in Philadelphia, Boston, and New York. Later came a burletta by Boucicault and a satire by John Brougham (*Po-ca-hon-tas; or the Gentle Savage, an Aboriginal, Erratic, Operatic, Semi-Civilized and Demi-Savage Extravaganza*) which attacked some of the less lovable traits of Raphael and his great sister.

Rachel went to the St. Nicholas Hotel, 519 Broadway, one of the best in New York, but disliked it at once. A private residence was therefore found for her at 5 Clinton Place. The rest of the family dispersed to various other hotels and, lastly, the company itself was put up at a secondrate place where Jean Chéry and Léon Beauvallet, both of whom wrote memoirs of the trip, complained bitterly about the food. Beauvallet marveled at the construction of the streets, at the poor sidewalks, at the expense of the hackney coaches, at the tremendous convenience of the large hotels, and in general at the largesse of Americans.

The United States of the early 1850's had twenty-five million inhabitants. Eight cities had more than 50,000 inhabitants. New York, by far the largest, had more than 600,000, almost all of whom lived below Thirty-Seventh Street. One-third of its inhabitants were foreign born, among them 30,000 Frenchmen.

The autumn season was under way at the New York theaters; thirteen were playing, and mostly doing well. Edwin Forrest was performing in town, as well as a French opera singer, Mme. La Grange. The normal prices of admission at the theaters were one dollar for box seats and dress circle, fifty cents for the orchestra, and twenty-five cents for the gallery.

The prices charged for Rachel's performances were considerably higher than any ever charged in New York, and compared to the highest prices in London. They ranged from four to two dollars, with an additional charge of twenty-five cents for reserved seats. This in a time when five dollars was a reasonable weekly wage. Besides that, the Metropolitan Theatre where Rachel was to perform was very large, too large for normal theatrical performances. In his prices, and in the selection of the theater, Raphael had laid himself open to a charge of greed, which was promptly made. On other counts he cannot be similarly accused. The company Rachel had brought was better than most touring groups. Jean Chéry was a *pensionner* of the Comédie Française, his brother Pierre came from the Odéon, as did Léon Beauvallet and most of the others. Two of Rachel's sisters were talented, though the public did not recognize the talent as much as the nepotism. Costumes and scenery were above the usual standards. Raphael had saved where he should not have—in his publicity—and spent when he need not have—on the production itself. The audience came to see Rachel, not Racine.

The income from ticket sales for the opening performance (*Horace*) was 26,000 francs, or more than five thousand dollars, five times the amount taken on a very good night in Paris. But, and there was the rub, it was only a fraction of the gold raked in by Barnum for Jenny Lind—17,964 dollars. Rachel felt cheated, not really understanding why the results were so different. Barnum had arranged that the best tickets for Jenny's first concert be sold by public auction. He had also persuaded a hat-maker named John N. Genin that the purchase of the first ticket to the concert, at fifty or a hundred dollars, would provide good publicity for him. He had suggested the same to the pillmaker Dr. Brandreth. The two were set therefore to bid against each other. As a result the first ticket went to Genin, in the end, for two hundred and fifty dollars. The auction brought in more than $10,000, and regular sales the remaining seven. The auctions of the first Lind tickets in Boston and Provincetown brought more than twice as much each as Mr. Genin paid for his seat. The first ticket for Rachel's first performance was sold at the regular price at the box office. A black market in tickets developed, but Rachel did not profit from that.

On Monday, September 3, 1855, at seven-thirty in the evening, the three thousand seats of the cavernous Metropolitan Theatre were nearly all filled. The curtain rose on Prémary's

Les Droits de l'Homme with Rachel's three sisters in the leading roles. The French portion of the audience enjoyed it, but the rest paid no attention. Then came a thirty-minute intermission in which a rather poor thirty-man orchestra played music from *Lucia di Lammermoor* by Donizetti. Then, at last, came *Horace*. The audience welcomed Rachel with a burst of enthusiastic applause, but after her triumphs in Berlin, London and St. Petersburg the reception was an anticlimax. Here was not the stubborn audience of Paris, always wanting to be reconvinced, and always reconvinced in the end; nor was it an awed crowd of foreigners to whom Rachel was the emissary of culture from the cultural capital of Europe. To the French part of the audience Rachel was a missionary from home, to be welcomed with enthusiasm and pride, to be shown off to the local, slightly inferior people. To most of the rest, however, Rachel was not a source of culture or pride, but a curiosity: Europe's major actress had come. She was not yet welcomed because of the pretensions to culture which enticed the socially prominent to the theater; she was merely a curiosity, an interesting spectacle. The American attitude was a source of continual bafflement to the members of Rachel's company.

A review in *Harper's Magazine* captured some of the atmosphere of that first night, and unconsciously foreshadowed the future. The audience, the magazine reported, was not more than one-third American; but some of the most distinguished American writers, poets and editors were there. Rachel was generously received upon her entrance. "There was no hooting, no whistling, no tumult of any kind. One indiscreet brother tried to yelp, and was instantly suppressed." The know-nothing attitude, which had done such damage to Macready six years earlier, was noticeably subdued. *Harper's* is proud of the audience, its appreciation and intelligence, and of Rachel who did not condescend to it. Rachel, on hearing of her lover's fate, "sinks fainting in her chair, after a pantomime of fluctuating emotion, which is the very height of her art." At that point someone in the audience flung a bouquet on the stage which crashed at the feet of

Horatius delivering a speech. The old Roman, not sure of what to do, picked it up to present it to Rachel, when a cry of "no" rang out in the theater. The audience had indeed behaved better than a provincial French audience years before, which had encouraged Rachel to acknowledge a crown thrown to her.

After an hour and a half of passionate intensity, the curtain fell on the dead Camille.

> Then came the judgment. . . . The curtain rose, and there [*Harper's Magazine* reports], wan and wavering, stood the ghost of Camille, the woman Rachel. She had risen in her flowing drapery just where she had fallen, and seemed to be the spirit of herself. But pale and trembling, she flickered in the tempest of applause. The audience stood and waved hats and handkerchiefs, and flowers fell in pyramids; and that quick, earnest, meaning "Brava!" was undisturbed by any discordant sound. It was a great triumph. It was too much for the excited and exhausted Rachel. She knew that the news would instantly fly across the sea—that Paris would hear of her victory over a new continent—that, perhaps, Ristori's foot would be found too large for the slipper. She wavered for a moment. Then someone rushed forward and caught her as she fell—and the curtain came down.
>
> There was no attempt at a recall. There was something too real in the whole scene. The audience silently arose and slowly departed.

The performance of *Horace* ended in the way Rachel usually performed it outside France: two-thirds of the way through Act IV, with the death of Camille. The rest, including all of Act V, was unimportant in a setting where Rachel was the only point of interest and the play as such a minor matter. Rachel also made the other concession to non-French taste: Camille died on stage, not in the wings.

The second night, on September 5, was *Phèdre*, and expectations were high. If *Horace* brought 26,000 francs how much more would *Phèdre* bring! It brought less than 20,000 francs, or $3,700. The shock was great. Chéry was scandalized, and no one among the cast could explain it. They all had mistaken the basic situation in the same way as Raphael had in providing good staging and competent acting for the tour. In Europe audiences had come to see Rachel as Phèdre. In America they came to see Rachel.

Adrienne Lecouvreur, on the following evening, raised the income above $4,000 once more, but the bafflement continued. Hugo's *Angelo*, on the nineteenth, for example, was well attended; for *Bajazet*, on the twentieth, the house was half empty. And Soumet's boring pseudo-classical tragedy *Jeanne d'Arc* made a powerful impact at the box office when it was first given.

Though Raphael and his company did not see it, there was a consistent pattern in the success and failure of the plays. The audiences were largest when Rachel did modern plays, and particularly when she did plays which aroused a sense of competition. *Adrienne Lecouvreur* was current in New York and Boston in a bowdlerized version. Charlotte Cushman, America's greatest tragic actress, had played *Angelo*, rewritten as *The Actress of Padua*. It also seems natural that an audience would be interested to see the greatest French actress impersonate the greatest French heroine: that explains the attendance for Soumet's *Jeanne d'Arc*.

Though the press continued to be ecstatic about "the greatest actress that ever lived," receipts continued to fall once Rachel had performed her whole repertoire. For the performance of *Angelo* on September 24 prices were reduced so that it now became possible to see Rachel for as little as fifty cents. More people came as a consequence, but the general level of receipts did not rise. On Tuesday, September 25, Rachel held a reading of dramatic speeches at the Tabernacle—admission $1.50. It had been arranged in order to give a view of Rachel to those many —mostly ladies—whose moral scruples prevented them from seeing Rachel in a theater. The English actress Fanny Kemble had done the same very successfully in 1849. As it turned out, the moral scruples clearly applied not only to the theater, but to Rachel: attendance was so poor that Raphael could not pay her the usual 6,000 francs after expenses. Publicity and locale were blamed, and the event was repeated on October 11 at Niblo's Garden; the results were no better.

During the repeat performance of *Andromaque* on October 1 Rachel caught a cold, which proved to be the beginning of the end. Yet throughout the month she managed to write cheerful letters to her mother at home, asserting that her health remained good. In adversity she became more considerate and her personal fortitude increased: "I eat and sleep like an infant; I act with herculean force in those tragedies and I am gaining weight!!!"

Far from attempting to safeguard her health, Rachel increased her exertions. In September a group of Frenchmen had written to Rachel and pleaded with her to sing the *Marseillaise*, as she had done at the Comédie Française during the early days of the Second Republic. She had declined. Early in October she changed her mind and added that attraction to her performances. On the first occasion, a performance of *Horace* on October 8, receipts rose above four thousand dollars once more; it was almost as much money as all the other twelve New York theaters combined took in that evening. The exertion, however, was too much for her. During the performance of *Jeanne d'Arc* on October 15 she coughed on stage for the first time. Yet, as if to tempt fate, she performed two plays on the evening of the 18th, *Phèdre* and *Le Moineau de Lesbie*. Two days later, on October 20, *Horace* and the *Marseillaise* concluded the first New York engagement.

Rachel had exhausted herself physically. She had performed even more than she had done on tour in earlier years. She had been generous; she had given one thousand dollars for the yellow fever victims in Norfolk, and four hundred dollars each to the French and Jewish Benevolent Societies. She had earned much money, though not nearly as much as hoped for, in the face of a series of considerable obstacles.

The most glaring obstacle was her brother. His minor acts of avarice damaged her reputation and income. New Yorkers objected more, perhaps, to the hidden charge of one quarter for reserved seats than to the abnormally high prices of admission.

By October 15 matters had gone so far that Ferdinando Wood himself, the Mayor of New York, wrote to Raphael and advised him strongly not to charge more for the seats of Rachel's benefit than had originally been announced.

The most serious obstacle was one that could probably not have been circumvented by a more adroit management: the moral objection to Rachel was deep-seated and transcended any objection to the theater or to her plays. Her plays were often found objectionable. La Tisbé, in Hugo's *Angelo*, is a courtesan and not, as in Cushman's version, an actress of Padua. *Phèdre* offended the audience deeply. Beauvallet poked fun at the American version of *Adrienne Lecouvreur:*

> In the English translation the Prince de Bouillon is called the Duc d'Aumont and the Princess is only his fiancée. The prudish Americans are offended to see Mme. de Bouillon, who is married, become the mistress of the Comte de Saxe. But they find it acceptable that this same woman should have a lover the day before her marriage to the Duc d'Aumont. This country has a strange way of understanding morals.

More than through her unadulterated plays, Rachel offended with her adulterated past, which was well known. To some extent Rachel's health forbade the kind of social exertions that Jenny Lind subjected herself to under Barnum's guidance. More than that, however, Rachel was snubbed by New York society. She had few visitors and appeared only on one social occasion, a party given for her by M. de Trobriand on September 21. He managed to collect some ladies of New York society for the event, but they were few. In more ways than one Rachel could not compete with Jenny Lind and her moving rendition of "Home Sweet Home."

On Saturday, October 20, Rachel gave her farewell performance in New York. On Monday she was scheduled to open in Boston. Sunday was used for travel because performances could not be given on that day. On Sunday, also, train connections were much poorer, and it took Rachel the whole day to reach her destination. Now some facts could no longer be hidden: "I felt cold on the train," she wrote a few days later, "and since coming to Boston I have been coughing like a tubercular patient; but that I am not, I want you to know, in spite of my pale complexion and apparent thinness."

Rachel stayed at the Tremont House while the company put up at the Adams House with its "unadulterated American cookery." She was very well received at the Boston Theatre, and played every night of the week. The box office receipts were as good as those in New York, and Raphael decided to extend the engagement. Then disaster struck: the receipts of the first evening of the extension, *Polyeucte* and *Moineau de Lesbie*, were $801. The reason for the sudden falling off may have been a certain antagonism aroused by Raphael's business methods, particularly in the sale of tickets. The extension was abruptly canceled, and farewell performances of *Adrienne Lecouvreur* and *Virginie*, with the *Marseillaise*, drew larger crowds. (Eliza Logan was performing *Adrienne* at the same time, in English.)

On the last evening in Boston, Rachel had perhaps the greatest ovation of her tour. The return to New York, however, was disastrous. On that same day the October 15 issue of the *Journal des Débats* reached New York. It contained an article by Jules Janin written when he had seen the first reports of Rachel's appearances in New York. He had written an appeal to her to stop that nonsense at once and return home. Lack of information was no deterrent to him, and his piece was chiefly based on one rather ludicrous report about American audiences and their behavior which, he indicated, consisted entirely of whistling, yelling, shooting and whittling with lethal knives on the armrests of the seats in the auditorium. Janin's main point was that he expected Rachel to fail because the glories of Racine were unsuited to an audience of tradesmen and a democratic society in general. The article was at once translated and widely reported in the press. Though she was of course not responsible, it damaged Rachel further with the public.

Now the disaster deepened at every turn. Rachel's return engagement was planned to take place in the Academy of Music, an opera house with no less than four thousand six hundred seats, with poor visibility, old, faded, dilapidated. Only two performances were given there, and both were yawningly empty. Raphael immediately tried to improve the situation, and managed to move the company to Niblo's Garden within four days. Niblo's Garden had no appropriate backdrops and other needed supplies, however, and some performances looked fairly ludicrous. Furthermore, Rachel's evenings had to alternate with those of Mme. LaGrange of the Paris Opéra.

By now Rachel's health was declining with considerable speed. Yet she went on, and opened on November 19 at the Walnut Street Theatre in Philadelphia in *Horace*. That, however, was the end: her health was wrecked. The rest of the engagement in Philadelphia was canceled; the engagements in Baltimore and Washington were canceled. On November 27, Rachel fled south in search of warmth and sunshine, to Charleston, South Carolina. Gradually, during the month of December, hopes faded that she would be able to recover and continue her North American tour. Charleston did not turn out to be as warm and healthful as had been hoped. It was decided to go farther south, to transport the company to Havana, and to undertake performances in a more hospitable climate and before a more appreciative audience. Before leaving, Rachel acceded to the request of some members of society and gave a single performance in Charleston, on December 17, 1855: *Adrienne Lecouvreur*. Here in this small southern town, so far from the centers of her world, Rachel took leave of her career, the greatest theatrical career, financial, geographical, and perhaps even artistic, the world had known to that time. It was a sad farewell; Chéry, who played Michonnet in that performance, reported that it was "the most painful spectacle I shall ever experience. . . . I saw her barely able to remain on her feet, barely able to speak, coughing at each word, holding her breath to stifle this cough, gripping my arm in order not to fall, and despite her suffering, I saw her find the energy to carry on to the end of her part with an indomitable courage." M. Félix was in tears. He too saw the end.

The flight continued, however, and so did the hopes. The engagement in the United States was ended for now. One would spend the winter in Havana, perform there and in the Spring— who knows. Raphael had preceded the company to Havana, and, with his usual disregard of facts, made commitments there. On December 23, upon her arrival on the *Isabel*, Rachel wrote, "My success will be great, I think. The subscriptions for the first dozen performances are already more than 60,000 francs." But two weeks later she wrote: "I am ill, very ill." Between Christmas and the New Year the truth could no longer be hidden.

On January 1 the members of the company went to see Rachel to wish her a happy new year. They found her weak but determined. In quiet tones she told them that the tour was over and that they were to be sent home. Raphael made his last budget for his sister: it would cost 67,000 francs to return the company to Paris. It was Rachel now who had to meet all expenses, including a fine of seven thousand pesos to a theater manager with whom Raphael had made a contract for some performances. For a moment Rachel hoped to stay in Havana with three actors, including Chéry, and make money with readings and scenes from plays. Then she decided against it. "I am unable to act any more. The actress is finished," she told Chéry.

Janin had criticized her journey *in absentia*. On her return to Europe, other voices were raised. Count Potemkin wrote to her from St. Petersburg: "You will recall that I begged you not to undertake that horrible journey," and asked her to return to Russia. That horrible journey, that disastrous odyssey was now held responsible for her illness. It is as if the insensitive, callous, democratic Americans were solely responsible for the fatality that was now generally anticipated. Even in 1855 medical science was far enough advanced, however, to know that her fatal tuberculosis was not of such recent origin. Rachel's health had never been good. As early as December 1839, in a letter to Déjazet, Rachel had complained about persistent coughing. Musset and

Janin both noted early how completely a full-length role exhausted her. In 1841 Fanny Kemble had judged her to be a
potential or actual consumptive. Time after time the critics
mentioned debuts after bouts with illnesses, and it is clear that
not all of them had been of a tactical nature. Rachel seems to
have been subject to attacks of bronchitis long before her final
illness. Throughout the 1840's and early 1850's references to illness increased in her private letters, until the shock of Rebecca's
death in 1854 brought her finally face to face with her own
weakening condition. The reaction was in keeping with her general behavior; instead of restraining herself, Rachel redoubled
feverishily her efforts to perform, to earn more money.

After her collapse in the United States and her failure to rally
in Havana, Rachel returned to Paris, no longer hopeful but
gathering a kind of moral courage that raised her higher than
the courage displayed in striking out in new directions in her
career. Ristori had her second season in Paris, while Rachel spent
the spring in the country at Meulan, visited by many friends.
In July she sought relief at Bad Ems, and in October she left
for the haven of tubercular patients who could afford it, Egypt.
On that trip she made her last friend, but in keeping with her
condition a spiritual friend only. The role Gabriel Aubaret
played in the last months of her life shows beyond a doubt her
tremendous appeal, an appeal which transcended the sexual, the
fashionable, and the glitter of success. Aubaret was an officer in
the French Navy, a spiritual, religious man whose long conversations with the invalid led him to a fervent devotion, which
expressed itself most signally in his attempts to save her soul by
converting her to the Roman Catholic faith. Such an attempt
was not a new thing. On the whole, the matter of religion or
race came up in connection with Rachel, not in anti-Semitic
fashion, but with the idea of conversion: someone so talented,
so charming, must go to heaven. Rumors that she had been converted spread so far at times that she once used a reception in
the aristocratic Faubourg Saint-Germain to deny them. The
Archbishop of Paris was present, and she recited the monologue

of Esther from Racine's play. When the Archbishop congratulated her, she replied: "Monseigneur, that is my faith." In New
York in September 1855, the *Tribune* reported that Rachel attended synagogue on Yom Kippur, and fasted. Aubaret was the
last, and the strongest, of these spiritually motivated friends, and
the one who almost succeeded.

From Egypt Rachel wrote many charming letters to friends
and to her children, whose welfare continued to be her most
important concern. One especially, written to Arsène Houssaye
"in the shadow of the Pyramids," indicates her mood of calm
after the storm:

> I have lived gluttonously. I devoured, in a few years, all my
> days and nights; well, it is done now, and I do not say like your
> penitents: I am guilty. I am guilty. . . . If I did not have two
> sons, who have all my love, I would die without regrets. The
> God of Israel will allow me, in the intermissions there above, to
> come down to kiss my children and to see once more my friends
> in that Théâtre Français which I loved so much. By the side of
> the Pyramids I look upon twenty centuries vanished into the
> dark. Oh, my friend, here I see the empty fate of actresses. I
> thought I was like a pyramid and I see now that I am no more
> than a passing shadow—a past shadow. I came here to find once
> more the life which is escaping me, and I see nothing but death
> around me. When one has been loved in Paris, one ought to die.

But she was still planning for life. She returned to Paris in the
spring of 1857, ready to spend the summer in France and to return to Egypt the following winter. That summer, her connection with the House of Molière ended forever. Her leave
from the Comédie, granted originally for the American journey
and extended pending her recovery, ended on May 31. On June
10, 1857, she wrote her final regrets. It may have been her hardest letter.

By the end of the summer it was clear that another journey
to Egypt was out of the question. Paris was also impossible for
her health, and the novelist Mario Uchard arranged for her to
be the guest of J.-J. Sardou, a cousin of the playwright, at his

house at le Cannet on the French Riviera. This was to be the last of her journeys. On her day of parting, in the early morning of a foggy, damp, cold day in fall, Rachel took a carriage from her house and let herself be driven to the Comédie Française. There she ordered the carriage to stop and, hidden deep in its shadow, she sat alone and quiet for a time, and contemplated silently the house which had been the center of her life, closed as yet so early in the day, gray, old, shrouded in the fog. Then she drove on to the Théâtre du Gymnase, where she also stopped for a short time. Then she went home to prepare for her departure. Some who recount this story say that she cried. One may doubt that, but the story itself rings true; it is in keeping with her character.

Sardou's house at le Cannet was in an almost inaccessible location, and Rachel, after her train journey, had to be taken there by boat. Prince Napoleon supplied his yacht. For the final steps she had to be carried in a litter. Rachel's biographer James Agate described a visit to le Cannet many years after her death. The house was unchanged:

> Here was the marble bed with its antique sculpture at the head and the figure of Tragedy at the foot. Here was the *salle-à-manger* with the decanters and glasses Rachel used. The salon is a very dark, long, narrow room with a ceiling representing the firmament. Exquisite stained glass windows everywhere. Rachel's piano. The fireplace, in the shape of the trunk of a marble tree whose branches enclose the whole room, still black with smoke. Ceremonial chairs. Statues in every corner. . . . It was all extraordinarily impressive, like a last act of Victor Hugo. We were shown round by a remarkable old lady of great age, who said, with finality: "Voici le lit de mort de Rachel. N'y touchez pas." No plaque. Nothing to tell the passer-by that here, jealously guarded, are the last links with the world's greatest actress.

The last days of the world's greatest actress were worthy of her. The calumnies and defamations that had plagued her as late as the preceding year were over. The fall of 1857 was quiet.

Aubaret, stationed at Toulon nearby, came, and made a last attempt to convert her. It is told that he almost succeeded one day, with a priest close at hand, when the sudden and unexpected arrival of a visitor interrupted his plans—as it turned out, forever.

The visitor was Prince Napoleon, who had journeyed across France merely to sit by Rachel's bedside for one afternoon and then to rush north again for military duties. The unique drawing power of that woman transcended her art and her beauty. In December, with the end approaching, she wanted to send souvenirs to all her friends, and with a supreme effort wrote seventeen notes in one day, to be sent out with oranges and flowers. In her note to Emile de Girardin she wrote: "January 1, 1858, I embrace you in this new year. I did not think, dear friend, that I would still be able to send you my sincere regards in 1858." As a more final gesture of farewell, she returned all their letters to her friends.

Dr. Tampier, her physician, received a telegram in Paris on December 31, asking him to come to le Cannet, and was by Rachel's bedside on Saturday, January 2. He saw at once that his duties as a doctor had been superseded by those of a historian; he left a record of Rachel's last twenty-four hours. J.-J. Sardou did the same, in a long letter to Mario Uchard. Towards midnight on Saturday Rachel roused herself, calmly, as after a long sleep; she talked and wanted to write to her father; when she found that she could not, she dictated a letter that contained her last wishes; a sudden attack interrupted her. But her prodigious strength of mind and will did not leave her until the very end. At 11 A.M. on Sunday her death was expected at any moment, but by the afternoon she had rallied enough to finish the letter to her father and to sign it. A little later she distributed some souvenirs among the people around her. At 10 P.M. a renewed attack, worse than the one in the morning, presaged the end; after an hour of struggle, her eyes closed and extreme pallor spread across her face. At that point Sarah gave up hope. She had asked a group of Jews from the congregation in Nice to come to le Cannet; they had waited in a room for many hours.

Now they were led in. And as they began their prayers, Rachel roused herself once more. Dr. Tampier says that he saw her lips move in prayer as her hand sought Sarah's.

"Hear Israel, the Eternal is our God, the Eternal is One."

Rachel died without struggle, without renewed suffering.

That same day, January 3, large packages arrived from Paris, presents she had ordered to be distributed among M. Sardou's household. He returned them unopened to the family, and received nothing from them for his kindness.

Rachel had herself given orders for an autopsy and the transfer of her body to Paris. At her funeral most of the great writers, actors and members of the Academy were present. A military guard of honor attended. Alexandre Dumas was among the pallbearers. The grand Rabbi of Paris prayed at her grave—and then, speaking in French, denied the rumor of her conversion. Not long after that the Félix family auctioned off every last item of Rachel's. Of the sum realized, 1,274,000 francs, half went to her children, all that could be given them according to law, a quarter to her parents, and a quarter to her brothers and sisters. Sarah was to have a special income of 6,000 francs from a fund that she in turn was to leave to Rachel's children. A few pieces, which Rachel had left to friends, escaped the Félix rapacity, among them, for Napoleon III, a bust of his uncle as First Consul, and a few items for the Prince Napoleon.

Rachel is one of a handful of actors and actresses whose memory remains and is revived constantly. The word of two of her contemporaries can be used to account for it, one social, one professional.

Prince Napoleon said after her death: "A woman who deceives you with such grace is irreplaceable. Where will we ever find another artist who can be Phèdre incarnate and a burlesque queen an hour later?"

Edmond Got wrote in his diary on January 5, 1858:

Mlle. Rachel was an incomparable theatrical structure, rather than a perfect artist in the widest sense of the word; for she was hardly ever any one but Camille in all her roles, especially after the provinces and the foreign countries had unbalanced in her the lesson of the masters, and driven her to the limits of her strength.

But what a voice! What pronunciation! What diction! What passion! What nobility! What rendition! What range! And even what beauty, no matter what is said!

Now, is this an irreparable loss for the Comédie Française? Personally, yes, because one will not find her equal again soon, if indeed one ever finds it. Administratively no, because she was a damaging factor, even a calamity for internal discipline.

Poor Got did not know what a calamity for internal discipline he was soon to be exposed to. In the year after Rachel's death, a girl of fifteen had her future disposed of by one of Rachel's old friends, the Duc de Morny: Sarah Bernhardt entered, or was pushed into the Conservatoire of the Comédie Française.

CHAPTER 6 / No Room at the Top

RACHEL had shown what an actress might do. Ristori was the first to travel the whole distance. She made four tours of the United States, she circled the globe; she lunched with King Kalahaua of Hawaii, was caught in a revolution in Peru, and was the object of violent student demonstrations in Moscow.

Paris in 1855 had been the turning point of Ristori's career. Since the days of the *commedia dell' arte* French actors and actresses had by and large been the only ones to transcend the boundaries imposed by language, and Ristori's trip to Paris was an act of considerable personal courage. After that, in the summer of 1855, Rachel was gone across the Atlantic, and Europe was curious to see the star who had driven her there—for the rumor that Rachel had actually fled to America because of Ristori's success could not be stilled, even though Rachel's plans had been made before Ristori's arrival. Ristori's rise began with that spring and summer in Paris. After that she first toured France: Le Havre, Tours, Blois, Orléans, Bordeaux, Toulouse, Marseilles, Lyon and more. Then she went to Belgium, then on to Dresden and Berlin, capitals of German Kingdoms, and finally back to tour her native country. The Italians received her with wild enthusiasm: in a few short months she had changed Italy's cultural reputation abroad. To a people starved for independence and a national role Ristori was a godsend. She continued to receive that support at home and went abroad each time strengthened by the belief that she was making an important contribution to the welfare of her country, quite in contrast to Rachel, whose trips abroad were resented by her Parisian audience.

In 1856 Ristori went back to Paris for the second of her stipulated seasons at the Salle Ventadour. The World's Fair had ended, Rachel was *hors de combat*, and the Parisians seemed to regret the heady enthusiasm and pleasant spite with which they had built up a foreign talent at the expense of their own. The whole atmosphere was like the morning after. Dumas could not arouse any enthusiasm for Ristori. Janin failed to repeat his feat of the year before; he wrote: "Arouse yourself, Rachel! The enemy is at your gates, your domains are being ravaged!" Rachel could not be aroused, and the critics who had baited her with Ristori the year before, now tried to belittle the talents of the Italian actress. They talked nostalgically of Mlle. Dorval, a much better romantic actress in their opinion. Ristori performed Alfieri's *Rosamunda*, to invite comparison to one of Rachel's plays, but nobody seemed interested. The only flicker of interest was Ernest Legouvé's *Medée*, the play Rachel had rejected earlier. Ristori returned to Paris in 1857 and 1858 as agreed. In 1858 she performed *Phèdre* there in Italian for the first time, but succeeded only in further offending the Parisian audience. It did not matter much; her triumphs were now in other places.

In 1856, from Paris, she went to London and on to Warsaw and then toured the Italian states as far south as Naples. From then on the rounds continued: Madrid, the Hague and Amsterdam, Budapest, St. Petersburg and Moscow, Egypt, Turkey, Greece and on and on through steady series of European engagements.

Paris, to its regret, had done its work and made Ristori an international actress. It had supplied the stamp of approval and Europe accepted the new star. Both as a personality and as an artist she was more in keeping with the temper of the time than Rachel had been. Her appeal was increased by the Italian struggle for independence, which culminated in the war of France and Sardinia against Austria in 1859, and the unification of most of the country in 1860. A great demonstration welcomed her in

Holland in 1859, for example, due in part at least to her nationality. Paris, too, welcomed her effusively in 1860, soon after the return of the victorious army of Napoleon III from Lombardy.

"There are two queens in Madrid tonight," the Queen of Spain said in 1857, during Ristori's performances in that city. The visiting queen had just persuaded the local queen to reverse the decision of her law courts and her government. A soldier had committed a rash, unpremeditated act of insubordination, goaded, like Billy Budd, to strike out at an officer who had insulted him. The soldier had been condemned to death. All the agitation of the people of Madrid and of the press had not succeeded in persuading the government to exercise clemency. On the evening before the soldier was to die, his mother came to Ristori's green room before her performance, threw herself to the ground and begged the actress to intercede directly with the queen, who was attending the play. It was the last hope. Ristori was moved, and during the intermission went to see Queen Isabella and ask for the soldier's pardon. She obtained it and, that evening, received one of the greatest ovations of her life by thousands of Madrileños massed in front of her hotel.

The Emperor of the French honored her, the Kings of Holland, Sweden, and Prussia personally conferred decorations on her, King Ferdinand of Portugal painted a water-color for her. King Kalahaua of Hawaii, to her great surprise not a savage, gave a party in her honor. The Emperors of Brazil and Russia, the kings and queen of countries too numerous to list became friends with her on a basis of equality unknown until the time of Rachel.

In part this new level of equality was the outcome of the French Revolution, and the shock of seeing the old royal order disintegrate. The Congress of Vienna in 1815 restored thrones just as the Japanese collapse in 1945 led to the restoration of the European colonies in Asia. Neither could re-establish the old order; after 1815 the monarchs, having been instated, deposed, reinstated and generally pulled about, were no longer in the position they had occupied in the eighteenth century.

At the same time, the status of the performing artist had changed fundamentally. In part it was a matter of official moral sanction. In 1730 Adrienne Lecouvreur, the greatest French actress of her time, was buried at night, without religious ceremony, in an unmarked grave. In 1905, Sir Henry Irving, Knight, was laid to rest in Westminster Abbey. The social stigma was still in effect in Rachel's time. The actor Joanny, for example, an older colleague at the Français, had changed his name when he went on the stage in order not to embarrass his respectable family. But in general performers knew that they needed no longer to wear the livery of a prince or nobleman, and the fruits of their labor were becoming very tangible and large. A vast new audience had been formed, consisting of the new middle class, the spawn of the Industrial Revolution. It was the class which Guizot, the French Prime Minister, admonished to enrich itself, the class typified by Rastignac's words in *Père Goriot:* "Parvenir! Parvenir à tout prix." It was the class that wanted to arrive, arrive at any price, which prompted William James to say that "the exclusive worship of the bitch-goddess SUCCESS —is our national disease." Around this worship it created a whole mythology of success. It stated and restated its gospel of wealth, as it was, for instance, formulated by Theodore Dreiser in 1897: "It is only the unfit who fail—who suffer and die. . . . They are unfit because, unlike the fit ones, they lack these peculiarities which aid one to survive. They are . . . too tired and weakbodied to risk seizing what is not their own." That "predatory culture," in Veblen's phrase, flourished nowhere more fully than in the New World, partly because a whole continent lay before the new nation of Americans, partly because the Industrial Revolution came late, and then came with full force as a result of the Civil War. In Europe established privileges, national rivalries and traditions hampered and impeded the flowering of the laissez-faire philosophy, made it less apparent and kept success and the class of its worshippers on a more subdued level. In the United States the Civil War had been the emancipation, not only of a race, but of a whole philosophy of life. The generation

NO ROOM AT THE TOP

after 1865 was in Kenneth Lynn's phrase "the most titanically successful generation in our history."

Ristori said late in life that her greatest triumphs had been won in England and the United States. All the international and near-international actresses toured the United States extensively, and made more money here, relatively, than anywhere else. All except Rachel: she had come too early. There were, for example, only nineteen millionaires in New York in 1855, and the richest, William B. Astor, had a mere twenty million dollars. Commodore Vanderbilt had, two years before Rachel's arrival, taken his first vacation in the first luxury yacht ever owned by an American. Between 1855, Rachel's tour, and Ristori's in 1866, more than a devastating war had occurred. Henry Adams, coming home about the time of Ristori's first arrival, wrote: "Had they been Tyrian traders of the year 1000 B.C. landing from a galley fresh from Gibraltar, they could hardly have been stranger on the shore of a world so changed from what it had been ten years before."

By 1866 the age of conspicuous consumption was in full flood. Astor's pre-Civil War fortune, Vanderbilt's pre-Civil War yacht were left far behind. When the Commodore died in 1872, he left $105 million, a sum that was eventually doubled by his son, William Henry, whose pronouncement characterized the era: "The public be damned"; less charitable than Marie Antoinette's comment on the breadless poor but much more realistic. The cake assumed phantastic proportions. The Credit Mobilier milked the Union Pacific enterprise. Another railroad, the Erie, was the battleground of the old, as represented by Vanderbilt, and the new: James Fisk, assassinated at the age of thirty-six, and given a military funeral of royal proportions; and Jay Gould, Fisk's partner in the grandest set of offices ever seen in New York, the Erie offices at the Grand Opera House. Gould tried nothing less than to corner the U. S. gold market, with the help of Abel Corbin, President Grant's brother-in-law. He was thirty-three at the time, two years younger than his partner Fisk.

Apart from these two Erie Railroad magnates there was Daniel

Drew, who acted the country yokel to perfection and went on lonely whiskey binges. And Jay Cooke, the inventor of the patriotic finance drive, perhaps an even more conspicuous consumer than the elegant Fisk. There was a more serious world of finance and industry, too, of course, Henry Clay Frick and Andrew Carnegie, Rockefeller, and the House of Drexel, Morgan and Co., all of which date their rise from the panic of 1873, which ruined Cooke. But the spirit which sent the Goulds and Fisks and Cookes forth from their poverty-stricken surroundings in small New England towns, and gave them the intrepidity and the opportunity to become rich beyond the wildest dreams, that spirit infected the whole age, and made tycoons in their own, smaller realms of the great actor-producers like Dion Boucicault, Augustin Daly, and David Belasco. Toward the end of the century the Klaw-Erlanger syndicate tried to corner the theatrical market just as Gould had tried to corner the gold market; in contrast to Gould, it succeeded for a time. Even the great Sarah Bernhardt was forced either to accept syndicate terms or be deprived of theaters across the country.

The captain of industry was, in Veblen's phrase, "the keeper of the national integrity," who "with a becoming gravity offered himself as philosopher and friend to mankind, guide to literature and art, church and state, science and education, law and morals . . ."

Into this heady atmosphere of ruthlessness mixed with moral preachments and sentimentality came the great actors and actresses, samples both of the myth of success and the lure of the forbidden fruit, examples as well as objects of conspicuous consumption. Their rise from obscurity to fame paralleled the rags-to-riches of the millionaire, confirmed the myths concocted by Horatio Alger in the 1870's, 80's, and 90's, and served the age both as an example of what to be, and, in moral terms, of what not to be as well.

They were also of use in turning the Fifth Avenue mansions and Newport palaces into havens of culture and refinement. Once the acquisition of money had ceased to be an all-consuming objective, the very rich, and especially their wives, began to find that they were also the very bored. They had no cultural background and few really absorbing social rituals, and the simple satisfaction of spending money had to pale eventually. They became avid collectors with wide differences in taste, giving rise to such captains of consumption as Joseph Duveen, Lord Millbank, who supplied them with works of art. They collected books, like Huntington and Folger, founded universities like Stanford and Rockefeller, or libraries like Carnegie, or simply collected, like Morgan or Hearst. Their mansions reflected their collector's instincts. Vanderbilt was so impressed with his block-long mansion on Fifth Avenue that he allowed an "art album" of it to be published that was solemnly bought by his friends and business associates, including J. P. Morgan. The album described the home as "a representative of the new impulse now felt in the national life." That new impulse was a great incoherent mixture of styles and periods: French tapestries, Florentine doors, African marbles, English china, and so on.

The theater fitted itself to this chaotic conspicuous consumption by the *nouveaux riches*. The drama and its production both catered to the aspirations and self-deluding hypocrisies of the age. It faithfully reflected its mixture of ruthlessness and sentiment. The great actors and actresses were themselves objects of conspicuous consumption, entertaining at and ornamenting the great receptions, banquets and other social events. The new society of the newly rich was as hard to break into as any old established aristocracy. It admired the exclusiveness of the European nobility and imitated it. Artists were pawns in that society, almost as much as the nobles and members of royal families in Europe. To capture a visiting prince for a soiree was a great victory for a New York hostess. To have a great star of the stage glitter at one's reception was more than just a consolation prize.

Adelaide Ristori was ready-made for that situation. She was the biggest and the best—the actress who had defeated Rachel, the international heavyweight world champion of the stage. And besides that, she was the Marchesa Capranica del Grillo, whose husband was a Roman nobleman. One did not have to worry about being outdone if one endorsed, entertained, and was entertained by her.

Ristori also was an excellent example of the Horatio Alger tradition, the child of obscure parents who by virtue of talent, hard work and love had risen to the pinnacle of success. She personified success in the arts, unhampered by the moral doubts that surrounded many of her professional colleagues. Rachel had not been respectable, mostly because of her life, but also because the women of her generation did not as yet accord respectability to actresses, at least in America. Ristori, though almost of the same age, came later and was, in both senses, respectable. She could personify in the age of the great middle-class Queen, Victoria, the aspirations of the middle class to respectability mixed with romance. She could also inject color into the drab existence of the lower orders. She supplied some of the gilt for the Gilded Age.

Ristori's choice of plays supported that mixture of respectability and romance. It largely consisted of the kind of drama that fell into disrepute before the century was out, and is now quite forgotten, even by Hollywood. Parts of it survive, however, in the operatic repertoire, where its romanticism and melodramatic starkness, enhanced and overshadowed by the music of Verdi, Puccini, Mascagni and others, is still attractive.

Two plays by a compatriot and contemporary were among Ristori's three or four main successes: Paolo Giacometti's *Elizabeth Queen of England* and *Queen Marie Antoinette*. Both are vehicles for star actresses, who are on stage in them almost all the time. *Elizabeth* is the better of the two, mainly because an internal conflict is involved. It treats the last fifteen years of the queen's life and the struggle between her love for the Earl of Essex and her need to remove him from power and, ultimately, from life, as a threat to her throne. Her sense of duty to England wins after long internal and external conflicts. Ristori performed Elizabeth more often than any other role, but she never ceased to hate the play. Her attitude toward any play was pietistic and

she hated the part of Elizabeth, not because of the role itself but
because of what the real Elizabeth had done to poor Queen
Mary Stuart. Even the opportunities of the tremendous, lonely
death scene could not reconcile her to the part.

Giacometti's other play, *Marie Antoinette*, was "written expressly for and by request of Madame Ristori." It portrays nothing but the slow decline of the queen who rises in fortitude and
magnanimity with each downward step forced upon her by her
persecutors. She is not the frivolous queen of the Trianon, but
an anxious, responsible wife and mother, a strong argument in
favor of conservatism and the *ancien régime*. The play is not a
study of conflicts but a set of effective scenes of pathos, in which
an almost endless series of farewells provided ample employment for the handkerchief trade. Ristori's own pietistic attitude
had repercussions on many of the plays in her repertoire. She
had at first refused Legouvé's *Medée*, not because of Rachel but
because she found the story morally objectionable. Legouvé,
however, persuaded her to read the play, and a reading convinced her of its beauty and, more important, of its essential
harmlessness in the light of contemporary morality; she says that
she undertook Legouvé's play because the death of the children
was concealed from the public, and not with certainty assigned
to Medea. Legouvé "had in this way succeeded in softening the
horror of this dreadful deed." Her *Medea* was an affecting, tear-
ful rather than a wild version, even though wild, passionate
scenes occurred in it. The children were unusually much in evidence. Ristori tells that she carried only one child with her
troupe on tour, for the speaking part, and relied on borrowing
the second one locally. On one occasion at least that local product got scared by "The Madam's" great outburst in the death
scene, and by the milling, threatening stage crowd and, officially
dead, made a screaming dash for the wings and the arms of his
own mother.

One role seemed worse than Medea to Ristori: Lady Macbeth.
To her the Scottish queen was "a creature worse than a wild
beast," "a monster in human likeness," and the prime mover of

the action of the play. It may have been an effective performance running the gamut of horror, in which Macbeth appeared
only "to serve as foil and contrast to his lady." "This woman,
this serpent, masters him, holds him fast in her coils, and no human power will come to rescue him from her." On tour the play
at times ended with her death, and Birnam Wood never had
to come to Dunsinane.

The stress on physical action, on movement, gesture, becomes
clear in reading Ristori's own description of her major roles.
With regard to Mary Stuart she says, for example: "I omitted
no opportunity throughout the scene with Elizabeth of showing
the torture I was undergoing. . . . Now I implored, by a gesture,
the aid of heaven, now I sought comfort from Talbot by a look
which entreated him to become the judge of the iniquitous
provocation I was enduring from my rival . . ." After she had
nearly collapsed, "I thanked them affectionately with expressive
gestures and signed them to retire as the moment of my weakness was past. But convinced by the harsh, haughty and insolent
tone Elizabeth employed——I turned my head slowly away from
her, with a fixed, penetrating look, accompanied by a slightly
ironical smile which seemed to say: 'You are vilely abusing the
power which superior strength has given you over your un-
armed prisoner.' "

Expressive action is even more significant in *Mirra*, the story
of a girl's incestuous love for her father. "I was very careful not
to meet my father's eyes, while at the same time I did not neglect
any opportunity of showing the audience, by my expression,
what jealous anger I felt at seeing my mother the object of his
tenderness. . . . In order to avoid his caress, I bent before him
in an attitude of simulated respect, allowing the terror with
which I shrank from him to be plainly seen."

The accomplishment of these visual double exposures must
have been a considerable feat; they were also necessary for an
actress who played mainly before audiences who did not understand her language. It is clear that the Italians excelled in this art.

Expressive body movement is an integral part of Italian conversation and social intercourse.

Both Ristori and Rachel were quite naturally inclined towards the use of physical action, though of different sorts. Rachel's achievement seems much more remarkable than Ristori's because she was frail physically, and because she built her reputation on a body of plays that almost entirely excluded physical action from the stage. Rachel was the first actress of tragedy to *jouer le mot*, to act out consistently what the lines said, and animate tragedy as an animated statue capable of sudden surges of tragic passion. Ristori, on the other hand, was much more volatile. She did not, like her lesser contemporaries, tear passion after passion to tatters. She was evidently able to dominate her scenes in subtler ways. Morley reports one example, from Ristori's performance of *Fazio:* "She is not the last speaker when she leaves the stage, but it is a rule with Madame Ristori never to quit the stage without making a point as she does go, and Fazio's last words were a jesting reference to Aldabella [his former love]. Bianca, therefore, turns towards him at her chamber door, and with two little parting gestures of the hand only—one representing playful but half-earnest warning, the other trusting love —impossible to any English actress, natural to an Italian, sums up in two instants the meaning of the scene." "Natural to an Italian"—this explains in part why Italians could achieve international status. The expressiveness of gesture and movement which were natural to Italian actors and, to a lesser extent, to the French, could transcend the boundaries of language.

Ristori crossed the Atlantic for the first time one year after the end of the Civil War. Jacob Grau was the manager who brought her, and the whole operation was in danger of collapse at the outset. At the point when Grau had to fulfill his preliminary commitments to her he lost most of his money in the fire that destroyed the old Academy of Music. But somehow he managed to borrow enough to get started. After a few weeks he had no further worries.

If Grau was penniless at the outset, Ristori certainly was not. She arrived with a personal entourage of nine, including her husband, son, daughter, manager, secretary and four servants, and took a suite at the Fifth Avenue Hotel. Grau had prepared the ground well, and success was not in doubt from the beginning. Ristori opened her engagement at the Lyceum Theatre on September 20, with the play that had become her curtain raiser as much as *Horace* had been Rachel's: Legouvé's *Medée*. As with Rachel, her compatriots formed a large part of the audience at the opening, and she had twenty curtain calls. In contrast to Rachel's experience, however, Ristori's appeal increased with each performance.

Ticket prices were approximately the same as for Rachel's performances, with a top of four dollars, but four dollars in 1866 were not the same as they had been in 1855. Like Rachel, Ristori went to Boston for one week from New York; then she performed in Baltimore for a week, and in Philadelphia for two. Then came Cincinnati, St. Louis, Chicago, Milwaukee, Indianapolis, Louisville, New Orleans, Washington, Pittsburgh, Detroit, Cleveland, Erie, Buffalo, Rochester, Syracuse, Utica, Troy and Albany. Each performance took in more than $2,000. The most spectacular financial success was in Chicago, where one night of Giacometti's *Elizabeth Queen of England* brought $4,800, and the total gross of one week amounted to $18,800, plus $1,800 from the sale of libretti.

A second engagement in New York was interspersed with the tour, and a third, farewell engagement came in May. At her last matinee, *Medée* on May 17, the house was so crowded that one hundred women paid two dollars each to see the play from the side of the stage. Twelve years before the middle-class women of New York had refused to be seen at Rachel's readings, let alone her dramatic performances. Now they were willing, not only to attend Ristori's plays, but to sit at the side of the stage in full view of everyone in the auditorium.

The *New York Times* estimated Ristori's net profit from her

tour at $270,000, and asked tritely but correctly: "What suc-
ceeds like success?"

From New York Ristori returned to Europe for a series of
previously planned engagements. In September, however, she
was back for an even longer series of performances, lasting until June of 1868. The statistics are impressive: In the first season
1866–1867 she gave 171 performances; in the second, 1867–1868
she gave 181, plus 57 in Cuba. Of the total 105 were in New
York and 16 in Brooklyn. Altogether more than half of them
were devoted to three plays: Ristori performed *Elizabeth Queen
of England* 90 times, *Mary Stuart* 67 times and *Marie Antoinette*
62 times.

It is pointless to recount in detail the endless series of tours
that occupied her for thirty years after her encounter with
Rachel in Paris in 1855. As a result of her North American
tours she undertook a tour to South America in 1869, performing in Buenos Aires, Montevideo, Rio de Janeiro and so on. In
1871 she went into the Balkans, performing in Rumanian cities
that had never seen a foreign actress; her caravan of horse-drawn
coaches, passing from Rumania into Southern Russia, lost its
way; the hotels were atrocious; but she went on to perform in
Kisinev, Odessa, Kiev, and elsewhere. By 1873 she had been to
about all the European countries and major cities except for
Scandinavia. From April of 1874 to January 1876 she made a
tour around the world, as usual accompanied by her husband
and a complete acting troupe. She recorded that they traveled
35,283 miles on water and 8,365 miles on land. From Bordeaux
they went to Rio de Janeiro, Buenos Aires and Montevideo.
There they took ship through the Straits of Magellan, and performed in Valparaiso and Santiago de Chile, where her reception
was particularly brilliant. In Lima, Peru, she was caught up in a
revolution without, however, being impeded in her performances for more than one evening. From there she went to Pan-
ama, crossed the Isthmus, performed in a number of Mexican
cities, and finally went on to New York. After a prolonged stay
there, she slowly toured across the United States to San Fran-

cisco, and there took ship for Hawaii. From there she sailed to New Zealand on a ship of only 800 tons, and went on to an extended tour of Australia: Sydney, Melbourne, Adelaide. The return journey via Ceylon, Aden, Suez, and Alexandria took her back to Rome in January of 1876. In 1879 she went to Scandinavia for the first time, and returned there in 1880. The students at the University of Upsala serenaded her and would not let her go.

In that year she first decided to retire from the stage, and then to learn English instead. She knew some English and as early as 1875, during her third American tour, she had performed the sleepwalking scene from *Macbeth* in the original, usually as an encore after the performance of a play in her Italian repertoire. Once she had decided, at nearly sixty years of age, to master English, she applied herself heroically to the task. On July 3, 1882, she was ready to issue forth as Lady Macbeth, a role she had performed in Italian for twenty-five years; characteristically, she bearded the lion in its den: the place was the Drury Lane Theatre in London. Of her original performance Joseph Knight, one of the most respected London critics of the day, had said that ". . . since Mrs. Siddons, Signora Ristori is unapproached as Lady Macbeth." Critical opinion of her English version was less enthusiastic; her acting style was going out of fashion; the young Sarah Bernhardt had just begun to gather her laurels. Her audience success was, however, as great as always, and she added her most popular roles, Mary Stuart, Elizabeth, and Marie Antoinette to her English repertoire soon after, bringing them to the United States for her last tour in 1884/5. The *New York Daily Tribune* found that "her use of English is surprisingly efficient." During that tour she performed *Macbeth* with Edwin Booth and participated in a strange experiment on May 12, 1885: at the Thalia Theater, the German language stage in New York, she performed *Mary Stuart* in English, with the rest of the cast acting in German. Ristori notes that she did not understand German: "During the solitary rehearsal I was able to have with them, I was careful to have the words immediately preceding my parts repeated very distinctly, accustoming my ears gradually to their sound. By this means everything went on correctly. The performance was a success; best of all, the greater part of the audience were persuaded that I was acquainted with the German language, and complimented me upon it." A few days later she said goodbye to her private Pullman car, the home on wheels that had always inspired her with respect for "the industrial genius which presides in America over all the locomotive enterprises." Her last tour was remarkable for several reasons, among them that her contract gave her forty per cent of the gross income of her performances, the largest percentage given to a single artist for a tour.

Ristorio was sixty-three years old in 1885. After her fourth tour of the United States her acting career was at an end. She never lost her concern for the stage and watched with interest, though not with approval the rise of the second generation of international actresses, Sarah Bernhardt and Eleonora Duse. In the last twenty years of her life she turned more to being the Marchesa Capranica del Grillo and less "la Ristori." Her son Giorgio, the new Marchese, was a chamberlain at the court of the Dowager Queen Margherita, and her daughter Donna Bianca a lady-in-waiting.

For her eightieth birthday, on January 29, 1902, tributes unique in the annals of theatrical history were devised. All Italian dramatic companies—about one hundred—devoted that evening to a performance in honor of the great actress. Special newspaper editions were published and medals coined in her honor. In the morning of the day, the King of Italy called at her residence. Prince Colonna, the Sindaco of Rome, brought her a bouquet of roses, with a tiny electric bulb in each bloom. In all schools of Rome the teachers delivered a lecture in her honor. The performance at the Teatro Valle, in the presence of the King and Queen of Italy, was an evening of unprecedented splendor. Princesses and duchesses bowed and kissed Ristori's hand. Similiar performances were held in Paris and Cairo, and she received 3000 telegrams.

Ristori died on October 9, 1906. At her funeral her most distinguished living colleague, Tommaso Salvini, delivered a commemorative address in which he spent a large amount of time and effort to deny that any rivalries had marred Ristori's career or life, and stressed especially that no struggles had ever taken place between her and Rachel. But in trying so assiduously to guard the good reputation of the departed, Salvini merely served to remind his listeners how central the issue of competition was in his day. Everything was conducive to it; the temper of the time, with its laissez-faire economy; its emphasis on competitive enterprise; the repertoire of the actresses, the plays in favor with audiences; the styles of acting and the stage practices in general.

Tommaso Salvini was not only Ristori's most distinguished contemporary in the theater, he was also the only international actor in the nineteenth century. His colleague Ernesto Rossi acted outside Italy, especially in Russia, but only Salvini had an extensive career spanning several decades and several continents.

Salvini, like Ristori, was the child of an acting family. A great patriot, he fought in the Roman revolution of 1848, and was often in trouble with the Austrian authorities. His international career began inauspiciously. Expecting to profit from Ristori's success, he went to Paris shortly after her in 1855. He had a very lukewarm reception which prompted him to give up the international field and spend the remainder of the 1850's and the 1860's in Italy. His international career really began, after some tentative forays, in South America in 1871. He had unparalleled triumphs. When he left Montevideo thousands lined the streets and marched with him to the ship. He followed that journey with one to North America, the first of five extended tours of the United States. During his second tour he performed in Washington and was invited into the House of Representatives by the Speaker. The entire House rose to welcome him; he shook hands with every Congressman present, and signed 278 autographs, including those for the House pages. Salvini also toured Europe repeatedly from Lisbon to Moscow, until his retirement in 1890 which he broke once, in 1902, when he performed in honor of Ristori's eightieth birthday. He died in 1916, at the age of eighty-seven. On the stage he developed a talent for bilingual performances that had wide appeal in the 1880's. During his third tour of the United States on April 16, 1883, he played one of his most successful plays, Giacometti's *Morte Civile*, in his usual role as Corrado, with Clara Morris (in English) as Rosalia. On some of his tours he acted almost exclusively with English-speaking casts, including performances as Othello to Booth's Iago and Mrs. Bowers' Emilia, and as the ghost to Booth's Hamlet.

Othello was Salvini's most impressive role. "Booth's was a melancholy, dignified Othello," Ellen Terry wrote in her memoirs, "but not as great as Salvini's was great. Salvini's Hamlet made me scream with mirth, but his Othello was the grandest, biggest, most glorious thing." His Othello was a barbarian with a veneer of civilization, who turns more and more animal as the poison of jealousy does its work. The barbarian triumphs in the end, an end as bloody and "realistic" as any in its time, and one that forced many of his admirers to divert their eyes. Joseph Knight, one of the foremost English critics, left a telling account (1875) of Othello's final moments:

> Staggering then to a seat, he commences, sitting and weeping, the final speech. Nearing the end, he rises, and at the supreme moment cuts his throat with a short scimitar hacking and hewing with savage energy, and imitating the noise that escaped blood and air, may together make when the windpipe is severed.

The great French actors never developed international careers. Talma was the first to act outside France with some consistency, but he did so more by demand of his Emperor than of any international-minded audience. Charles Fechter's international career was largely confined to England and America, where, however, he acted in English, not in French. Apart from Fechter,

who really changed rather than internationalized his career, a
few French actors gravitated towards Russia. Lemaître gave
some performances as Robert Macaire in London, and Coquelin
made an extensive tour of Europe and America in 1886, shortly
after the second international French actress, Sarah Bernhardt,
had achieved her international status. He also toured with her
once in the United States, and paid visits to the London stage
in the first decade of the twentieth century. That was the closest
a French actor came to an international career.

Mlle. George and Mlle. Déjazet, born in the eighteenth century, had been too early for consistent international careers.
Both performed abroad on occasion, but could not compete
with Rachel. Rachel's crown might have fallen to Aimée Desclée, who made her debut at the Théâtre du Gymnase in June
of 1855, when Rachel was about to give her final performances
at the Français. But Desclée was indolent and not sure of herself,
and inclined to substitute an existence of amatory adventures
and luxurious living for the singlemindedness needed to pursue
an acting career to its ultimate reaches. She left the stage for a
time and was afraid after that to face a Parisian audience. Instead
she went to Italy for a triumphant tour, and then to Belgium.
Her foreign successes were due to a fear of Paris, rather than an
extension of her career at home where she never succeeded completely. Her repertoire was that of the international and near-
international actresses after Rachel. It contained many of the
plays, especially those of Alexandre Dumas *fils*, which were also
performed by Bernhardt and Duse.

Déjazet was too early, and Desclée too lazy. Réjane, on the
other hand, was too late. She was born in 1857, thirteeen years
after Sarah Bernhardt, and when she entered the international
arena, the top position was firmly committed. Sarah Bernhardt
became an international star in the early 1880's, near the end of
Ristori's career. For nearly a decade she remained in solitary
eminence, until the appearance of the second Italian: Eleonora
Duse.

Besides the French and the Italians there were none. The critic

Grein saw the reason in the case of Mme. Mann, "the greatest actress of Holland—one of the greatest of the world. But for the
bar of language she would have been as renowned as Sarah Bernhardt and Duse." The ones who tried most often were the German actresses. Fanny Janauschek had great appeal, but she did
not become a star on the American stage until she had retired
from the theater for a year, learned English, and changed her
entire repertoire—a typically international repertoire—to the language of the country where she performed for most of the remainder of her life. Though she had been called "the German
Rachel" in her earlier days, this was merely a matter of publicity.
Rachel was unique; she had few imitators and no successful followers at all. Some actresses could perform items of her repertoire to elicit the idea of competition, like Eliza Logan who
performed Adrienne Lecouvreur in Boston in 1855, but there
was no "school of Rachel."

There was, however, a definite "school of Ristori," to which
Janauschek, the American actresses Mrs. Lander and Mrs. Bowers, and several others belonged. Her style as well as her repertoire were imitable. Macready thought that it was "not difficult
to act like Signora Ristori" and to imitate her "melodramatic
abandonment and lashing up to a certain point of detachment."
Like the vast majority of critics and experienced observers, he
found her inferior to Rachel.

The actress Helena Modjeska, on the other hand, said: "I was
in rapture over Madame Ristori, and came to the conclusion that
Italians are the best actors in the world. They can impersonate
characters from all the plays in the world. The French are at
their best in French plays, but the Italians are universal."

Modjeska, who grew up in the heyday of the Ristori tradition, transcended it to become a great star in her own right. Of
her, as much as of any actor or actress, it is true that except for
her language of origin she would have been an international actress. Even so she came close. She was born in 1840 in Cracow,
a city in Austrian Poland, and early became the first actress of
Warsaw, the center of her country as well of its Russian part.

Like Ristori, she became an object of suspicion to the three foreign powers who divided and ruled Poland: Russia, Prussia and Austria. Like Ristori, she was an ardent patriot who felt stifled by the atmosphere of censorship, suspicion and suppression. In 1866, in Poznan, she was the focus of a great patriotic demonstration that forced the police to call on the Prussian Army for help. When the greatest actress of Poland visited the West, she found that she compared favorably with the great actresses of the free world of Paris. She spoke French well, and acted so well that Dumas *fils* asked her to do *La Dame aux Camélias* in Paris. She refused, but the Comédie Française successfully invited her for a guest performance in *Iphigénie*. Here, however, the comparisons with Ristori ended. An actress who played in Polish, or in French with an accent, could not make her way internationally.

In 1876 Modjeska, with family and friends, emigrated to California to become farmers in the land of plenty. They knew nothing about farming, however, and the rustic idyll ended quickly. Forced to look for some other means of support, Modjeska learned English with singleminded energy, and after many difficulties obtained the grudging consent of a manager to give one matinee performance. On August 13, 1877, Modjeska performed *Adrienne Lecouvreur*, in English, in San Francisco. It was a spectacular triumph that led to an immediate engagement in the city, and an equally spectacular triumph in New York in December. When Bernhardt came to the United States for the first time, Modjeska was considered her chief rival. She remained an American favorite for a quarter of a century, toured with Edwin Booth, Forbes-Robertson and Maurice Barrymore, and was admired by Longfellow, Grant, Sherman, Lowell and Tennyson. She was constantly compared to Bernhardt and, later, to Duse, but she could not hope to go where Bernhardt or Duse went. Neither Polish nor English were languages on which an international career could be built.

CHAPTER 7 / Quand-Même

Q<small>UAND-MÊME</small> is a phrase hard to translate: it means something like *nevertheless, just the same, in spite of everything*. Sarah Bernhardt had it as her motto and inscribed it on her stationery. She chose it at the age of nine, she writes. Someone had dared her to jump across a ditch that was much too wide for her. She jumped and hurt herself, and immediately asserted that she would do it again, *quand-même*, if anyone dared her.

Rachel's motto was similar: *tout ou rien*. In the new iron age that believed in individual struggle for survival, the ambitious man and woman wanted all or nothing; anything in between had little meaning. It was an appropriate motto, and for much of her short life Rachel did have all, all that could be gained in her sphere. Sarah Bernhardt's motto is appropriate, too: it implies the struggles to reach the top, and Bernhardt clawed her way to it with a singlemindedness that Rachel had never needed.

Rachel had another advantage over Bernhardt. She was not alone. Her family, rapacious and hardheaded, were closely knit and gave their most famous member calculated but powerful support. Sarah Bernhardt's family did not exist as such. She was an illegitimate child, whose mother was overshadowed as a woman and a cocotte of the Second Empire by her more successful and beautiful sister Rosine, and in turn preferred her younger, more beautiful daughter Jeanne to Sarah. Jeanne turned into a morphine addict, probably a nymphomaniac, and died young. Their other sister, Régina, died of tuberculosis at eighteen.

In her autobiography Sarah is ambiguous about the circumstances of her birth, and most of her biographers have accepted her certificate of baptism as telling the true story of her parentage. According to it Sarah was born on September 25, 1844, the daughter of Edouard Bernhardt of Le Havre and Mme. Judith van Hand of Paris. The birth date is clearly wrong. Sarah herself celebrated October 23, and several other documents give October 22. Some biographers have doubted also that the year was 1844, a lack of chivalry often called for with regard to actresses, and they have been aided in this by Sarah in her later years, when she cast doubt on it herself in order to make the miracle of her eternal youth all the more miraculous. But as the documents that date back to her youth agree on 1844, it is likely that that is the right year. In that case Sarah was in her twelfth year when she was baptized at the convent of Grandchamps on May 21, 1856.

Who were her parents? Obviously the father was Edouard Bernhardt, as stated by the Chaplain at Grandchamps, who obviously would not lie, and this story was later reinforced by Sarah, who obviously ought to know. Sarah presumably knew, but it suited her well to go along with the little deception practiced on the Chaplain. After all, she had a son who in turn had two teen-age daughters at the time Sarah wrote her autobiography, and if speculation could be set at rest, it should be. The truth, is, however, that Edouard Bernhardt is Sarah's uncle and her mother's brother, not husband; and Hand, or Hard, or van Hand, was the maiden name of her grandmother, inserted presumably, together with a false birth date, to make detection of the real circumstances harder.

The real circumstances still elude us to some extent. It seems certain that Judith or Julie Bernhardt or Bernardt, Sarah's mother, spent some time in Le Havre. The Civil Registry of that city contains an entry for Saturday, April 22, 1843, noting the birth of twins to Julie Bernardt, musical artist, the daughter of Maurice Bernardt, oculist, and the late Jeanne Hard. The twins were named Rosalie and Lucie, and both died within three weeks. Probably they were Julie's first children.

As there is no record of Sarah's birth in Le Havre, one can believe other documents that state that she was born in Paris and that the record perished in the burning of the City Hall, together with thousands of other documents, during the Commune in 1871. It is very likely that her father was a resident of Le Havre. Sarah had a strong attachment to that city, and some other evidence points that way. An attorney from Le Havre represented her father in the matter of a legacy left to Sarah, and also in some decisions made earlier about her education. Some near-contemporary accounts say that her father was a one-time naval officer and son of a ship owner in that city, named Morin. Considering the practice of wealthy young men of that time, it is not unreasonable to conjecture that Sarah's father met Julie in Le Havre, and later set her up in an apartment in Paris, visiting her there periodically. The apartment must have been fairly humble, at 5, Rue de l'Ecole-de-Médécine, in the university district on the Left Bank, but Julie, like her sister Rosine, had at last made her way to the Promised City of Paris. Both became cocottes in the early years of the Second Empire, leaving such provincial benefactors as Morin behind. Rosine became a very successful practitioner, mistress of the Duc de Morny, the Emperor's half-brother, among others. Julie had to content herself with lesser fare and remained in her sister's shadow. Sarah was her oldest surviving child, followed by Jeanne-Rosine in 1851 and Régina in 1854, none, it is fairly clear, by the same father.

Sarah told Reynaldo Hahn, in old age, that once when she was a little girl, her mother took her for a walk in the Tuileries where they came upon an enormously obese woman who occupied two chairs at once. Sarah screamed and ran from that much ugliness. It was the old Mlle. George. The story is fictitious, to be sure, not because Mlle. George was not fat enough to need two chairs, but because Julie Bernard (as she called herself in Paris) is unlikely to have taken Sarah for a walk in the Tuileries.

Shortly after her birth Sarah was boarded with a peasant woman near Quimper in Brittany, who nursed her and took care of her for some years. She did not see her mother often, and usually under exceptional circumstances. Once, so Sarah tells, she fell accidentally into the fireplace, and was badly burned. Her nurse threw her into a large pot of warm milk, and butter was amassed in huge quantities to cure her burns. Far more important to her than being cured was the fact that Julie Bernard came post-haste from Paris, with her lover Baron Larrey, who was also a physician, and with another doctor. They were followed by several of Sarah's aunts, including the beautiful Rosine. After long neglect, Sarah was suddenly the center of her family's attention; she was to remember that lesson. Presumably as a result of this reminder of her existence, Julie transferred the nurse, her husband and Sarah to a pleasant little house in Neuilly, a suburb of Paris. But, as Sarah said "she was as sincere in her despair and her love as in her unconscious forgetfulness." Julie stayed as far and as long from Neuilly as she had from Quimper. Eventually the nurse's husband died, the nurse married a *concierge* in Paris and moved there. Sarah found herself suddenly shifted from pleasant country surroundings to an airless, closet-sized room in a dark, small, foul-smelling apartment. Julie was not notified, and one can suppose that Sarah, ill-kept as she was by the *concierge,* was also no longer paid for by her mother. Sarah was desperately unhappy at 65 Rue de Provence. She felt trapped physically and otherwise, forgotten and lost at the age of five. Then, one day, an elegant lady came to look at an apartment in the building, and when she turned her head, Sarah recognized her Aunt Rosine. She let out a scream, ran to her and clung to her sobbingly. The elegant lady recognized Sarah and was embarrassed. She promised to call for Sarah the next day, but Sarah had already learned her first major lesson in life. Her belief in promises was small; she was sure that only an action could rescue her, and that only if it were sufficiently disastrous. The five-year-old child threw herself down into the street from the window of the apartment, broke an arm in two places, and injured her knee. After that Aunt Rosine simply had to take her along at once. Sarah spent the next two years at her mother's home in the charge of a servant.

In the fall of 1851 Sarah was sent to boarding school, first to Mme. Fressard's in Auteuil, and subsequently to the Augustine Convent of Grandchamps, where she was baptized.

Sarah came into a legacy from her father in 1857, and it may have been his death that prompted Julie Bernhardt to remove her daughter from the school. Now her education was to be in the hands of a governess, Mlle. de Brabender, who filled one half of a mother's place in her life. The other half was soon to be taken by a charming and selfless friend who lived in an apartment in the same building, Mme. Guérard.

The Paris of the late 1850's, and her mother's house, were unlikely to give Sarah the sense of order and the feeling of tranquillity she desperately needed. The political and moral turbulence of the Second Empire was at its height. *L'Empire c'est la paix* (the Empire means peace), the Prince President had said before he ascended the throne as Napoleon III. In the six years since that happy advent of peace, France had gone through the three years of the Crimean War, and was just about to enter the war of Italian liberation against Austria. Yet it all seemed a splendid beginning of a new era. France was once more the first power on the Continent, industry was developing, railroads were being built. Baron Haussmann was tearing down the old Paris to build his splendid boulevards, and the city had rivaled the great London itself with the second World's Fair. The Emperor and his splendid court seemed as solidly golden as their ornate dinner service. Actually the dinner service was gilt electro-plated on silver, a brand-new process, and the gilt veneer of the new-process Empire was as thin.

Julie Bernard, the cocotte, was part of that veneer. Sarah hated her mother's friends and her parties and would do what she could to avoid them. She would pour ink on her dress in the last minute, or turn her ankle until she could not walk straight. She was at the same time very conscious of being neglected, and aware that her mother preferred her pretty sister Jeanne, whom she raised herself, to Sarah with her unruly hair and her wild fits of temper. Strong contradictory feelings about her mother permeate Sarah's autobiography, published in 1907; they emerge even more clearly from Sarah's conversations in old age recorded by her granddaughter Lysiane. Again and again she cites her mother's antipathy, her constant belittling of Sarah's accomplishments. She often makes light of her situation, as in the opening sentence of the autobiography: "My mother was fond of traveling: she would go from Spain to England, from London to Paris, from Paris to Berlin, and from there to Christiania; then she would come back, embrace me, and set out again . . ." The feeling of bitterness is still there after sixty years of effort to make up for a childhood of neglect. "It was very evident," she says on a later page, "that mamma loved my sister more than me, and this preference, which did not trouble me ordinarily, hurt me sorely now." "Not trouble me ordinarily"—two pages later she cites her mother's preference again, and one page further on she asserts that her mother did not like Mme. Guérard because she "did not prefer my sister to me." Only major actions and disasters elicited attention and compassion, and those Sarah learned to produce. It is not surprising that she, like Ristori, enjoyed funerals and developed a fascination for coffins. She threw out an early suitor, an undertaker's assistant, because he refused to let her see an embalming.

Julie, for her part, found Sarah a continuous trial. The girl was not beautiful in the usual sense, though even then her appeal had a certain intoxicating quality. She was not permitted to shine in the salon of her mother, who was in her early thirties and at the height of her appeal as a woman. It was considered much more appropriate that the inconveniently grown-up girl be married off, and so the butcher, baker and candlestick maker, in their more genteel forms, were imported to lay their hearts and money at her feet. Marie Colombier, an actress and part-time novelist who later wrote a scurrilous biography of Sarah, cites long lists of them, and hints at extensive and orgiastic immorality. Nevertheless it appears that the honest citizens were highly unsuccessful in their propositions, moral or immoral, and that Sarah rejected them with the utmost impoliteness. What should Julie do? Sarah was too young to live by herself in 1859, too old for the usual schools for girls. Sarah reports that a family council was held on the matter, and that the Duc de Morny, as Aunt Rosine's lover a *quasi* member of the family, decided the matter with an offhand remark: "Send her to the Conservatoire."

It is more likely that the Duke was bored with the discussion than prescient of her talent. Sarah had to be disposed of, an occupation had to be found as she did not have an independent income, and there were few occupations for women in 1859. He was probably sure that he could arrange her admission without much trouble and quite irrespective of any talent. So, in spite of the shocked objections of Mlle. de Brabender and Mme. Guérard to the whole scheme, Sarah was that evening taken to the Comédie Française for her first plays: *Brittanicus,* which bored her, and *Amphytrion* which made her cry so loudly that she had to be taken home at once before the closing curtain.

In her autobiography, interesting to note, Sarah presents herself at the age of fifteen as a child. She was furious at the idea of going to the Conservatoire. She pouts, she raves, she pulls out all stops to prevent the decision, simply because she once more has no part in the making of it. She is still threatened with punishment by her mother, and once more retreats into sullen submission. It was for the last time.

Daniel François Auber was the director of the Conservatoire in 1860. He was seventy-eight, a prolific and popular operatic composer whose main work had been done thirty years earlier. Sarah makes it a point in her memoirs to tell that Mlle. de Brabender and Mme. Guérard accompanied her to the entrance examination, and that all other girls, about thirty of them, were accompanied by their mothers or other close relatives. From the first moment Sarah felt at a disadvantage. Shyness, lack of knowledge of the nature of the examination—one does not know, but at any rate Sarah had no one to give her cues when she finally appeared before the judges. They were a formidable group upon which the shadow of Rachel lay heavily: Samson, Rachel's teacher; Beauvallet, her partner; Augustine Brohan, her rival in some roles; Regnier and Provost, who were there before she even came, and Bressant. Instead of a dramatic scene from Racine or Corneille she recited a fable, "Les Deux Pigeons," by La Fontaine. Beauvallet wondered softly if the Conservatoire was being turned into an elocution class, but actually it was not a bad choice. Adrienne Lecouvreur recites it in Act II of the play that bears her name, one of Rachel's plays, and Sarah put herself thereby in line with the first as well as the last (so far) of the great actresses of French tragedy.

Morny's intervention assured the girl of a place in the Conservatoire, but the fact that both Beauvallet and Provost volunteered to have her in their classes indicates more than acquiescence. Auber expressed his regret that so charming a voice was not destined for opera.

Sarah, however, attributed her admission solely to the influence of the Duc de Morny. Once more some forces beyond her control had decided her future, and merit had not been the main factor. It seems that she hated the Comédie from the day of her admission to its school. At the end of the first year she won the second prize in tragedy, and never forgot that it had not been the first. At the end of her second year she won no prize in tragedy at all—a fact she attributed to Provost's illness, which had landed her in Samson's class—and won second prize in comedy. She never forgave the beautiful Marie Lloyd for preceding her here, too. The fact that a second was very good meant nothing; to her it meant only that it was not the first.

The winners of the first prize were assured a debut at the Comédie, while those who came second were generally given the opportunity to act at the Odéon. That Sarah in 1862 was nevertheless given a contract at the Comédie was probably due to a further intervention by Morny. The young girl felt no pleasure, only resentment that she was still rising on her mother's (or aunt's) merits.

Only seven years had passed since Rachel's final performances, but tragedy had fallen into disuse again. The Comédie glittered along with the glittering Empire, but its strength lay in comedy alone. The new serious drama, realistic in intent if not in result, was passing it by.

Sarah's engagement at the Comédie began badly. Things went wrong from the day she set foot in the House of Molière. Her mother ought to have accompanied her, a minor, to the Director's office for the signing of the contract. She did not. Instead, Sarah came with Mme. Guérard. As if to compensate herself for her mother's neglect, Sarah came decked out in the height of fashion, very inappropriate for a novice. She arrived moreover in the carriage, complete with footmen, that belonged to her aunt Rosine. All this is unlikely to have appealed to Thierry, the Director. The news of the big dinner that Rosine gave to celebrate her engagement is also unlikely to have endeared her to her future colleagues and superiors: Morny was present of course, and Camille Doucet from the Ministry of Culture, who had helped him to smooth the way for her impending career; and Count Walewski, the Minister of Culture himself. Sarah recited *L'Âme du Purgatoire* by Delavigne, and repeated it, at Walewski's request, to an improvised piano accompaniment by Rosine's neighbor, Giacomo Rossini.

On August 11, 1862, Sarah made her debut as Iphigénie, in Racine's play. Samson and Provost, black coated and frightening rather than reassuring, were in the wings. She was, as usual, fearfully afflicted with stagefright, *le trac*. The most feared critic, Francisque Sarcey, was kind: "Mlle. Sarah Bernhardt . . . carries herself well and speaks with perfect clarity. That is all one can say at this moment . . ." Her other debuts were no better, and a few months later Sarcey finally pronounced her insufficient.

For Sarah it was a nightmare. She was no longer second even; she was a failure, pronounced dead by the critics, if indeed they noticed her at all; disparaged as usual by her mother and her circle; neglected, it seems, even by her first lover, the Comte de

Kératry, a dashing young cavalry officer who seemed constantly
to be away from Paris. On January 15, 1863, her pent-up emotion, her disgust at being disregarded, vented itself. It was the
occasion of the annual homage to Molière, when the actors and
actresses advanced onto the stage of his theater two by two,
were greeted by applause (presumably a measure of their individual popularity for that season) and placed palm fronds at the
foot of his statue.

Sarah had brought her small sister Régina along back stage.
In the excitement of preparation Régina stepped on the train of
one actress' gown. Mme. Nathalie was fat, aging, probably
nervous about the volume of her applause. She turned and
pushed the child so hard that Régina fell against a column and
cut her face. Sarah turned around and impulsively slapped Mme.
Nathalie's face. Nathalie fainted, the entire company was in an
uproar, the ceremony was interrupted, and Sarah was at least no
longer an *anonymous* failure.

Sarah liked to remember in later years that she was called into
Thierry's office the next day, ordered to apologize, refused, and
tore up her contract. In reality, however, she simply left the
office after her refusal. In the end it was her lack of roles at the
Comédie that caused her quite undramatic resignation.

Within a few weeks Sarah had obtained a new position, at
the Gymnase, Rachel's first theater, where she also failed, or
thought she failed, in less than a year.

Maurice Bernhardt, Sarah's only child, was born on December
22, 1864. When she left the Gymnase precipitously at the end
of April and fled south with the faithful Guérard in tow, she
may well have been aware of her pregnancy, and the knowledge
may have contributed to the precipitousness of her break and
her flight. The child's father was most likely the Prince Henri
de Ligne, a Belgian nobleman she had met in 1862.

The next two years were very difficult. Sarah was out of
work, and though she looked hard, she could not obtain more
than an occasional role. Beset with financial worries, leading a
hand-to-mouth existence, Sarah had many short-lived liaisons,

and the dissipation of her life is quite evident. But throughout the two years after the birth of Maurice she never ceased to try to find her way back to the stage, in contrast to many who gave up quickly and became cocottes. She finally succeeded in obtaining an engagement at the second imperial theater, the Odéon. The Odéon did not have the stature of the Comédie, but it was also much freer and less encrusted with tradition. The great romantic plays had been performed there in the 1830's and 1840's when the Comédie proved inhospitable, and its actors were often better than those of the senior house.

Rachel had been the actress of the *grande bourgeoisie*, which was trying to be aristocratic. At the Odéon Sarah became the idol of the rising bohemian world of Paris, of the students, artists and musicians. She was not beautiful, but she had a beguiling nonchalance about her, a fresh charm. She dressed with impeccable taste to suit her appearance and the occasion; she was not afraid to be unusual and daring. She radiated a vibrant energy and intelligence. She was still thin, and not at all fashionble in that respect; but rather than hide it, she used it to telling effect in her dress and manners. She had large expressive eyes, and considerable grace in movement. Above all, she had a strong, evocative voice, to which the epithet "golden" was beginning to attach itself, a voice that, with its flexibility and with its owner's perfect sense of timing, could seem to transform prose into poetry. That voice played a large role in her first major success.

The Empire was gradually sliding into a less and less enviable state in the late 1860's. Its external position was becoming more precarious. It had forfeited the good will of Italy without gaining the good will of the Pope. The Pope never forgave the Emperor Napoleon for losing most of the Papal States when Italy was unified after the defeat of Austria in 1859. Italy resented that it had had to buy France's help with Savoy and Nice, and that France had prevented complete unification by protecting the Pope in Rome. Prussia had defeated Austria in 1866 and was now the dominant power in Central Europe. The French-sponsored Empire in Mexico had failed and its Emperor, Maximilian, had been shot. Internally, the restlessness of the bourgeoisie had led to repressive measures and more restlessness in turn. The opposition was becoming more numerous every year.

Victor Hugo, the greatest poet of France, went into exile when the Empire was established. As a constant reminder of lost liberties, he lived proudly, stubbornly and uncomfortably on the Island of Jersey, a British possession just off the French coast. As long as the Empire was new and the Emperor successful, he did not matter. But now the gilt was coming off as reverse followed reverse, politically as well as economically, and with it Victor Hugo's stubborn resistance received new prominence. By 1868 there were the usual demonstrations in the theaters, and in one of these Sarah became involved. Insistent demands were being voiced for a revival of the Romantic drama, especially the plays of Hugo, as a political rather than an artistic gambit. As Hugo was in exile it was manifestly impossible to revive his plays, but the Odéon decided to treat the demand as a purely artistic matter, and to revive a play by Dumas, the second most important of the Romantic playwrights. Dumas had acquiesced to the Empire, and for that and other more or less pertinent reasons was no longer as popular as the management of the Odéon supposed. His *Kean* was the choice for a revival and there were loud objections that had their climax on the night of the first performance. Ostensibly the riot was directed against Dumas, but the undercurrent was the protest against the government. The noise began even before the performance got under way, and one could hear more and more loudly the cries *"Ruy Blas . . . Ruy Blas"*—a demand for one of Hugo's most significant plays. The curtain finally went up, pandemonium reigned, and nothing said on stage could be heard. The performance proceeded dismally while the audience enjoyed its rowdiness and Dumas sat pale and haggard in his box—until Sarah entered and began to speak. "Mlle. Sarah Bernhardt," wrote *Le Figaro*, "appeared in an eccentric costume which only served to increase the storm, but her vibrant voice, that stunning voice, moved the public. She had tamed it, like a little Orpheus." Chiefly she succeeded by stepping forward and giving her lines right at the public, but without her magnificent voice, and the strength of her appearance, she could not have calmed the crowd.

Her first artistic success in a more normal manner came almost one year later. An unknown young poet, François Coppée, had brought a play to Agar, the tragic actress who was a member of the company at the Odéon at that point. The play was a one-act called *Le Passant*. It was in verse and had only two characters, the great courtesan Silvia and the page Zanetto. Agar's role was Silvia, and for Zanetto Agar suggested the actress who had played Aricie to her Phèdre: Sarah Bernhardt. Sarah was enthusiastic and together the two persuaded a doubtful management to put on the play.

Le Passant was a triumph that marked a change in the taste of the audience. For more than fifteen years prose drama on contemporary life had dominated dramatic development in Paris. The plays of Dumas *fils* and Augier had replaced both Rachel's classical revival and the romantic drama. Now, in the late 1860's, verse drama with a historical setting was reasserting itself, and that romantic revival fitted Sarah Bernhardt very well. She spoke poetry "like the song of the nightingale," de Banville wrote, "like the sighs of the wind, like the murmurs of the water, like the poems that Lamartine once produced."

After *Le Passant* Sarah was the undisputed queen of the Left Bank, of the students, the shop-girls, the young and gay. They came to be known as the "Saradoteurs," a kind of cheering section, claque and bodyguard, who would handle critics roughly if they dared to speak unkindly of their object of affection.

In 1869 Sarah also suffered a misfortune, which, at least in part, worked to her benefit. Her apartment at 16 Rue Auber caught fire, and the place burned to the ground while she was in the theater. Nobody was hurt, but all her belongings, her clothes, her new furniture, her beginning jewelry collection, and even her two pet tortoises Zerbinette and Chrysagère (the latter particularly resplendent with its gold back set with small blue, pink and yellow topazes) were lost. Some of her friends

organized a benefit performance to help her financially. In itself
that would not have been sensational or particularly lucrative;
she was, after all, just at the beginning of stardom. But Adelina
Patti, the most famous singer of her generation, was in Paris just
then, and she was prevailed upon to participate, a completely
unexpected coup which guaranteed a sold-out house. Patti, not
always famed for the goodness of her heart, might not have done
so had she not also been the Marquise de Caux. Her husband,
the Marquis, may have had some influence on her decision, and
affairs past or present were sufficiently public in Paris to admit
the added piquancy of seeing Patti perform at the benefit for
her husband's former mistress. At any rate, she acquitted herself
royally, and sang *Una voce poco fà* three times.

The outbreak of war with Prussia on July 19, 1870, was met
with great patriotic fervor. Sarah nightly sang the Marseillaise at
the Odéon, and contemporary accounts say that her voice out-
soared the entire audience. As she was not musical and could not
really carry a tune, she probably chanted rather than sang. But
she must in some way have dominated that audience, a further
demonstration of her emerging vocal and histrionic power.

The enthusiasm for the war did not last, for there were not
even the initial successes to keep it going. The disaster at Sedan,
where the Emperor and most of his army surrendered to the
Prussians, came within weeks of the beginning of the conflict.
The road to Paris was suddenly open to the enemy, and the ex-
aggerated confidence of the French people turned to sudden
panic. The railway stations were invaded by thousands attempting to escape, and essential transportation services began to break
down almost at once. The theaters closed, lines formed before
food stores, the unimagined possibility of a siege of Paris was
suddenly upon the city.

Sarah would not be idle. She would play her part, and did so
with that mixture of heroism and theatricality that characterized
her whole life. Her patriotism and her wish to help were great
and genuine, but her resourceful mind also hit upon the right
role Sarah Bernhardt could play in that great real-life drama of

the siege of Paris. Emile de Girardin and Duquesnel, the manager of the Odéon, were called on first of all to assist her in her
plan to turn the Odéon into a military hospital. After that had
been done she really went to work. Her first request was to the
Prefect of Police, to get his support in obtaining food and supplies. She was immediately successful, for the new Prefect was
none other than Comte de Kératry, the dashing lieutenant of her
earlier life. He not only put his resources at her disposal; he even
let her take his overcoat as a blanket. She remembers that he
also sent her ten barrels of wine and two of brandy; 30,000 eggs,
and hundreds of bags of coffee, boxes of tea and cans of preserves. That was only the beginning. M. Mercier, the chocolate
manufacturer, sent her five hundred pounds of his product. M.
de Rothschild sent two barrels of brandy and one hundred bottles of his own wine. An old schoolmate from Grandchamps
sent two hundred pounds of salted butter, and on and on.

In spite of all the misery that surrounded her, and all the constant news of military reverses, Sarah found a kind of heady
happiness in this effort, a happiness that emerges still in her autobiography. All this frantic activity, all this private initiative and
private help, all this ingenuity and often chaotic free enterprise
gave her, and thousands of others, a sense of importance, or at
least of relevance, which later, more organized efforts would
not produce. Every dozen eggs was a victory, every bottle of
wine a successful skirmish, every blanket the result of a victorious patrol. And everywhere, indefatigable in the midst of all the
egg victories, the brandy battles, was Sarah; Sarah the provider,
the nurse, the administrator, the aid and comfort. She obtained
all; she found the overworked doctors to come to her wounded;
even the old Baron Larrey, the friend of her mother's when
Sarah was an infant in Brittany, came and put his medical skill
to use once more.

She did help hundreds of soldiers, and her hospital was better
provided than most. Her resources of energy were immense, and
for the first time now they were being put to the test. She no
longer coughed into her handkerchief or threatened her man-

agers with the imminent outbreak of galloping tuberculosis. She
now had arrived at a faith in her own strength, a faith that was
not to leave her again.

Among the soldiers who came to her hospital was a young
lieutenant whom she liked and to whom she gave an autographed
picture of herself when he left the hospital as a convalescent.
He remained her friend, and forty-five years later, during another war, when she herself was in the hospital after the ampu-
tation of her leg, he took time to come down and visit her. He
was the then commander in chief of the Allied Forces, Marshal
Foch.

Her absorption in the work of the hospital did not obscure
her view of the world outside, and of the worsening situation.
She saw the women lined up for the steadily diminishing rations
of food. She sometimes gave brandy to some who, half-frozen,
waited through the night to get half a loaf of bread in the morning. The bombs were now falling around the Odéon, and the
wounded had to be kept in the cellars. The Prussian lines were
drawing more and more tightly around Paris, and Sarah realized
that the city could not hold out much longer. In January the
armistice came, and the Prussians marched down the Champs
Elysées.

When, on one cold autumn morning, she ascended the steps
of the Tuileries for the first time since the fall of the Empire,
she shed a tear for Napoleon III, who had surrendered his sword
rather than shed unnecessary blood, and for his lovely Empress,
who had fled in the carriage of her American dentist, "for it was
not even a Frenchman, but a foreigner, who had had the courage
to protect that unfortunate woman." Her feelings, like Rachel's,
were for the established order, and particularly for the monarchy.

Victor Hugo's exile had ended with the end of the monarchy.
He had come home in triumph, and as soon as the theaters reopened in the fall of 1871, the Odéon was preparing the long
awaited revival of his work.

The first performance of *Ruy Blas* was on January 26, 1872,

Bernhardt as Mrs. Clarkson in *L'Etrangère,* in the late 1870's

A portrait group of Parisian celebrities by Alfred Stevens (1828-1906)

1. Joseph Lockroy (actor, dramatist) 2. Ernest Reyer (composer)
3. Antonin Proust (journalist) 4. Léon Cladel (writer) 5. Georges
Ohnet (playwright and novelist) 6. Paul Hervieu (writer) 7. Henri
Becque (playwright) 8. Sully Prudhomme (poet) 9. Jules Massenet
(composer) 10. Juliette Adam (writer) 11. Henri Meilhac (librettist)
12. Ludovic Halévy (writer) 13. Emile Augier (playwright)
14. Francisque Sarcey (critic) 15. Jeanne Bartet (actress) 16. Jules
Lemaître (writer) 17. Victorien Sardou (playwright) 18. Sarah Bernhardt 19. Edouard Pailleron (writer) 20. Jules Claretie (journalist and
playwright) 21. Unknown 22. Emile Reich 23. Georges Bizet (composer) 24. François Coppée (playwright) 25. Edmond Got (actor).

Bernhardt as Hamlet, about 1900

Bernhardt as the Duke of Reichstadt; death scene in the sixth act of
L'Aiglon, 1901

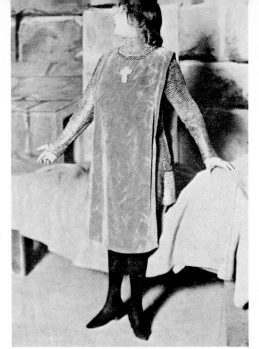

Bernhardt as Joan of Arc, in
1911, at the age of sixty-seven

Bernhardt as Queen Elizabeth; death scene in the film made of
Moreau's play

Bernhardt in her dressing room in 1922, a few months before her death

Duse in 1884, at the age of twenty-six

Duse in Goldoni's *La Locandiera*

Duse as Cleopatra, probably in Shakespeare's play, 1880's

Duse as Francesca da Rimina

Duse in the letter scene of the final act of *La Dame aux Camé- lias*, 1890's

Duse in *La Città Morta,*
about 1900

Gabriele D'Annunzio

Duse in 1923 before her final
American tour

Bernhardt's funeral procession passing down the Rue Royale

with Sarah as the queen. It was an unheard-of success, and more than one hundred performances were given before it was removed from the repertoire again. The cast was the best that could be collected at the Odéon, and that probably meant the best cast in Paris. Sarah was not the main star by any means, but one of four, and it was her outstanding performance rather than the prominence of her role that made her the center of attention.

The critics, with one or two exceptions, were enchanted with her. Sarcey said of one of her main speeches: "Mlle. Sarah Bernhardt sighed that delightful ballad with a mournful voice; she did not search for shades of difference; she gave us one long caress of sounds which had in its very uniformity I do not know what sweetness and appeal. She merely added the music of her voice to the music of the verses." It was still her voice more than her acting that captivated the audience, "that languishing and tender voice, with its perfect delivery of rhyme so that not one syllable is ever lost." *Le Passant* had established her talent. Now, after the war, the role of the Queen in *Ruy Blas* made her a star.

The Comédie Française could not ignore her any longer. In the spring of 1872 Émile Perrin, its director, offered her a contract at 12,000 francs a year. Although her contract at the Odéon, at 9,600 francs, had one year to run, Sarah decided to accept the offer. She left the Odéon in characteristic fashion, managing not only to break her contract but to feel completely in the right about it.

Théodore de Banville thought Perrin's offer "a serious, violently revolutionary decision. Here is poetry entering the home of dramatic art, and, to be frank, the wolf coming into the sheepfold." He was wrong in one respect. At the Comédie Sarah was a wolf among wolves. No one could out-intrigue her, but she was unnerved at times by the wall of hostility she encountered. She was genuinely concerned with her art and took great pains with her roles and costumes. She soon found that too much eagerness was not welcome in the businesslike atmosphere of the

Français. Perrin soon came to dislike her and sided generally with those members of the company who did what they could to show the star who had come from an "inferior house" that she was no star at the Comédie.

Her roles were failures and she might have passed out of theatrical life once more if the artistic element had not been overshadowed by her rivalry with Sophie Croizette, which, in the best tradition, was built up by the press and the gossip on the boulevards to enhance the excitement of an evening at the Comédie.

The rivalry led to quarrels and to long-drawn-out intrigues. When both of them received roles in an eagerly awaited new play by Octave Feuillet, *Le Sphinx*, in March 1874, the author and the director both had to intervene in the quarrel because the two actresses were locked in bitter battle about the light of the stage moon, which both insisted should be falling on one to the exclusion of the other in a certain scene. Matters went so far that Perrin suspended Sarah and tried another actress who was, however, found to be insufficient. As a result the decision had to be moonlight for both Sarah and Croizette, which satisfied neither.

The performance itself became a battle between the two, in which Sarah was at a disadvantage because she had the smaller, less spectacular role. As Berthe de Sevigny she won the applause of the connoisseurs. She played discreetly and with noble dignity, and managed to elicit prolonged applause with a few words, or a gesture of her outstretched hand. "In the last act," as Sarcey wrote, "where she is the outraged wife who forgives, she displayed an intensity of passion, both dignified and vehement, which aroused real shouts of admiration."

Sarcey admits, however, that Croizette, to his disappointment, took the lead in the race, even though the role of Blanche de Chelles was not well suited to her. She captured first place by means of her death scene: Croizette drank her poison and collapsed into a chair. Then the real spectacle began. Croizette's face suddenly turned green and decomposed visibly. It became furrowed with fearful contractions; her eyes, glazed and haggard, rolled in their sockets, her hands and mouth shook convulsively, her head was caught in the convulsions of lockjaw. It was a revolting spectacle, but it was also sensational. (The newspapers subsequently revealed the tricks of lighting that had given Croizette her green complexion.)

Here, too, Sarah learned a lesson. One could do a crude thing on occasion and be crassly sensational, though the rest of the performance might live up to very high standards. The new plays that Sarah performed in the 1880's contained death scenes much more accomplished and shocking, though more subtle than Croizette's.

At the end of 1874 Perrin was in difficulties with Roselia Rousseil, who was to play Phèdre in a new production, and was forced to substitute Sarah. She prepared her part in four days and, at last, had a chance to play the greatest role of a French stage actress.

Rachel had played Phèdre as a woman possessed by her passion and wrecked by it mentally and physically. Ristori, a more amply built woman, and a more Victorian character, played Phèdre to arouse pity rather than terror. Her Phèdre was a martyred woman, an object of sentimental anguish in an almost anti-Rachel performance.

Bernhardt upheld Rachel, but, in keeping with the development of acting since Rachel's breakthrough, played Phèdre in a more human, less demonic and also less statuesque manner. Rachel lacked tenderness, a feeling that Bernhardt could add to her interpretation. She depicted real love perverted by a great, pervading sense of guilt. Phèdre, in Bernhardt's hands, became a woman destroyed by her own uncontrollable drives, more a study in psychology than in demonism. To some of the more conservative critics her interpretation seemed too natural and simple at first, but eventually she obtained universal acceptance for it.

Sarah played Phèdre for forty years, refining and rephrasing her role until she had transformed it into as perfect a work of

histrionic art as any ever created, one that fascinated the generation of 1910 as much as it did that of 1870.

In 1874 Sarcey said: "She has forced the old experts to admit
that, in the second act at any rate, she was the equal of the memory of the great tragedienne [Rachel]."

On June 28, 1896, Reynaldo Hahn described a performance
of *Phèdre* in London: "Both [Rachel and Bernhardt] (the proof
is in Ristori's memoirs) had a similar conception [of Phèdre's
entrance in Act I]. But I can hardly believe that Rachel was
able to give, as Sarah does, the idea of a woman mortally
wounded by love. Her entry is entirely individual and is one of
the most beautiful things ever seen: All that has been conceived
in the purest type of sculpture is here combined with the ravages,
the tortures love can impose on a human being."

May Agate, the actress, saw Bernhardt as Phèdre in 1912,
and still considered it one of the supreme acting achievements
she had ever witnessed.

Sarah Bernhardt was far too restless and ambitious to accept
the pace the Français imposed on her. In her increasing frustration she turned to arts other than acting. She had displayed some
artistic inclinations earlier, in the aimless months between the
Convent and the Conservatoire. Pronier records a favorable
notice in the *Mercure de Paris* of October, 1860, of her painting
"Les Champs Elysées en Hiver," which won the first prize in
an exhibition at the Academie Colombier. She seems to have
dropped her interest as soon as she entered the Conservatoire,
and did not return to it during the hectic 1860's. In 1873–1874
she took up sculpture, which she studied briefly with Mathieu-
Meusnier, who had sent her a statue of herself in her role as
Zanetto in *Le Passant*. In 1874 she submitted the bust of a young
girl (presumably her sister Régina) to the annual Salon; Rodin
succinctly described it as "une saloperie." Undeterred by Rodin,
and praised by a number of critics, she continued to sculpt, and
regularly submitted works to the Salon. In 1876 she sent her
most ambitious work, a group called "Après la Tempête," which
received an honorable mention. There also were busts of Girar-

din and Rothschild, a bas-relief of a dimple-chinned Ophelia, head and shoulders, floating on the river, and others.

In the middle 1870's, Sarah spent more time in her studio than at the theater. Her feelings about her art were presumably genuine. But the way she did it was typically Sarah, and left her open to the accusation that her artistry was a search for publicity rather than art. Her studio was scenery, a dramatic setting for the sculptress, rather than a useful workroom. It had its bohemian aspects, but mainly it strove to be the perfect studio, the perfect setting for the artist. In it Sarah wore the perfect clothes, which may have been less perfect to work in—a white blouse or vest, and white pants, all made of silk, adorned with a large lace collar and cuffs, and rounded out with a white tulle cravat. The clothes accentuated her unfashionable slenderness, something she enjoyed doing not only in her studio. In public she wore tight fitting sheath dresses, quite unlike the fashions of her time, that scandalized society at least as much as the trousers she wore in her studio.

After a few years of sculpting, she suddenly conceived a passion for painting, and, as with her sculpture, began on large-scale compositions almost immediately.

Sarah did not only sculpt and paint and act in these years. She also read voraciously and often discriminatingly, she discussed and argued, she went to concerts, lectures, openings of art exhibitions, she was seen and heard everywhere. Clearly she conceived herself as being a renaissance woman—or rather a renaissance man, one should say, a person of unbounded versatility and iconoclastic tendencies. And though the artistic and cultural world of Paris did not take her that seriously, it would have found it impossible to ignore her—even had it wanted to.

As the proper setting for her role Sarah built herself a renaissance palazzo in 1875, at the intersection of Rue Fortuny and Avenue de Villiers. It was the most sumptuous setting of her career, and she built it without any knowledge of how she would pay for it. The year before Sarcey had broken his vow to review only plays and not the lives of players, and commented at length on her spending habits. She herself says that she inherited 100,-000 francs in 1875, but as the mansion cost at least 500,000 francs, the source of the rest remains unspecified. Her salary had risen from 12,000 francs to 20,000 francs, not a small sum, though little compared to the income of Rachel. It was not enough to maintain her standard of living. And while Rachel took care to have Walewski supply her with a mansion, Sarah seems to have had no such single source.

Sarah always took great joy in luxuries of all kinds and wanted a sumptuous setting for its own sake. But she also gloried in her publicity, and the new palazzo was part of her public face. She was fond of collecting all she could find written about her. The extent of her publicity is unequaled before her time, even by the great Barnum. While Rachel may have encouraged a few of the stories that epitomized her rise from rag-picking to riches, Sarah encouraged almost everything that published her name and everyone who spoke of her or was likely to. All her homes were always filled with dogs, cats, monkeys, fish, tortoises and other beasts. She was genuinely fond of them and unafraid, but she also used them for her ends, as she used her art, her house and her friends. In addition to her menagerie her house contained other items that interested her and gave food for articles to reporters. There was a skull, for example, autographed and inscribed with verses by Victor Hugo. And there was of course her famous coffin. We do not know when she had it made, but it was there, in her bedroom, by the middle 1870's, and it traveled with her around the world wherever she went on tour. Dozens of stories are told about it. One she told herself—that she slept in it while her sister Régina, dying of tuberculosis, lay in Sarah's own bed in the same room. This aberration of taste, possibly a true story, was embroidered and embellished by later writers, and by those who knew her. According to these stories the coffin contained more than fifty pictures of Sarah in costume; she is supposed to have played the piano at a mock funeral of herself built around the coffin; and so on.

Her life was such that relatively innocent actions would be

news, and small, newsworthy acts became sensations. The most
sensational among the true stories was that of her ascent in a
balloon, during the International Exposition in Paris in 1878.
The publicity was enormous; all minute details of her equipment, supplies and actions were described, her food and drink
and the whole momentous course of the journey. She returned
to Paris a hero after the balloon, which had drifted off course,
finally landed in a field near the city. The journey had two consequences: The Théâtre Français fined her 1,000 francs for
leaving the city without prior notice. And she wrote a rather
charming book describing the whole ascent.

By the late 1870's publicity was not only Sarah's daily life;
Sarah's publicity was part of the life of Paris and even of France.
Thérèse Berton, whose husband had been one of Sarah's leading
men on and off stage, says quite simply: "She was by now the
greatest feminine personality—I say it in all seriousness—that
France had known since Joan of Arc."

Like that more saintly predecessor she had people around her
who wanted to see her burned as a witch, though they posed as
friends rather than enemies. One of them, for example, Albert
Milland, wrote in *Le Figaro* in August, 1878, that Paris talked
only of the actions and gestures of Mlle. Bernhardt, turning her
into a goddess whose

> slenderness is merely the result of the dissolution of matter. She
> is as uncorporeal as possible, all dreams, all vapor, all spirit. . . .
> For my part, I believe that Mademoiselle Sarah Bernhardt is
> surrounded by clumsy people who, with their insistent adver-
> tising and the stories they peddle, end by injuring their favorite
> artist. Nobody more than I appreciates the grace, the charm of
> the young actress. Everywhere people praise her wit, her educa-
> tion, her noble artistic aspirations. Why do some of her courtiers
> succeed in spoiling all that by giving her a reputation for
> strangeness and eccentricity which, I like to hope, she does not
> care for in the least? They say that she sleeps in a coffin, that
> she dissects dogs and cats, that she dresses like an undertaker,
> that she produces both pictures and statues, that she dyes her

hair blonde because her cheeks are too fresh for her to remain
brunette. Such stupidities can only hurt Mademoiselle Sarah
Bernhardt . . .

Sarah replied that it was not clumsy friends, but clever enemies, who hurt her: "It exasperates me to be unable to do anything without being accused of eccentricity. I had great fun
going up in a balloon, but now I dare not do so. I assure you
that I have never skinned dogs or burned cats. And I regret that
I cannot prove that I am a natural blonde. . . ."

Significantly, the one aspect of her life that others used in-
cessantly to publicize themselves Sarah kept largely to herself.
In her old age she once said to her friend Suze Rueff: "I have
been one of the greatest lovers of my time." But her autobiography is completely without hints, and those who supply long
lists, such as her archenemy Marie Colombier, are too unreliable
to be believed. There were lovers, for profit rather than pleasure, in the 1860's. She could not have survived the lean years
between the Gymnase and the Odéon without them. But they
were, except for the Prince de Ligne, not of a stature comparable to Rachel's. In truth, they were bourgeois more often than
noble, and not even as infamous as Doctor Véron. After all,
Sarah was still small fry in those years, and the value of her scalp
in a collection was exceeded by those of dozens of other actresses
in Paris, from Agar on through the alphabet.

Sarah never used these men to publicize herself. The Prince de
Ligne never suffered those consequences, and the Marquis de
Caux was used for no more than the benefit performance after
the fire in the Rue Auber, at which his wife Adelina Patti sang,
if he was used for that. Moreover, once the lean years were
ended, even some of her enemies admitted that Sarah had no
lovers taken for the sake of position and wealth. That, in fact,
is, for her time, a completely exceptional situation. It is not
known if any rich men helped to build the mansion on Avenue de
Villiers; if they did, their names were not divulged. Sarah had
many lovers, but after her success was assured they came from

the world of the stage or the arts, for pleasure, not profit. She was of course suspected with everyone; with the critic Sarcey, because he was one of the earliest converts to her art; with the Emperor Napoleon III; with various Princes, theater directors, critics, writers; with anyone who spoke well of her; and with the rich and famous who thronged her green room. All one can say is that in an age when scalps were worn in public, quite a number of men who exhibited no reticence in other cases had nothing at all to say about her.

She did love, ephemerally and hotly it seems, among the successful men in her sphere of life. Mounet-Sully, whom she had ignored when he was an actor at the Odéon, became her lover after he had become her successful partner at the Comédie. She took him away from Maria Favart—a trophy. He in turn was succeeded by George Clairin, the painter, who remained her devoted friend decades after they had ceased to be lovers. Like Rachel, Sarah managed to retain the friendship of most of the men who had loved her.

In Rachel's day the Comédie Française had frequently gone to England for series of performances. Since 1855, however, the interest of the English public had waned. Now, with the stories about Sarah Bernhardt and her rivalry with Croizette the interest was reviving, and the impresarios Hollingshead and Mayer engaged the Comédie to appear at the Gaiety Theatre in London from June 2 to July 12, 1879.

The engagement was arranged on very favorable terms, but the Comédie proceeded to complicate matters immediately. Neither Bernhardt nor Croizette were as yet full members of the Comédie; that is, they did not have full shares in the company. Knowing that the London engagement was made mainly on their account, they used the occasion to demand that they be given full shares. They were refused and thereupon declared that they would not go to London. The committee of *sociétaires*, under the chairmanship of Edmond Got, accepted their decision; the Comédie Française was, in their opinion, not subject to blackmail. At that point Messrs. Hollingshead and Mayer balked. If the Comédie proposed to come without Bernhardt and Croizette, they declared, then they would consider the contract void.

Thereupon Sarah submitted graciously to her colleagues: she did not, after all, want to ruin the profitable tour; she merely wanted her rights. And the Comédie, gracious in return, and much relieved, gave her and Croizette full memberships. Peace reigned once more—that is, until the Comédie announced the selection of plays for opening night: two comedies by Molière, one with Delaunay, one with Coquelin, and both among the most admirable (and most easily understood) pieces in the current repertoire. But Messrs. Hollingshead and Mayer objected: Sarah Bernhardt was not scheduled to perform in either play. At the last minute, therefore, a compromise was reached, and the final act of *Phèdre* was incongruously sandwiched between the two comedies.

In this unnatural setting Sarah made her international debut. Actually, the disadvantage of having to perform one act of a play out of context was more than compensated for by the attention that all the preceding disagreements had drawn to her. The public, fully informed of the actions of the Comédie, and of Messrs. Hollingshead and Mayer's stout defense of the public interest, came to the opening highly interested and much disposed to admire. It gave Bernhardt what John Murray, an eye witness, considered the greatest ovation in the history of the English theater. "Enthusiasm such as is rarely witnessed in the theater followed the fall of the curtain," wrote the *Standard*. The foremost critic of the day, John Knight, wrote:

"Mlle. Bernhardt realized fully the passionate, febrile, and tortured woman. Her supple frame withered beneath the influence of mental agony and relentless desire, and her postures seemed chosen with admirable art for the purpose of blending the greatest possible amount of seduction with the utmost possible amount of penitence . . ."

In one evening Sarah had reached a point in public favor where she could simply do no wrong any more. The redoubtable Knight actually felt apologetic, it seems, when he had something adverse to say about her. After *Hernani* he suggests that Sarah, "looking admirably picturesque in a medieval costume, with slashed sleeves and frills round the neck . . . took, as it seemed, but a moderate interest in the scenes before her. Hypercriticism might almost have suggested that her attitudes, supremely graceful as they seemed, were not quite unstudied." Knight redeems himself for this temerity of criticism by stating that in Act V she excelled "in one of those electrical displays of passion which, since the disappearance of Rachel, have been unknown upon the stage."

Francisque Sarcey had been sent to London by *Le Temps* to observe the tour. As a French critic he spoke quite differently from Knight and his colleagues. To Sarcey, of course, Sarah's Phèdre was not new when he saw it in London. After citing the lyrical praises of the London press, he wrote about the Phèdre of her first night:

> She took, as is natural in moments of great emotion, her first note too high and once having started on that pitch, as experienced actors know well, she had to keep it up. She had to start from the high note and rise higher as the sentiment she had to express became stronger and stronger. She was obliged to scream. She hurried her delivery. She was lost. You think perhaps the English audience experienced that sense of discomfort we should have felt in Paris? On the contrary, they were delighted, applauding with frenzy, and when she reappeared half dead on the arm of Mounet-Sully they gave her an ovation.

The performance of the following evening, *L'Etrangère*, with Sarah as Mrs. Clarkson, was mediocre, according to Sarcey. But it did not matter any more. "She could have splashed about in the part as she pleased. The audience had made up its mind to admire her, and this enthusiasm was reflected in the press. . . . What will they say when they really see her act well?"

Little more, actually; and herein lies the secret of the international actress. Sarah to the end of her days continued her battle for Paris. But from the first day in London she also learned, as Rachel had learned before her, that a foreign audience, once it had made its collective decision, was more easily pleased, won, retained than a Parisian audience.

During that performance of *L'Etrangère* Sarah actually had a lapse of memory and left out one whole key scene. Everyone on stage and behind the scenes was consternated; any audience in Paris would have made audible its displeasure. The London audience never knew the difference—another point in favor of performing in foreign countries.

Sarah's immediate success had another consequence. Paris, in 1879, had still been a battleground between Croizette and Bernhardt. London was not. Sarcey reported that Croizette, admirable in *L'Etrangère* and *Le Misanthrope*, could not succeed with the public, which had eyes for Sarah alone.

English society also loved Sarah from the start, and pardoned her eccentricity, her unreliability and lack of punctuality. At first those who gathered around her were perhaps not as illustrious as those who had dined and entertained Rachel, but they were enthusiastic. After the constant intrigue and infighting of Paris, London was heaven. Hostesses forgave if Sarah forgot to come, were delighted when she did come, no matter when. Moreover, London, the largest, richest city on earth, was also a heaven of a different sort after Paris, still not entirely recovered from the war and the Commune. Sarah loved to drive in Rotten Row, to dine at English homes where, she found, one could eat very well, and talk to Englishmen who, it turned out, did not conform to the stereotype of the aloof eccentric. Sarah not only performed at the Gaiety. She received large fees for dining and then reciting at great houses, fully accepted as a guest as well as an artist. In addition, her works of art were put on exhibit; the Prince and Princess of Wales, and Mr. Gladstone, came to the opening, and Prince Leopold of Belgium (later King Leopold II) bought her "Jeune fille portant des palmes."

Like Rachel, Sarah would not rest. She went from performance to dinner to exhibition to performance, and both her health and her acting suffered. But the public did not know and did not care. She was the star of the season. When she did fall ill sufficiently to have to cancel a performance, the evening's receipts at the theater took a disastrous plunge. *Tartuffe*, without Sarah, took the place of *L'Etrangère*, and receipts fell from 500 pounds (advance sale) to 84. The resentment and jealousy in the company were considerable.

Her exploits were as usual half willful, half calculated. She did, as always, what she wanted to do, and, as always, what she wanted to do was sufficiently spectacular to attract the attention of the press. Her most famous exploit was a trip to Liverpool, to the Cress Zoo, from which she returned with a cheetah, six chameleons and a white wolfhound, all to be added to her collection of monkeys and dogs that already inhabited and enlivened Chester Square, the decorous quiet neighborhood where she had taken a house.

Meanwhile, back in Paris, rumors had it that she smoked cigars, wore men's clothes (and could be seen dressed in them for the payment of one shilling), fenced and boxed, threw a kitten in the fire and poisoned two monkeys. More seriously, Sarcey accused her of jeopardizing the Comédie and her colleagues through her neglect of duty and her mad exploits. Finally, Albert Wolff, in *Le Figaro*, wrote a lengthy article accusing Sarah of a large variety of misdeeds, moral and professional. The chorus of critics of her behavior swelled constantly at home while she was still in London, drowning out the one voice that suggested that Sarah Bernhardt should be permitted to lead her own life. The voice was Emile Zola's, and Sarah was to remember it later.

In his summary of the season of the Comédie in London, Knight had called Sarah a genius who stood out from the rest of the company and must be permitted to do so. He invoked once more the memory of Rachel and admonished the Comédie to give Sarah her pre-eminence, no matter how uncomfortable and demoralizing it would be for her colleagues. Decidedly that was not the opinion of Perrin and the *sociétaires* led by Got. He in particular did not want to be reminded of Rachel—he had suffered, and seen his Comédie suffer, from her exceptional status. Such a thing was not to happen again.

Maurice Rostand writes that Sarah returned from England "covered with English laurels and French calumnies." She felt insulted, almost ostracized. The press was against her, her colleagues shunned her for the most part, and she felt that the management would oppose her at every turn in the future. Even the public was largely hostile.

Sarah had learned one thing from Rachel's career. The theater public of Paris did not like its stars to curry favor elsewhere, but it could be won back by a superb performance or a daring act.

Bernhardt chose the daring act and bided her time. She waited for Molière's birthday. Sarah had had one bad experience with that festivity, at the time when Régina stepped on the hem of Mme. Nathalie's gown. Now the conflict swirled around Sarah: should she attend the ceremony? Should she risk being hissed? She had received several anonymous letters warning her to stay away, among them one which said: "My poor skeleton—you will do well not to show your horrible Jewish nose at the ceremony day after tomorrow. I fear for it because it will serve as target for all the apples being boiled for your sake in the good city of Paris. Let it be known that you are coughing blood and stay in your bed to reflect on the consequences of your outrageous self-advertisements."

After that Sarah of course decided to go, *quand-même*. But she told the authorities that she refused to let anyone go with her across the stage, so as not to expose him to danger. When the time came, she went on, alone. She advanced slowly towards the statue, dressed in a perfectly simple white dress; the entire audience was deathly silent. Then she slowly turned, stepped forward, toward the footlights, confronted the audience full on, and instead of bowing she slowly raised her head. At that moment pandemonium broke loose and she received one of the greatest ovations of her career at the Comédie. Paris liked a brave woman.

In the spring of 1880 Sarah was scheduled to appear in a new role. It was *L'Aventurière* by Émile Augier, a playwright whom Sarah disliked. She also disliked the play and her role in it. The first performance was to be on April 17, and though Sarah declared that she was unwell and unready, the schedule was kept. Clearly the role of Dona Clorinde was not suited to her; clearly she made no effort to rise above it, or to do even moderately well. The costume, which made her look like an English teapot, did not help. Sarcey, the friendliest critic, said that her Clorinde had no face. Vitu, more explicitly, said that she resembled la Grande Virginie in *L'Assomoir*, Zola's book about whores and brandy shops. On April 18, Sarah sent her resignation to Perrin, citing her mistreatment on the occasion of Augier's play as her reason. To make her decision irrevocable she sent copies of her letter of resignation to *Le Figaro* and *Le Gaulois* by special messenger, but let it go to the Comédie by mail. She left the same day and went into isolation at Sainte-Adresse near Le Havre.

So, at the age of thirty-six, Sarah, having left the Comédie Française for the second time, returned to the city that always had a special attraction for her. The manner of her departure indicated that she considered it final. She may have been very angry about *L'Aventurière*, but she was no longer the girl of twenty who had left both the Comédie and the Gymnase impulsively within a year. Her move was not sudden: It had been contemplated; it had to come sooner or later. At the Comédie she could not occupy the unique position of Rachel, in spite of her artistic abilities. Rachel had the basic asset of having brought to life again the main reason for the existence of the Français—the classical tragedies of Corneille and Racine. In Sarah's time the situation was different. The classical drama was no longer a battle ground because it was no longer tied to artistic and political issues. It was accepted, and the public recognized its position as an honored heritage—no more. The romantic drama, the technique of which Rachel had used, in part, to revive the classical, had joined the older form in the exalted status of a heritage. The Comédie was transforming itself from a defender of the faith into a museum. It still occupied an important place, but its importance had been on the decline since the romantic era half a century before. In this setting Sarah could be famous, accomplished, acclaimed—but she could not be unique.

By temperament Sarah was a child of her era. The axiom of success, as yet unspoiled by doubts, by considerations other than the concept of the survival of the fittest, was still the pristine promise it had seemed at first. Moreover, the summit of artistry in the theater, the one supreme international crown open to women was vacant. Rachel had held it when Europe was still the only crown worth having. She had died trying to add the New World to her realm. Ristori had taken over from her. In 1880 she was still performing, still touring, but she was now nearing sixty, a portly Lady Macbeth, Medea, Mary Stuart, Marie Antoinette.

One cannot say if the role to which Sarah would aspire, the role of supreme actress of the civilized world and its outposts, was clear to her at the beginning. It is sure, however, that she did not take long to learn. To her great artistic ability she could add two indispensable attributes. She had a flair for doing everything in a spectacular way, a grand manner that transcended the narrower aspects of publicity and advertising. Henry James had recognized that fact during her first stay in London. Writing in *The Nation* on July 31, 1879, he said: "She is not, to my sense, a celebrity because she is an artist. She is a celebrity because, apparently, she desires with an intensity that has rarely been equalled to be one, and because for this end all means are alike to her. She may flatter herself that, as regards the London public, she had encompassed her ends." Second, she was French, stamped with the hallmark of Paris and the Comédie Française, world representative of the capital of culture and the fountainhead of fashion. With her talent, her flair and her background she could be unbeatable. London in 1879 had assured her of her power, given her a taste of pre-eminence that the Comédie or, in fact, any purely Parisian role could never give her. She had received ovations for performances that would have been cold-shouldered in Paris. Her voice, her manner carried all before her, no matter at what pitch she intoned her Phèdre. She would never really leave Paris behind; wisely, though perhaps unconsciously, she always retained her roots, always returned to Paris to face and reconquer the Parisian audience. But from Paris she went out into the world, and particularly to America, time after time, for forty years.

Now, however, at the end of April, 1880, she was almost in hiding. After some of the hubbub had died down, she returned to Paris, declaring that she would devote the rest of her life to sculpture. Her sculptures were selling briskly and providing a substantial annual income. But the 20,000 francs of her annual salary from the Comédie, insufficient as they had been, were no longer there. Furthermore, what would happen to her appeal as an artist if the appeal as an actress receded into the past? She had broken her contract with the Comédie, she was the defendant in a suit that the theater had brought against her on that account and she was rapidly running out of money and credit.

Sarah was of course not serious about leaving the theater. New contacts were already made. Hollingshead and Mayer, having imported the Comédie the year before, offered to import Sarah with a newly collected troupe. She therefore went to London for the second time, with four old plays, and two she had never done before: *Phèdre* was her bow to the classical, *Hernani* to the romantic repertoire, *Le Sphinx* and *L'Etrangère* were contemporary works in which she had scored great successes. The new plays were *Frou-Frou*, the greatest role of Aimée Desclée, with whom she thereby invited comparison; and *Adrienne Lecouvreur*, which challenged the memory of Rachel herself. It was a formidable repertoire, now that she at last had the chance to choose her own roles. The range was immense. Her Phèdre was beginning to achieve real mastery and renown. Her Dona Sol was exactly the contrary of that guilt-ridden, passionately unhappy woman of antiquity: a young, adoring virgin, romantically in love with danger as well as Hernani. Then the snake-like Mrs. Clarkson in *L'Etrangère*, the

frivolous Gilberte in *Frou-Frou*, the great actress Adrienne—a
more formidable display of talent and versatility can hardly be
imagined.

Sarah opened at the Gaiety Theatre on May 24 and conquered
once more, and even more completely than the year before, because all her competition came from without the Gaiety, not
from within. She no longer fought with Perrin or competed
with Croizette, but with Henry Irving and Ellen Terry at the
Lyceum, doing Shakespeare, and with Patti singing at Covent
Garden. She was unique in her own place.

If Sarah had any doubts about her success without the venerable cloak of the Comédie, it was dispelled on opening night. On
the contrary, it seemed as if release from the Comédie had enabled her to develop to the fullest extent. She not only retained
the position of eminence gained the year before. She also acted
brilliantly. Several important critics, Sarcey and Vitu among
them, had come to London sent expressly to see how Sarah
would do. After *Frou-Frou*, Sarcey, quite overwhelmed, went
to congratulate her in her dressing room and topped his praise
with the declaration that Sarah's performance of that evening
would re-open the doors of the Comédie to her. Sarah suggested
politely that he not refer to that idea again.

Perrin sent a messenger to London to persuade her to return.
It was no less a man than the dean of the *sociétaires*, Edmond
Got. Sarah let him cool his heels for some time. Then she finally
granted him an audience, and let him give her his argument. He
did not plead with her to be generous for the sake of the House
of Molière together with a considerable raise that might perhaps
have swayed her. No, he argued that she was giving up a good
thing, a steady job with a pension at the end, and that the company would in its goodness forgive and forget, and withdraw
its lawsuit. Wrong man, wrong argument. The lawsuit proceeded, and in the end Sarah was condemned to lose her part of
the pension fund, and to pay the huge sum of 100,000 francs
damages.

When Sarah's season at the Gaiety ended on June 27 she returned to Paris. She had already signed an agreement with William Jarrett, an American impresario, for a tour of the United States. Between the end of June and October 16, when she was scheduled to leave Le Havre for New York, she was free. Characteristically, she did not rest.

After a few days in Paris, Sarah went on to Brussels to perform *Adrienne Lecouvreur* and *Frou-Frou* at the Théâtre de la Monnaie. From there she went on to Copenhagen, to the Royal Theatre where she was at first frightened by the shouting crowd of two thousand Danes who welcomed her at the train station. DeFallesen, the manager of the theater, had to enter the train to entreat her to come out. Only then she overcame her fear of disappointing, with her thinness, "those magnificent men and those splendid and healthy women." In the evening the King and Queen of Denmark, with the King and Queen of Greece and the Princess of Wales came to see *Adrienne*. The queens threw their bouquets on the stage and the public was delirious. The King placed the royal yacht at Sarah's disposal when she expressed the wish to see Elsinore, Hamlet's castle.

After her return to Paris, Sarah still had a few weeks before her Atlantic crossing. Again she did not rest. Duquesnel came to ask her if she would undertake a tour of the French provinces, a thing she had neglected (or declined) to do before. He was remembered: he had brought her to the Odéon, had kept her there, and was therefore responsible for the real beginning of her career. She agreed to travel under his management. Within a week a company was assembled and Sarah began to tap a source which Rachel had always found profitable. Beginning on September 4 she gave 25 performances in 28 days of *Adrienne* and *Frou-Frou*. She earned 50,000 francs, much more than her annual salary at the Comédie.

William Jarrett had approached Sarah originally in 1878, but she had turned down his suggestion of an American tour. She turned him down again when he came several months later—but not quite, for she permitted him to arrange a series of appear-

ances for her in private homes during the stay of the Comédie
in London. When Jarrett, three days after Sarah's resignation,
came for the third time with his American proposition, Sarah
accepted.

Sarah later described Jarrett with obvious awe. He was old,
sixty-five or seventy, looked like King Agamemnon, and had

the most beautiful silver-white hair I have ever seen on man's
head. His eyes were of so pale a blue that when they lighted up
with anger he looked as though he were blind. When he was
calm and tranquil his face was really handsome, but when gay
and animated his upper lip showed his teeth, and curled up in a
most ferocious sniff, and his grin seemed to be caused by the
drawing up of his pointed ears which were always moving as
though on the watch for prey. He was a terrible man, extremely
intelligent, but from childhood he must have been fighting with
the world, and he had the most profound contempt for all mankind. Although he must have suffered a great deal himself, he
had no pity for those who suffered. He always said that every
man was armed for his own defense.

In 1879, during Sarah's visit to England, Henry James had
written: "I strongly suspect that she will find a triumphant
career in the western world. She is too American not to succeed
in America." Unlike Rachel, who was in tears, Bernhardt was
very excited and expectant when the *Amérique* left Le Havre
on October 15. She celebrated her birthday on board, visited
the unfortunates in the steerage, met Mrs. Abraham Lincoln, so
she tells, and landed in New York on October 27. The advance
publicity had been colossal, and the reception was according to
it. Ships with journalists and sightseers came out to meet the
Amérique. When she stepped on American soil, a band played
the *Marseillaise*, and the French consul and a large welcoming
committee extended the honors; the only thing missing was the
twenty-one-gun salute for a visiting sovereign. There were, in
recompense, so many speeches that Sarah, tired and bored, gave
a convincing performance of a faint and was quickly carried to
her hotel. Jarrett refused to spare her the ordeal by interview.

She saw the reporters one by one, as she had learned to do in London, as she would do year after year, decade after decade, answering the same stupefying questions about personal habits, impressions, views, about what she ate for breakfast, about pet dogs, current public figures, critics, and above all the theater. It is not surprising that she gave her invention free reign from time to time. The monotony must have been overwhelming.

Rachel's mistake was not repeated. Henry Abbey, Sarah's American manager, had sold tickets for the opening performance at the Booth Theatre by auction, à la Jenny Lind. They had fetched $20 to $40 each. The financial arrangements were spectacular: $1,000 per performance for the star, 50 percent of the receipts over $3,000, and $200 for expenses per week, together with a private Pullman car complete with two chefs and a piano. One hundred performances were guaranteed. The repertoire consisted of eight plays: *Phèdre* and *Hernani*, *Adrienne Lecouvreur*, *L'Etrangère*, *Frou-Frou*, *Le Sphinx*, and two works she had not done before, *La Princesse Georges*, and the greatest of her future successes, *La Dame aux Camélias*. Her company was mediocre—who cared?—except for her leading man Angelo, a good actor whom she had remembered gratefully from her first days at the Odéon. It was to include Jeanne Bernhardt, her sister; but she had fallen ill before the departure and Marie Colombier replaced her, at least until she caught up with the company a few weeks later.

On November 16, Sarah first performed what was to be the most popular role of her career—Marguerite Gautier, in *La Dame aux Camélias*. "Camille," as it was called, had been seen in America before; Modjeska had done it and several others, but Sarah's success permanently eclipsed all of them. Years later even Duse could not break Sarah's hold on that role in the United States. The public and the press went wild and never recovered. Sarah had twenty-seven curtain calls after the last act.

The matinee on December 4, which ended the New York run, was an indescribable scene. Bernhardt's carriage could not come near the Booth Theatre—hundreds of people blocked the way. She finally managed to get to the stage entrance on foot, shaking innumerable hands, writing autographs (a novelty then), accepting presents, flowers. One lady tried to cut a lock of her hair, but only got as far as a feather in her hat. The play was *La Dame aux Camélias* once more, and Sarah counted seventeen curtain calls after the third act, and twenty-nine after the fifth. Sarah was exhausted, but when she wanted to go to her carriage Jarrett reported that about 50,000 people were blocking the street. Sarah finally made her escape by another door.

The company left for Boston that evening, but Sarah did not travel until the next day. Instead, her strength recovered, she went during the night for a visit to Menlo Park, to meet Thomas Edison. Sarah reports in her memoirs that she could see at once that Edison was bored and that her visit was an inconvenience to the inventor, a necessity imposed by considerations of politeness and publicity. She rose to the challenge, charmed him completely, and they became good friends. He showed her his fascinating machines, recorded her voice, and sent her on her way with a supper in the early hours of the morning.

After two weeks in Boston and a few performances in cities of New England, the company went north to Montreal. The arrival was undimmed by sub-zero temperatures. Sarah suffered again through the *Marseillaise,* the patriotism of a French-speaking people, flowers, speeches, an interminable dedicatory poem; this time she seems to have fainted in earnest, and recovered only when she was finally permitted to thaw out at the Windsor Hotel.

Between performances she visited Ottawa, was a guest of the Iroquois, and nearly lost her life climbing over ice floes in the frozen St. Lawrence River. Jarrett's reaction was in keeping with his character: "If you had lost your life, Madam, you would have been dishonest, for you would have broken your contract of your own free will."

After Montreal the company traveled south again, visiting, among others, Baltimore, Philadelphia and Chicago, where Sarah stayed at the Palmer House, liked Mr. Palmer, and was appalled at the pig-slaughtering in the stockyards. Then came St. Louis in the week of January 24-31, 1881, a very dirty city in Sarah's opinion, then Cincinnati and New Orleans, which she liked very much. There were always smaller cities between as Sarah wended her triumphant way across much of the United States east of the Mississippi, with forays across the river. The large cities were resting points in a dizzy round of one- and two-night stands in the smaller towns, from New York to Canada, to the Gulf of Mexico, and up to Canada again until the tour ended in April and May in New York.

It had been a wild tour, made wilder by Jarrett's and Abbey's abilities as publicists, and by Sarah's flair for the bizarre. Even before the opening in New York, the gladiatorial element had been stressed. Clara Morris was performing at the Park Theatre in a French play, adapted as *Alix* in English. It was decided that Sarah should attend a performance and pay her respects, and the press was informed accordingly. As she told it later on, the event was executed with the care of a royal visit. Sarah, flanked by Abbey and Jarrett, did not appear at the performance until it was well under way, but before Clara Morris was to make her first appearance. When she entered the stage box, the performance stopped and the orchestra intoned the *Marseillaise*. A minute or two later Clara Morris appeared and was applauded by the crowded house. Instead of giving her first lines, she walked down to the footlights, threw a bouquet of flowers into Sarah's box, and blew her a kiss. Sarah, in turn, pressed the flowers to her heart and then threw a bouquet of her own to the stage, wrapped in ribbons of red, white and blue, colors that make up the French as well as the U. S. flag. There was great excitement, and nobody remembers what happened to poor *Alix*. It hardly mattered.

That was only the beginning. There were lots of stories about Sarah and the crowds of admirers. On one occasion a girl is supposed to have cut a vein in her arm, have dipped a plume from her hat in it, and obtained Sarah's precious autograph in that way. In Chicago the welcoming crowds got out of hand, and

Sarah had to be rescued by the police and by a gigantic stranger to whom she wanted to show her gratitude when he had safely delivered her to the Palmer House. He turned out to be an escaped murderer. Chicago—what else? Near Chicago, in Joliet prison, she performed an act of *Hernani* for the convicts and was upset to find out that the prisoner who movingly expressed their collective thanks was condemned to be hanged the next day. Or so she tells.

Other stories abound. In St. Louis she consented to an exhibition of her jewels, and Mme. Guérard, her companion, found that they had been added to lavishly for the show. As a result of that exhibit there were sudden, not unjustified fears of a great train robbery *en tour*, and extensive protective measures were taken, with more publicity. In Mobile, Alabama, the scenery collapsed; in New Orleans Sarah suffered competition from Emilie Ambre, the soprano who sang Verdi's *La Traviata* on the same day as Sarah acted in *La Dame aux Camélias*, the play on which that opera is based. Most pungent, however, was the story of Sarah and the dead whale. From Sarah's highly colored accounts and somewhat hazy notions of time, distance and geography it is not clear exactly what happened, and the newspapers of the day do not help much. A man named Henry Smith, it seems, owned a whale, evidently no longer alive, and moored in Boston Harbor. He persuaded Sarah to visit the whale, to walk on its back, and to pull out part of a whale bone, provided, one assumes, by the management. That little stunt was the source of considerable inconvenience. When Sarah arrived in New Haven, there was a brass band, Henry Smith and the whale, complete with advertising that linked Sarah, the whale, the whalebone, and a large corset manufacturer. Sarah threw Henry Smith out of the hotel, but that made no difference. Two days later it was Hartford, and there again was Smith with his whale, salt filling its insides, ice encasing its outside, preserved to be paired once more with the Great Bernhardt. How the whale got to Hartford, thirty miles inland, we do not know. Only when Sarah reached Montreal she found to her relief that the whale had not succeeded in following her. Presumably Smith, who had charged one dollar admission to the thousands who wanted to see Sarah's whale, had permitted the beast to disintegrate.

Publicity by Sarah, or at Sarah's expense, was considered good no matter how pungent. Sarah also posed several problems, however, that could not be shunted aside as easily as a whale, though they could also, at times, be put to surprising use. It is clear that the role of the actor had changed since the early part of the century, due perhaps more to Talma, Rachel and Ristori than anyone else. Social respectability had come, even a kind of royal treatment, the first inkling of the new aristocracy of the theater and later the film, which would in time replace the older aristocracies. Sarah was welcomed everywhere in America, as Rachel had never been, for America had changed considerably in a quarter of a century, though the theater was still considered a place of immorality. An actress like Sarah Bernhardt was, because of her repertoire and her flamboyant behavior, particularly subject to attack. *Adrienne Lecouvreur*, which had been denounced in 1855 when Rachel had performed it, was still being denounced from the pulpit in 1880. Sarah's first performance attracted a glittering crowd, but it consisted mainly of men, and there were very few women and almost no young girls. A Boston clergyman displayed his tolerance when he said that he did not think one must consider himself inevitably damned to hell fire for having attended a performance by Mlle. Bernhardt. Scurrilous pamphlets preceded her, though one cannot be sure that they were all due to her enemies, and that Jarrett's advertising genius played no role in them. One described her as a monster who had seduced the Tsar, Napoleon III and Pope Pius IX. Another said that she had four children, including one by the late French Emperor and one by the Pope. A pamphlet called *Too Thin* asserted that she owned the skeleton of a man who had killed himself for her sake which she now used to rehearse with, and so on.

Sarah survived the calumnies, the whale, the one-night stands in Mobile, and Decatur, Leavenworth and Erie, Newark and

Memphis, the adulation, the reporters. She returned to New York in April for a last series of performances, including a special matinee for actors and artists, in which she was acclaimed in *La Princesse Georges,* and received presents and a total of 130 bouquets, including a casket from Salvini and a medallion from Mary Anderson. The same evening she gave her farewell performance as Marguerite Gautier.

The next morning on the *Amérique* Sarah set sail for Europe. As she came to the door of her stateroom, an elegant little man approached her, bowed, and presented her with a magnificent casket of jewels. Before she had quite recognized him he had vanished. Then she knew—it had been Henry Smith, the owner of the whale. Jarrett was barely able to prevent a tantrum, but Sarah refused to keep the jewels. She could afford it. She had given 156 performances, including 65 of *La Dame aux Camélias,* 41 of *Frou-Frou,* 17 of *Adrienne Lecouvreur* and six of *Phèdre.* The repertoire of the international actress, as distinct from that of the star of the Comédie or the Odéon, was taking shape. The total receipts had been more than 17,000 francs per average performance, or more than two and a half million francs in all: more than half a million dollars in a time when six or seven dollars a week was a living wage.

She had finally surpassed Rachel and was returning home a full-fledged international actress. She could reflect also that she was thirty-seven, and that, at that age, Rachel was already dead.

CHAPTER 8 / International Actress

On MAY 15, 1881, a large number of boats—almost a hundred according to Lysiane Bernhardt—sailed out of Le Havre to welcome Sarah on her return from America. She had agreed in advance to give a performance for charity in Le Havre that evening. It seemed a good way to make her return to the stage in France. She had reason enough to feel uncertain about the reception a French public would give her, and a provincial city, notably her second home-town, was less risky than Paris. Curiosity had brought hundreds from Paris to see her as the Lady of the Camellias for the first time on French soil. The audience received her warmly, though the applause was tame after London and New York.

Two days later she was back at her mansion in the Avenue de Villiers. If the reaction of the press was any indication of the public reaction in general, she had reason to be disquieted. The writers preferred to recall her last performance in the city— *L'Aventurière* at the Comédie—more than a year before, rather than dwell upon her triumphs in foreign countries. On the day after her return she received a visit from the playwright Victorien Sardou. He had just completed a new play, *Fédora*, clearly intended as a vehicle for her. What happened next is not certain; either he did not make her a firm offer of the role, or she felt that she should not act in Paris at this point—at any rate, she made commitments for tours of Europe immediately after her return, and Paris had to wait.

Within a few weeks she was off to London with her company, for the third season in as many years. Through the intervention of the Prince of Wales, the Lord Chamberlain as the official censor of plays granted her permission to perform *La Dame aux Camélias* in the capital for the first time. A performance of that play in English was still out of the question in London, but in French it could, with royal patronage, somehow be tolerated.

Paris had been cool towards her when she came back from America that spring, and Sarah knew that something needed to be done to regain popular favor. She resolved to do it with a daring act once more, as she had two years before, on her return from the first engagement in London. The occasion was the national holiday, July 14. This was a special fourteenth of July, for it also commemorated the first ten years of the Third Republic. At the Opéra a gala performance of Meyerbeer's *Robert le Diable* was to take place, in the presence of *les deux Jules*—Jules Grévy, President of the Republic, and Jules Ferry, the Prime Minister. As a climax Agar was to chant the *Marseillaise*.

At 11 P.M. the backstage area was in a turmoil. Agar was to recite in a few minutes, and Agar could not be found. A pleasantly smiling Sarah Bernhardt had just come back stage and greeted a few acquaintances. When the hubbub was getting frantic she suddenly dropped her large cloak and displayed a white, classic dress with a tricolor sash. Agar, she said matter-of-factly, was unavoidably detained and had asked her to perform. The manager felt between the devil and the deep blue sea. To let the devil go on stage meant risking a riot; but not to have the *Marseillaise* at all seemed worse, and Sarah was sent on. There was a loud murmur; one will never know what would have happened if the two Juleses had not been there. But the end result was—of course—a triumph.

Even the two Juleses might not have prevented a protest if the audience had known what had really happened. Agar's love life was still vigorous and complex in spite of her age, and at that point a mustachioed captain of dragoons was much on her mind. Sarah, it is reported, arranged for Agar to receive a message that her captain was about to undergo a serious operation in Tours, and while Agar was on the train to Tours, Bernhardt was on the stage of the Opéra.

Sarah had inserted herself again into the theater world of Paris. Now Deslandes, the manager of the Vaudeville, joined with Sardou in urging her to perform *Fédora*. Yes, said Sarah, but they would have to wait until her return from a European tour of fifteen months' duration. Deslandes offered her 1000 francs per evening with a guarantee of 100 performances, an unheard-of contract for Paris. Sarah, in reply, demanded 1500 francs per evening, plus twenty-five per cent of the box office sales. The stunned Deslandes agreed to everything, even a year's postponement.

One more thing happened before she left Paris again. She received a visit from a young stranger, Aristide Damala, the son of a rich merchant in Greece. He had served his country, more or less, as an officer and a diplomat. His habits and behavior, his affairs and indiscretions had finally forced him out of the Greek diplomatic service, and he now wanted to make a career of acting.

Sarah was quite possibly intrigued not only with the superb handsomeness of the man but also with his apparent imperviousness to her charms, which were played upon him full force. He was enlisted in the company to go to Brussels; at the time Angelo, who had toured with Sarah since their departure for America, was presumably still her lover. In Brussels Damala performed satisfactorily in *Hernani*, and was engaged as second lead for the tour. Later events gave rise to the assertion that Damala was a completely incompetent actor, kept on merely because of Sarah's infatuation with him. That is not likely; though her artistic judgment was often beclouded by love, it was never obliterated by it. Clearly several of her partners served for both bed and boards, but almost all of them were good actors: Pierre Berton, Philippe Garnier, Mounet-Sully, Angelo. And some of her partners, like Lucien Guitry, were chosen for their talent alone.

After the performances in Brussels the company went to the Netherlands, then to Scandinavia and finally to Russia. Sarah's success in Russia was very great, though not as great perhaps as Rachel's. The reasons had less to do with Sarah's ability as with the general situation in the country. Russia had opened herself to Western culture in the twenty-five years since Rachel's tour, and the novelty was not as great. In addition to that, the Russian aristocracy and upper class, which made up a large part of the audience, had taken to traveling to the West and to spending a considerable amount of time in France in particular. An actress from that country, though very welcome, was no longer an outstanding event to them. The Czar in 1881 was Alexander III, a reactionary, anti-western autocrat, quite a different man from his grandfather Nicholas, the Czar of Rachel's time. Nevertheless Bernhardt performed twice at the Winter Palace in Petersburg, doing *Le Passant*, the death scene of *Adrienne Lecouvreur*, and two acts from *Phèdre*, and was congratulated by Alexander III.

From Moscow and Petersburg Sarah went to Warsaw and on to Austria, and from there to Italy, first traversing the north in a series of performances to reach Lyon in February, and then returning to Italy via Turin to tour the whole peninsula.

The voyage through Austria was a triumph, but the Italian tour was not too well received, and the ovations of the rather independent cities of Italy may have seemed a little pale after those in Russia and Austria with their glittering capitals and subservient provincial centers. It may also have been that Sarah, thirty-seven years old, felt her hold loosening on the twenty-seven-year-old Damala. At any rate in Naples on March 30, she decided to marry him. Her decision was impulsive and, once made, she insisted that the marriage had to take place at once, and in England, for only there could the formalities, and the difficulties of a marriage between people of different nationalities be kept to a minimum. So to England went first a stream of telegraphed instructions, and then the happy pair. Sarah instructed her company to go to Nice and await her there. After a dash by train and boat across the Apennines, the Alps, the plains of France and the English Channel Aristide Damala and

Sarah Bernhardt were married at St. Andrew's Church in London on April 4.

Sarah's Italian tour had another consequence, one she did not know of until much later. In Turin she performed at the Teatro Carignano in her usual repertoire of Dumas *fils*, Scribe and so on. Sweeping through dozens of cities and their theaters in a few months, she paid no attention to them or to the local actors and actresses who, temporarily displaced from their dressing rooms and stages, stared at the great lady from Paris who moved in a different world from theirs and who commanded applause, attention and fees that they had never dreamed of. At the Teatro Carignano Sarah therefore did not notice the dark-eyed twenty-three-year-old local actress whose dressing room she occupied for a few days. But the little local actress watched and drew her conclusions from her observations. Her name was Eleonora Duse, and she became the last of the international actresses.

The precipitous marriage to Aristide Damala, which caused the dash from Naples to London in April of 1882, turned out to be no more than an episode in Sarah Bernhardt's life, though a painful one. The marriage was precarious from the first. Damala continued to have affairs with other women, and there were frightful scenes of jealousy. More than that, Damala was a dope addict. He had been introduced to Sarah through her sister Jeanne, also an addict, and she did not find out, it seems, until it was too late. Sarah loved Damala, but she loved him as she loved her cheetahs and pumas. She wanted to possess him as long as it pleased her to do so, and quite possibly the marriage itself was the result of her realization that she had not succeeded.

Angelo had been discarded after the marriage, and now Damala reigned supreme on tour as Sarah's leading man when both rejoined the company in time for a tour of Spain. On their way from Spain to London for the usual season Sarah and Damala stopped off in Paris to give one performance of *La Dame aux Camélias* at a benefit. It was an occasion of unusual interest. Sarah had never performed the play in Paris before; Damala was a

powerful added attraction. Sarah was frightfully nervous and
may not have played with the verve she showed in that role elsewhere. Nevertheless she was a success, especially in the final acts.
The press was very cruel to Damala, though, and on reading the
comments one cannot avoid the feeling that some reviewers,
unable to criticize Sarah, vented their antipathy on him.

After her English season, an annual event by now, Sarah returned to Paris to give Sardou's *Fédora* its much delayed premiere at the Vaudeville. Before that event took place, however,
Sarah entered into yet another role—or rather, her son did. After
rather brief negotiations Maurice Bernhardt assumed the management of the Théâtre de l'Ambigu and produced his first play
in November: *Les Mères Ennemis* by Catulle Mendès, a drama
based on the collapse of Polish independence in the eighteenth
century. The leading role was played by Aristide Damala.

It is clear that Maurice, not yet twenty years old, did not
manage the Ambigu; his mother did. It is almost as clear that the
whole undertaking was originally intended to provide a stage
for Damala, because Sarah either did not want to, or could not
obtain the role of Ipanoff for him, the male lead in *Fédora*.
Sarah, who saw Damala slipping away from her, evidently hoped
that by this means she could avoid a scene or even a break.
Damala would be playing a major role at another theater and
therefore regrettably not be available for *Fédora*. Damala may
have seen through the scheme, especially as she in an unguarded
moment offered him the role of Ipanoff on tour, after the Paris
run. Or he may simply have been angered by the tremendous
success of *Fédora* compared to the mild interest shown by public and critics in *Les Mères Ennemis*. On December 17, after a
series of convulsive quarrels with Sarah, he suddenly left the
Ambigu, and her.

Five days before his departure, on December 12, *Fédora* had its
premiere. It was a huge popular success, though the critics did not
warm to it. It is a superbly constructed, suspenseful melodrama
in which the audience found constant opportunity to concentrate its interest on the leading actress. The plot was suited,

furthermore, to foreign audiences because it was simple to follow and demanded considerable virtuosity of mimetic play. The words were much less important than the self-explanatory actions and the business on stage. Sardou was no poet, but Sarah's marvelous voice was enough, combined with plot and stage activity, to carry the evening to a successful conclusion. Finally, it was a bloody and sexy story. William Winter, the conservative American critic who disliked Sarah artistically as well as morally, said of *Fédora:* "The distinguishing characteristic of this drama is carnality. . . . Almost it exhales rankness like that of a menagerie."

The first week of performances of *Fédora* was filled with quarrels between Sarah and Damala, and ended in his departure. She must have suffered greatly. But she performed *Fédora* every night, for one hundred and thirty times, until April 25, 1883, when it closed in Paris—not because it had ceased to attract audiences, but because Sarah needed money and could earn much more by going on tour. She needed the money chiefly because of the Ambigu. It had failed to hold Damala. It was now to be a vehicle for the drama of a higher kind than the one performed by most boulevard houses. Its second play was by Jean Richepin, a handsome heavy-built poet. It was called *Le Glu* (the Snare), a realistic play in the tradition of Dumas. It had a marvelous cast, including Agar and Réjane, was elegantly staged, and so its failure has to be blamed on the play itself. Richepin produced several expensive theatrical failures for Sarah, but as he was handsome and consoled her well, and quickly, for the loss of Damala, he had to be forgiven.

Sarah's successes all over Western Europe were not enough to atone for the financial sins committed at the Ambigu. By the time the management of Maurice Bernhardt ceased to exist, it was 400,000 francs in debt. The debt had to be paid; on February 8, 9 and 10, 1883, a public sale of Mme. Bernhardt-Damala's jewelry attracted a huge crowd.

Sarah's first experience with theater management did not deter her from further attempts. Maurice, with Derembourg by his side, was installed as manager at the Théâtre de la Porte-Saint-Martin. Sarah opened with *Frou-Frou*, for which she was condemned—not because she did badly but because she thereby desecrated the memory of Desclée. In December it was followed by another expensive failure by Richepin, *Nana Sahib*, a play on the 1857 uprising in India. To rub salt into Sarah's and Richepin's wounds Damala had returned—cured, it seemed—and was performing with enormous success in Ohnet's *Le Maître des Forges* for a long run of performances at the Gymnase. The story goes that he once came to one of Sarah's matinees and very deliberately and obviously counted the half empty house, and that the very frustrated Richepin threw him out bodily.

Richepin was also involved in another, much more sensational encounter, which concerned Sarah, his play *Nana Sahib*, and a scurrilous book. The rise of Sarah Bernhardt, and the flamboyance of her life had led to a number of *romans à clef* in which she figured. In 1882 Edmond de Goncourt published *La Faustin* and Felicien Champsaur *Dinah Samuel*. The most notorious of the books about Sarah, however, was not by a novelist, but by a fellow actress with some talent at writing, innuendo and prurient inventiveness. Marie Colombier had been engaged by Sarah for her first American tour, to replace Jeanne Bernhardt, who had fallen ill. When Jeanne recovered and rejoined the company, Colombier was put on the sidelines, and finally left to return to France. In 1883 she published *Memoires de Sarah Barnum*, with a preface by Paul Bonnetain. In this fictitious biography—the name Barnum was well chosen and would stick to Sarah for the rest of her days—Sarah's rise and fame are accounted for on two grounds, publicity and sex. In fact, the book fully accomplishes the feat of not seeing her as an actress at all, but merely as a cocotte of the vilest sort: being pandered for by her mother since the age of sixteen; pandering extensively for her sister Jeanne; having a succession of paying customers, all described in detail with thinly disguised names and much circumstantial matter; being cheated by Damala twice a day on the average; and much more. What might have been a collection of judiciously chosen, believable points about the less public aspects of Sarah's past is so completely perverted by Marie Colombier that the whole becomes not only vile but completely ridiculous. The press was silent at first about the book until Octave Mirabeau could not restrain himself any more at its increasing circulation, and published a violent attack on it, on its author "Marie Pigeonnier" and on Bonnetain, with whom he fought a duel. The young Maurice Bernhardt then challenged someone—anyone—to fight a duel with him on behalf of Marie Colombier, the first of many such duels he wanted to fight to defend his mother's honor. Marie Colombier not only refused to have anyone champion her cause; she also ridiculed Maurice in public.

Sarah had the final say, however, and in Sarah-fashion. Some time after these events Sarah and Richepin went to Colombier's apartment. The scene, one cannot help thinking, was more than mere retribution: it was a Barnum-like stroke of public revenge, on which the reporter of the *New York Herald* cabled six thousand words to New York that evening. It also happened to be December 19, 1883, the day before the opening of Richepin's *Nana Sahib*.

Marie Colombier attempted to hide when Sarah and Richepin broke into the apartment. But Sarah found her behind a curtain and horse-whipped her through the length of the house while Richepin occupied himself with smashing the furniture, knick-knacks and anything else he could find. After that the publication of *La Vie de Marie Pigeonnier*, with a preface by "Jean Michepin" was an anticlimax. So was *Nana Sahib*.

Richepin's failure on the stage had its repercussion elsewhere as well. Philippe Garnier became Sarah's new leading man, so much so that he could make her act Ophelia to his Hamlet in 1886. His Hamlet was hissed, and one can hope that some of these hisses were directed not at his acting but at his cruelty in making Fedora-Theodora-Tosca-Phèdre act Ophelia at the age of forty-two.

Sardou's *Théodora* was first performed the day after Christmas, 1884. It is entirely concerned with passion and intrigue, completely unallayed by shades of characterization or moral issues. Its sumptuous setting astonished the audience. Sarah had several changes of costume, and the train alone for one of them cost 7,000 francs. The play is set in the Byzantine Empire; the Empress Theodora, a former prostitute, rules jointly with, and vigorously intrigues against the Emperor Justinian, her husband. The fictitious plot is a maze of complications involving one Andreas, Theodora's lover. The play ends with one of the most sadistic execution scenes ever shown on stage: the victim is held by two burly men, each pulling a rope tied to his wrists; with his arms thus outstretched, he is then slowly strangled to death by a woman. *Théodora* was an enormous success with the public. Its uninterrupted run of two hundred performances was one of the longest in the history of the Paris theaters to that time. It was seen in hundreds of performances all over the world.

After *Théodora* Sarah's repertoire for the 1880's was established: with a few additions, it consisted of the work of two contemporary playwrights: Alexandre Dumas *fils* and Victorien Sardou. Dumas provided her with her greatest single success, *La Dame aux Camélias;* Sardou with major costume dramas, one of which he wrote for her every second year, on the average. At first glance their plays appear to differ fundamentally: Dumas deals with the present day, and with moral issues, Sardou with the past, and with intrigue in high places. In reality, however, they are of one piece, and reflect accurately the desires, hidden and overt, of the audiences that came to see them all over the world. The basic formula contains two ingredients: sex and money. As money equals power in the society for which they wrote their plays, power may take the place of actual money, especially in the "historical" drama. But sex and money it remains, ever since, in Rachel's day, the great middle class tired of the excesses of Hugo's romanticism and the simple brutality of the plays of Dumas *père.*

In 1858 François Ponsard, one of Rachel's last playwrights and lovers, wrote his most successful play, not about the past like *Lucrèce* or *Charlotte Corday,* but about the present, bourgeois world of Paris. It was called *L'Honneur et L'Argent*. Honor and money seemed a tremendously appropriate title and theme for its age. Play after play followed it—*Francillon, La Femme de Claude, Le Fils Naturel, Le Demi-Monde, L'Etrangère, Le Mariage d'Olympe, Les Lionnes Pauvres* and so on—all depicting various aspects of this double theme. Take, for example, *La Princesse de Bagdad*, by Dumas *fils*, the play in which Duse first made her name in Turin. The title is meaningless except that it involves the past of Lionette, the heroine, who is the daughter of an oriental prince and a courtesan. Presumably that is the reason why she spends too much money. The first ten minutes—all of them—are taken up with such fascinating matters as overspending, loans, inheritances denied and changed, interest charges. Nourvady, who has forty million, loves Lionette to distraction and attempts to compromise her by various means, such as buying, furnishing and staffing a mansion in the hope that she might consent to use it and thereby give him a hold on her. When Lionette enters the mansion she finds a trunk filled with a million francs in gold, and meditates over it: "That is really beautiful, like everything that has power. There it is, ambition, hope, dreams, honor and dishonor, the undoing or the saving of hundreds, perhaps of thousands of human beings . . ." and so on for more than one printed page.

Money is power, as Lionette realizes, but honor is no adequate counter to it. In all these plays the real counter to money, the real concern in the interplay of power, is sex. Dumas, Augier, Sardou and the others wrote play after play in which they dazzlingly displayed sex and money, for a tantalizing, fascinating, utterly absorbing and earnest ninety-five per cent of the time until an honorable moral is quickly introduced before the final curtain.

Dumas managed to capitalize on the beliefs and attitudes of his time better than any other dramatist of the nineteenth century. *La Femme de Claude* (1873), which was carried through the world by Bernhardt and Duse, shows both his talent and the reflection it casts on his time. He wrote a preface of Shavian

size to it, in which he defended his work as an eloquent preachment against immorality. The graphic presentation of immorality as a preachment against it is an old idea, and Dumas restates
it as eloquently as anyone.

In 1873, when *La Femme de Claude* was first performed, the
lost war against the Germans was still fresh in everyone's heart.
The play deals with a great scientist, Claude Ruper, about to
deliver a powerful new secret weapon into the hands of France.
In defense of his work Claude says that the new weapon was
moral because it would avert rather than foster war; its very
destructiveness would prevent the recurrence of armed conflict.
(That argument, of course, is as time-honored and as valid as
the one regarding the virtue of depicting immorality.)

In any case, the invention and the patriotic fervor are plot
devices. The play is really concerned with Césarine, Ruper's
wife, who is called Claude's wife because of the resemblance of
her moral proclivities to those of Messalina, the wife of the Roman Emperor Claudius. At the start of the play she returns home
after an escapade of three months, one, it is clear, in a series of
many. Divorce is not legal—another of Dumas's concerns—and
husband and wife have been on terms of frigid politeness for
years. Césarine's character—despicable—is talked about with
great frankness by all, including Césarine. The first scene of the
play is once more almost entirely devoted to the subject of inheritances, the sale of the house, mortgages, and legal problems
of joint property. We never lose sight of these, but they share
the center of the action with sex. The catlike Césarine is in
league with a foreign agent, Castagnac, who has a financial hold
on her. At his orders she attempts to seduce Antonin, her husband's confidential assistant. She succeeds and he, suddenly
stricken with love, steals the secret documents for her. She is
caught by Claude *in flagrante delicto*, and shot by him.

The world of Dumas is populated with men and women who
have made money or have lost their money or have inherited
money (this last is much the best and most frequent), but never
any who are actually in the process of making money except

illegally, like Césarine. They love to distraction, if they love at all; and they are almost always aristocrats or at least on the fringe of the nobility. Even Césarine comes of noble stock. (German, of course, else how could she be so depraved?) Their rank is not necessary to the plot, as is Hamlet's or Phèdre's, but an adjunct to arouse interest. The middle class preferred to watch plays, not about the middle class, but about the upper class to which they aspired, and which, for the occasion, was given a middle-class outlook and middle-class concerns.

The audience could indulge its aspirations even more fully in the plays of Sardou, though it could presumably not feel as moral about seeing them, as they did not, like Dumas' dramas, deal with supposedly serious contemporary problems.

Sardou wrote some realistic plays in the Dumas sense, but he is remembered, if at all, for his spectacular plays in historical or at least foreign settings. They share with the here-and-now plays their basic plots, their concern with sex and money, and the ubiquitous fallen woman: Fedora (not a historical character, though made remote by being a Russian) is not a fallen woman, but ends up a murderess, giving her at least a minor sin; Theodora, La Tosca, Cleopatra, Gismonda, are. All are encased in a cocoon of historical events: the Russia of the Czarist aristocracy and the Nihilist revolutionaries, the Byzantine Empire, Papal Rome on the verge of Napoleonic conquest, Egypt on the verge of Roman conquest, Athens under the heel of the Turkish conqueror.

La Tosca is the most plausible of these plays. La Tosca is a famous singer in Rome, lover of Mario Cavaradossi, a painter. The Papal city is in the grip of fear spread by Baron Scarpia, the head of the secret police, who works feverishly to stamp out the flames of revolution which threaten to engulf it: the armies of the French Revolution led by General Napoleon Bonaparte are advancing on Rome. Mario becomes involved in the revolutionary underground, is taken to Scarpia's quarters and tortured in the back room while Scarpia extorts some crucial information from Tosca. He succeeds only when he arouses la Tosca's jealousy for a moment through a complicated maneuver involving a fan that belonged to another woman and was supposedly found among Mario's possessions. Scarpia loves la Tosca to distraction and she agrees to spend a night with him in return for a safe-conduct pass with which she and Mario will be able to escape from Papal territory. When the pass is signed and Scarpia comes to collect, she stabs him to death with a carving knife. But he got the better of her: the safe-conduct was false. Mario dies in front of a firing squad in the Fortress of Saint Angelo and Tosca jumps to her death from the ramparts after witnessing the execution.

This magnificently contrived set of logically arranged events almost seems plausible when it happens on stage. In moments of calm we get glimpses of human characters in Dumas' and Sardou's plays, and get a sense of reality. When the great scenes come and the star launches into *émotion forte*, all that is lost; but the previous development and, above all, the visual continuity on stage make the audience forget that. Césarine talking confidentially to her maid at the start of *La Femme de Claude* seems like a normal sharp-witted woman. It is the same Césarine —visibly Duse, Bernhardt—who makes a fevered attempt first to deceive Claude and then to regain his love, and who seduces Antonin in a matter of minutes. La Tosca, half in love, half jealous, banters with Mario in Act I; the same woman murders Scarpia with a carving knife she just found on the dinner table in the next act and jumps to her death in the last.

Césarine: love, blackmail, seduction, theft, high treason, incitement to kill, murder. Tosca: love, jealousy, torture, high treason, attempted rape, murder, imprisonment, false papers, execution, suicide. A mere listing of the chief events swirling about the heroine in these plays indicates the scope of the plot. In each case a large moral issue is involved; the use of the secret weapon for France; freedom or dictatorship for Rome. But in neither case is the moral issue in any way the determining factor; the causes are personal. Césarine betrays her husband and goes on to crime and death because her husband has refused her last, feverish declaration of newly rising love. La Tosca betrays her lover and goes on to crime and death because of jealousy.

The list of the ingredients of *La Femme de Claude* and *La Tosca* also shows something else: the wide variety of the obvious spectacular elements involved, and the range of acting opportunities open to the stars in the main roles.

The tightly constructed well-made play with its plentiful physical action made a clear understanding of the lines themselves rather superfluous. With Shakespeare and Racine what is said is the most important element. With Dumas and Sardou what is done is most important. Language is an accompaniment rather than the main carrying factor, and a good, interesting voice was needed more than the interpretation or creation of a character. At key points in these exciting, eventful plays words were in any case often replaced by screams, gurgles and the sounds of anguish.

The most famous and most successful play of Bernhardt's and Duse's repertoire, and of the second half of the nineteenth century, was Dumas' *La Dame aux Camélias*. It does not contain the physical violence of Sardou or of some of Dumas' later plays, but in every other respect it has the ingredients of the successful play of its time.

La Dame aux Camélias has first of all the right combination of subservience to morality and justification of immorality to suit the age. The whole age was absorbed in romantic stories about fallen women and tuberculosis, and here they were in conjunction. The courtesan who loves selflessly and, moreover, gives up her lover for selfless reasons just because she loves him, struck everyone as romantic and pitiful. The poignancy was increased by the fact the story had autobiographical overtones. In September, 1844, Alexandre Dumas *fils* and the actress Eugenie Déjazet went to the Théâtre des Variétés, where they saw Marie Duplessis sitting in one of the boxes. Marie, whose real, more prosaic name was Alphonsine Plessis, was a great beauty, one of the foremost kept women of Paris, intelligent and well-read in spite of her lower-class origin and poor schooling.

vivacious and charming. A great giver of parties who spent 100,-
000 francs a year, she was then twenty years old and already
afflicted with tuberculosis. She was allergic to the smell of flowers, and liked only camellias. Her first great protector, Antenor
Duc de Guiche, had given way by that time to Count Stackel-
berg, the former Russian ambassador, and others. Dumas was
fascinated; a theatrical dresser arranged a meeting. They became
lovers.

Her way of life was such that he had the choice either of being a kind of back-stairs lover or of keeping up with Marie's
public life. For the former he was too proud, for the latter he
was not rich enough. Marie cared for him sincerely and made
no demands—or hardly any—but even so he could see clearly
that she was socially and financially kept quite out of his class.
In August, 1845, torn between his pride and his desire, he finally
broke off the affair. Some time after the break he accompanied
his father to Madrid, and from there he wrote to her, half trying
to re-establish the relationship. From Spain father and son went
on to North Africa, and the journey stretched into months.
When they returned, Alexandre heard in Marseilles that Marie
had died during the Carnival season. At an auction of her effects
Dumas bought a gold chain, and in May of the same year went
to St. Germain, where he had gone riding on the day of his first
seeing Marie at the Variétés. In St. Germain he took a room in
a hotel and began to write his novel *La Dame aux Camélias*.
Much of Marie remains in the character of Marguerite Gautier:
her romantic inclinations, her camellias, her parties, and the constant sexual competition swirling around her. In his own place he
invents a hero, Armand Duval who, unlike himself, attempts to
reform her; and Armand's father, who goes to Marguerite and
pleads with her to let Armand go so that his sister, a pure young
girl, can make a suitable match in society. (Any thought of a
similarity between Duval *père* and Dumas *père* is unwarranted.)
Marguerite sacrifices herself for the sake of her love for Armand;
she not only leaves him—she makes him think that she has returned to her old life so that he will stay away from her in dis-

gust. She remains steadfast even when the deeply hurt Armand humiliates her in public by hurling his winnings at cards at her feet, as payment for past services. In the final act Marguerite is dying of consumption, alone, abandoned, without money. It is the Carnival season, a sad contrast to her present state. But her true love is being rewarded. Armand's sister has made a respectable marriage, and his father, who admired Marguerite's steadfast adherence to their agreement, tells all to his son and sends him back to her. He comes and embraces her; moments later, she is dead.

Dumas believed that he wrote moral plays that faithfully represented natural human behavior. He asserted that the theater must have truth as its aim, and that truth is discovered by observation. The story of a famous courtesan who falls in love with a good young man and leaves him at his father's request so that his sister can marry another good young man, was to Dumas an observation of nature. He tells the story charmingly against a setting devoid of all viciousness, and with proper attention to the moral code. Apart from sex or love (and honor as a cloak of the plot) money is the dominant element. Money is present in a different incarnation in each act, and serves as the symbol or setting of the mood. In Act I a gay party shows the expensive tastes that Marguerite sacrifices in the second act for the love of Armand. Armand's father is stunned to find that, far from taking Armand's money, Marguerite supplies the means for their idyllic summer at Auteuil. From that moment on he is convinced of her sincerity. Armand throws the money he won gambling down at Marguerite's feet as the crowning insult when he meets her again after her supposed betrayal. Marguerite, almost destitute at the point of death, is still generous with money.

The play which Dumas based on his novel was ready for performance in 1849, but one theater after the other refused it. Rachel declined to do the title role. She did not like prose drama, and she objected to the role because Marguerite, in contrast to the many other courtesans in Rachel's repertoire, was placed in a contemporary setting. (Sarah Bernhardt, in moving the play back to its original 1850 setting in the 1890's, finally removed those qualms, the same as had hampered Manet with some of his major paintings in the early 1860's. His *Olympia* and *Le Déjeuner sur l'Herbe* put nudes in a contemporary setting and caused a great scandal. Nudes in a safe, historical setting could be as fleshy as they pleased.)

In 1851 Bouffé, the manager of the Vaudeville, finally agreed to perform the play, only to have it banned by the Minister of Culture of the Second Republic. The Second Republic was about to expire, however; after Prince Napoleon's *coup d'état* in December the Duc de Morny was put in charge of the ministry which had banned the play, and it was first performed in February 1852 to become, eventually, the single most popular French play of the century.

In 1886 Sarah undertook her second transatlantic journey, thereby concluding the first phase of her international career. In the six years since her departure from the Comédie she had established herself on both sides of the Atlantic and journeyed as far as Russia. With Sardou and Dumas she had acquired the properly effective international repertoire. In the next few years she was to extend her sphere as far as Australia and Peru, to play in East Africa and Hawaii.

There seemed to be no end: a long tour, followed by a new play or two in Paris, followed by another long tour. Interspersed with these were the usual spring seasons in London, her usual summer vacations in Belle-Isle, the revivals of *La Dame aux Camélias* or *Théodora*, and the occasional performance of *Phèdre*.

Edmond de Goncourt gives a picture of Sarah in these years of the height of her success: "Sarah arrives in a pearl-grey tunic braided with gold. No diamonds except the handle of her lorgnette. A mothlike wisp of black lace on the burning bush of her hair; beneath, the black shadow of lashes and the clear blue of her eyes. . . . She must be nearly fifty. She wears no powder and her complexion is that of a young girl."

That was the public Sarah who wore a perfume so penetrating that a gentleman's sleeve, if she took his arm, smelled of it for hours after.

Off stage, and in private, Sarah was sensible and shrewd, generally kind, and had a good sense of humor. She took for granted of course that she was the greatest actress in the world and would be jealous of everyone, large or small, who could in any way affect that claim. She was kind to her family and loyal to her friends. She looked after her sister Jeanne until her death, and after Jeanne's daughter Sarah (Saryta); she loved Mme. Guérard, who remained a member of Sarah's household until her death in 1890. One of her most singular acts of kindness came in May and June, 1889, when Damala, dying of his drug addiction and penniless once more, turned up for the last time. For several weeks she patiently performed *La Dame aux Camélias* by his side, to give him the illusion of life and spare him the shame of downright charity. A few months after that he died at the age of thirty-four.

Her greatest love always was, not Damala, but her son Maurice. "What does it matter to us who his father was! With a mother like that . . ." wrote Maurice Rostand. That was partly the problem. With a mother like that the charming, handsome Maurice never emerged from a charmed, lovely boyhood. Psychologists may interpret Sarah's reported reply, when asked her age once: "Twenty-three, like my son." Or when she said that she always thought of him rather than of her Mario of the evening during the torture scene in *Tosca*.

Maurice had married the Princess Therese (Terka) Jablonsky on December 29, 1887, and had two daughters by her: Simone, who married an American industrialist, Edgar Gross; and Lysiane, who wrote a book about her grandmother and married and divorced the playwright Louis Verneuil, also the author of a book about her grandmother. The Bernhardts lived around the corner from Sarah, on the Rue de la Neva. Life was not easy for Terka in the shadow of her mother-in-law.

On October 23, 1890, Sarah performed her fourth Sardou

play, a natural choice of subject: *Cléopâtre*. It was sumptuously done, full of oriental splendor, but, comparatively speaking, it was a failure. It did not even reach one hundred performances.

It was not the fault of the play itself. Cleopatra was another Fedora, another Theodora, another Tosca, as expertly contrived; but the public was tired. Sardou had represented Sarah in rage: the rapacious lioness clawing her enemies, her lover and finally herself. The audience had enjoyed the complete abandonment of restraint, the freedom of vicariously experienced high emotion, lascivious, gluttonous, bestial. Tosca had been the best of them, giving Sarah her greatest chance to act. The English critic Scott wrote of Tosca's "cries of agony, her wild shrill screams of despair in the torture act; never in my memory so nearly rising to the height of great tragedy, as in the murder of Baron Scarpia." Her cries sent "a shudder of horror round the house" and "once, maybe by accident, the two cries, the cry of the man, the cry of the woman, met in a wail of piteous unison, causing an indescribable effect." "Sarah Bernhardt should be painted knife in hand over the dying Scarpia, for it is the nearest thing to great tragedy that has ever been seen in modern times." Tragedy seems hardly the term one would apply to *Tosca*, but it was exciting theater, well acted, theater that could readily speak to foreign audiences.

Even before *Cléopâtre* Sarah had realized that she needed changes in her established repertoire. She was sure that she could go on for some time to bring Sardou to Moscow or Melbourne or Milwaukee, but she knew also that she was losing her hold on Paris. That hold was a matter of personal pride but it was also more than that: she was the great international actress from Paris. She could not afford to lose Paris without risking her dominion everywhere. While the rounds of triumph continued into the last decade of the century, one can notice also more and more her search for a new base of appeal, a new drama. On this would depend whether she would continue her conquests or become a popular institution, treated eventually with nostalgia by the elderly critics and playgoers, and disregarded by the rest. She had seen that treatment accorded to the elderly Ristori when she herself had set out on her international career.

In 1889 Sarah had received an explicit warning that her repertoire was on trial. A petition appeared in the newspaper *Le Gaulois*, signed by fifty prominent personalities of the cultural life of Paris, which said: "You who are acquainted with Sarah Bernhardt should tell her that many women and young girls would like to applaud her, but that the kind of play she acts prevents them from going to the theater where she has her triumphs. She creates either a vicious queen, or a strumpet, or a great lady of doubtful virtue. Many of us would acclaim her with enthusiasm if she acted a pure heroine in a moral play."

While preparing for Cleopatra Sarah was also looking for the right play on Joan of Arc, for what would be purer or more natural for women and young girls than the national heroine of France? The French stage had not been lucky with its Joans. Rachel and Mlle. Georges had done the tragedy by Soumet, a poor play. Schiller's play, the most famous, Sarah found ridiculous. In the end she decided on *Jeanne d'Arc*, libretto by Barbier, music by Gounod, which had been performed at the Gaieté in 1873, with Rachel's sister Lia. Barbier's *Jeanne d'Arc* was a chronicle, a panoramic view rather than a play, but Sarah managed to infuse a dramatic element into it that the work would have lacked in any other hands. On January 3, 1890, at the age of forty-five, a grandmother, she interpreted for the first time a girl who had never seen the age of twenty. Somehow it all seemed very right. Anatole France said of her Joan: "She is poetry herself. She embodies that reflection of the stained glass windows which the apparitions of the saints have left behind. . . . She is a legend come to life."

La Tosca and Theodora therefore became Joan of Arc in January before becoming Cleopatra in October. Between these two plays she inserted one other essay in purity which, however, aroused more controversy than the most impure Sardou heroines.

On April 5, Good Friday, Sarah played the role of the Virgin
Mary in the sacred drama *La Passion* by Edmond Haraucourt. It
was not really a performance but a dramatic reading, and it was
given in the Cirque d'Hiver, in part because she could not obtain
a regular theater for the play. To Sarah, Haraucourt's play was
"du bon théâtre," good theatrical material. It was also a play of
elevated sentiments and noble intent, and therefore seemed better than Sardou. She refused to listen to those who counseled
her to abandon the project. Once she sensed opposition, she was
going to perform *La Passion* all the more—*quand-même*. Official
opinion said that it was a sacrilege to put the Virgin Mary on
stage. Unofficially it was added: to have the Virgin Mary put
on stage by a Jewess.

The events of 1890 made Sarah realize that she had probably
lost some of her public appeal. In January 1891 she therefore
embarked with her company on the longest and most extensive
tour of her life. Except for two very brief return trips she was
absent from the French capital for two years and nine months.
She performed on all continents except Africa, and had all the
adulation and triumphs which Paris now denied her.

The first part of the world tour was devoted to North America. Sarah moved without pause through the major centers of
the continent covering the great cities between the two coasts
in three months.

New York, February 6–March 14, at the Garden Theatre
Washington, March 16–21
Philadelphia, March 23–28
Boston, March 30–April 4
Montreal, April 6–11
Detroit, Indianapolis, St. Louis, April 13–18
Denver, April 20–22
San Francisco, April 24–May 1
Departure for Australia, May 2.

Then, for eleven weeks, Sarah toured the principal cities of Australia, a triumph that ended when 5,000 people sang the *Marseillaise* as her ship sailed out of Sydney harbor.

On September 10 she was back in the United States to perform across the continent, west to east. In May Sarah was back in Paris, long enough to rest briefly, to go to a few parties, and to perform at a benefit. By the end of the month, she left again for a tour of Europe. In London she rehearsed Oscar Wilde's new play *Salome*, the performance of which was, however, banned by the Lord Chamberlain. Then she went on to the French provinces, the Low Countries, Austria, Russia, Poland, Scandinavia, Italy—all had been done before, all the successes repeated themselves, the same reviews, the same interviews, the same plays, the same. After a few days at home in March, 1893, giving *Phèdre* at another benefit, she left once more for the east, Budapest, Bucharest, Constantinople, and back, before embarking for South America, giving performances in Rio de Janeiro, São Paulo, Buenos Aires and Montevideo.

On October 1, 1893, she was back in Paris to stay at last. She was more famous and richer than she had ever been. The tour had been so stupendous and its success so unprecedented that even Paris forgot its sense of superiority and gave her a welcome such as it had never given a returning star.

Jules Lemaître, writing of her after her return said: "More than any other [woman] she must have known enormous, manifest, intoxicating, infatuated homage, the homage given to conquerors and Caesars. She has been given that homage in all lands of the earth, with welcome not given even to kings. She has received what will never be accorded to the princes of the world." And Sarcey wrote when Sarah returned in 1893, from her ten thousands of miles of travel: "It is a strange thing, unheard of, inexplicable, but nevertheless true, that Mme. Bernhardt today looks younger, appears to us more dazzling, and, to speak the truth, more beautiful than ever."

Sarah's experiences during the dozen years since her first

American tour had been unprecedented: The twenty-nine curtain calls after *La Dame aux Camélias* one evening in New York, when fifty thousand people—or so it seemed to Sarah—waited for her outside the theater, and Jeanne Bernhardt had to be disguised as Sarah to distract the crowd and let her sister escape. Or the necklace placed upon her by the Emperor Franz Josef of Austria after a performance of *Phèdre*, or the presents from King Alfonso of Spain and King Umberto of Italy. Or the château lent to her by the Archduke Frederick, or the yacht King Christian IX of Denmark lent her to take her to Elsinore Castle. Or the dinner she gave to the Prince and Princess of Wales, and the German shepherd dog she gave the Prince—as one member of royalty to another. And all the gifts, tangible and intangible, like Oscar Wilde's sonnet "To Sarah Bernhardt":

> How vain and dull this common world must seem
> To such a One as thou, who shouldst have talked
> At Florence with Mirandola, or walked
> Through the cool olives of the Academe;
> Thou shouldst have gathered reeds from a green stream
> For a goat-foot Pan's shrill piping, and have played,
> With the white girls in that Phaecian glade
> Where grave Odysseus waked from his dream.
> Ah, surely once some urn of attic clay
> Held thy wan dust and thou hast come again
> Back to this common world so dull and vain,
> For thou wert weary of the sunless day,
> The heavy fields of scentless asphodel
> The loveless lips with which men kiss in hell.

And all these millions of francs that had sifted through her hands. They continued to sift: On May 25, 1893, during a short stay in Paris, she had bought a theater. Undeterred by past experience she was now to be a producer once more. At the Porte-Saint-Martin Sardou and Duquesnel had jointly produced her great successes. At the small Théâtre de la Renaissance she would be able to produce what she wanted and control not only what would be done but how it would be done. In the next five years, under her management, the Renaissance was to see twelve new plays, nine of which would fail and only one which would reach beyond one hundred performances: *Gismonda;* by Sardou, of course. Time and again she had to fall back on *Fédora, La Dame aux Camélias* and *La Tosca* to recoup her losses. That, however, must not obscure the fact that some of her most interesting later work was done here, in old as well as new plays, in the gem-like setting of this intimate, well-decorated house. In December 1893, as if to recover from her tour, she did twenty performances of *Phèdre* in one run, about as many as she had done in her seven years at the Français. That achievement revealed a new *Phèdre,* and an actress at the summit of her powers. Paris watched with fascination and, for once, without reservation.

She revived *La Dame aux Camélias* that season, set back to the 1850's, the time of its writing, for the first time—a costume play and a classic. After the opening Alexandre Dumas paid her the final gesture of homage. He sent her the original of his famous letter to Marie Duplessis in which he broke off their liaison, for Sarah to have and keep as the only document left of that old story. He believed that it was due her; Sarah was now the in-carnation of Marguerite Gautier.

CHAPTER 9 / Our Lady of the Quivering Nerves

THE years in which Sarah Bernhardt made her greatest world tour, 1891 to 1893, were also the years in which Eleonora Duse became an international actress of first rank. No Italian actor or actress of the generation after Salvini and Ristori had achieved that stature. The only ones who aspired to Sarah's pre-eminence were French, and even the most persistent of them did not come close.

Duse was fourteen years younger than Bernhardt. Like Adelaide Ristori she came from an old professional acting family. When the Ristoris were travelling through Venetia with their small daughter Adelaide, one of several companies of actors in the Austrian north of Italy, the foremost member of their craft was Luigi Duse, Eleonora's grandfather. The son of actors, he was born toward the end of the eighteenth century in the port city of Chioggia, and became the last great interpreter of the *commedia dell' arte*, and producer of the Goldoni and Gozzi repertoire. In the small and large towns of the Italian north-east Luigi Duse made the final determined attempt to adapt the declining Venetian theater to the changed tastes of the nineteenth century. He almost entirely discarded the masks that had been the mark of its stylization. He eliminated most of the improvisation; and he created a new character, Giacommetto, the last popular addition to the stock figures of the *commedia*. George Sand and Musset saw him in Venice and admired him greatly. For some reason he fell into disfavor with the Austrian authorities, and at the time of his death in 1854, he was poor and forgotten.

Eighteen members of the Duse family were strolling players in the later years of Luigi's life, including his four sons. The least happy of them was Alessandro, never more than a mediocre actor, who would have preferred to be a painter. Besides that, the life of the strolling players was becoming more difficult with each passing year. The wars and revolutions in the 1840's and 1850's were affecting their audiences, their itineraries, their travel permits, and led to increasingly strict government supervision of their repertoires and movements. As these difficulties increased, their audiences decreased further. The costumes and scenery deteriorated and the money to replace them had to go more and more into the barest necessities of food and shelter. The Duse family company, descendants of the great Luigi who lived out his days alone in Padua, were among the poorest and saddest groups fighting the losing battle for audiences in small towns in the final years of Austrian rule in Italy.

In 1858, a year before that rule ended for most of the peninsula, on October 3, Alessandro Duse was presented with a daughter by his wife Angelica Cappelletto. The place was the small town of Vigevano, where the company had arrived only the night before, giving rise to the persistent story that the little girl was born in a railway train. The company had put up at a modest inn, the *Cannon d'Oro*, and the little girl was baptized Eleonora.

1858 was the year of Rachel's death, but the Duses are not likely to have noticed her passing, even if they knew of it. They were too busy trying to feed themselves, and to find new engagements and the means to get to them. They rarely could afford the train; more often they traveled on river barges, or in gypsy-like carts, in the rain or scorching sun, through mud and snow. They carted with them their torn and rumpled costumes and their paper scenery, for one-night stands and some hurried sleep in third-rate inns before moving on the next day. For the child Eleonora these first years of her life meant constant movement and irregularity, a rootless existence in cold, dark, dank rooms, a different one almost every night, where the child was often left alone because both of her parents were needed at the theater.

Her troubles increased as she got older. Since the Duses were constantly on the move, leading the lives of itinerant fruit pickers rather than those of men and women of the stage, the child could get no consistent schooling or training of any sort. And when Eleonora could get to a school for a while, the other children would make life a hell for the small, pale, shabbily dressed girl. She was, after all, a *figlia di commedianti* in an age when to be an ordinary actor's child still meant to be little better than the child of thieves or vagrants.

The Ristoris, Adelaide's parents, had been reasonably prosperous, and acted on the road in better days than those of the new Kingdom of Italy in the 1860's. The Félix family had been just as poor as the Duses, but they worked together with single-minded devotion to better themselves. Sarah Bernhardt was born into an unhappy family situation, but at least there were money and connections. Eleonora had nothing—no money, no future, only a disintegrating trade, a father who carried it on unwillingly, and a mother afflicted with tuberculosis who dragged herself from place to place, and finally from hospital to hospital. From her father Duse inherited a certain dislike of her profession, from her mother weak lungs, and from her general situation a neurotice disposition, shy, erratic, self-centered, temperamental, pessimistic.

She was needed on stage long before she could understand what she was doing. By 1863 her name appeared on programs. At twelve or thirteen she had to take over the roles of her mother, who was no longer capable of fulfilling any obligations on stage. She had to be Francesca da Rimini, Pia de Tolomei and others, leading roles in plays of violence, desperate romantic love and adultery; she performed adult love scenes with uncles and other relatives. At an age when the young girl should have had the peace and quiet of an ordered existence she had to scream her heart out on stage, interpret unnatural and equivocal situations, starve and worry, without anyone in whom she could confide.

Shortly before Eleonora's fourteenth birthday, Angelica Duse died of tuberculosis. Her daughter could not even be present at the deathbed. Angelica was buried at public expense in an unmarked grave and Eleonora did not have enough money to buy herself the obligatory black dress. One of her female colleagues advised her to sell herself in order to get money for the dress, but Duse, in her usual withdrawn way, simply turned away and left the woman standing alone. But she carried a picture of her mother with her for the rest of her life, and never showed it to anyone.

After Angelica's death Alessandro Duse saw no reason why he should have to bear his hated work any longer. For a short time he took employment, together with his daughter, with other traveling companies. Then he told his daughter that he wanted to leave, go to Chioggia, his home town as much as he had a home town, and to turn to his real love: painting.

Eleonora does not seem to have objected; she was too young to assert herself, and too crushed already by the uncertainties and privations of her life. She does, however, seem to have borne her father a lasting grudge or, rather, she seems to have suffered, silently but for a long time, at his abandonment of her. She took employment with a succession of minor companies and began several years of restless, fruitless search—hardly for a career, more likely for a sheltering niche in the only trade she knew. She acted doggedly, and doggedly went from company to company until a leading actress, Giacinta Pezzana, saw something in her that others did not yet see, and took her in to join a resident company in Naples.

Duse felt secure for the first time in her life during that season of 1878–1879 in Naples. The future looked reasonably bright, she acted with a good company and she was no longer an unimportant member of it. She made friends for the first time. She met Matilde Serao that year, a young intellectual who was to become a well-known novelist and remained one of Duse's most devoted friends all her life. The young actress became interested in art and literature and in good conversation. Among her new acquaintances was one Martino Cafiero, a well-to-do man about town, who soon began to take her to dinner, to museums and galleries, and on moonlight sails in the Bay of Naples. Cafiero talked very well. Duse was fascinated by his easy culture, and surprised that a man of such background and intelligence should consider it worth his while to spend so much time with her. She did not realize that she was on the way to becoming a local celebrity, and Cafiero was about to add a scalp to his collection. She did not realize it for a long time. After he had seduced her, she was so completely in love that the future seemed to hold only one thing she desired: marriage to Cafiero. Cafiero did not discourage her feelings and hopes.

At the end of the season Pezzana accepted an engagement in Turin, and urged Duse to sign a contract for the same theater. For Duse it would be a considerable advance in her career because Turin was much more important than Naples, perhaps the most important theatrical city in Italy, and Cesare Rossi one of the better managers. Duse was too young and shy to discuss the future openly with Cafiero, who remained strangely silent on the subject of marriage. In the end she signed the contract, hoping to force the issue with him. She continued to hope until the last minute, until the train to the North actually pulled out of the station in Naples. Cafiero had not even come to say good-by.

Shortly after her arrival in Turin Duse found out that she was pregnant.

Under these conditions she had little chance to repeat her Naples success. Rossi considered her a failure, gave her small parts and, out of personal kindness, made provision for her to have her baby in quiet in the country. Before that, however, she made one more attempt. Surely, she thought, Cafiero would marry her now that he was to be the father of her child. She wrote to him, and the length it took him to reply, as well as the tone of his letter, should have convinced her that the world of her ideals had little basis in reality. It did not, and it took a shabby meeting in a hotel in Rome with the shabby Cafiero to convince her. After one day, during which he seduced her once more and then declined to give any but the most marginal financial assistance, she returned, in her third-class carriage, to Turin, with one more chalk mark against the world in general, and against the world of men in particular.

For the final stage of her pregnancy she was quartered with a peasant family at Marina di Pisa. The child, a boy, died within a week, and the disconsolate girl was watched over by Matilde Serao, the first of a number of occasions when she acted as Duse's selfless best friend.

An accident rescued Duse from her despondency. Pezzana had left the Carignano, and Rossi, without a leading lady of any stature, fell back on Duse. It may also be true that he liked his comfort and preferred a quiet obscure actress to a famous and temperamental one. By default Duse took over the roles of her former protectress. In the following year she married a fellow actor, Teobaldo Checchi, as quiet as she, and a rather pleasant man in that he was one of the few who did not consider her fair game as a fallen woman. She soon bore him a daughter, Enrichetta.

Duse may have suited Rossi's convenience, but her drawing power was small. The Città di Torino Company at the Carignano played to empty houses. At times the evening's income did not exceed 30 lire. Rossi might have had to give up if an outside event had not come to his rescue.

Sarah Bernhardt, sweeping through Europe on her first great tour, was moving into Italy. Rossi hastened to offer her the Carignano for her performances in Turin. She accepted and gave four performances: *La Dame aux Camélias*, *Adrienne Lecouvreur*, *Le Sphinx* and *Frou-Frou*. The reviews ranged from somewhat reserved (for *Dame*) to ecstatic (for *Frou-Frou*).

The boxes at the Carignano, which usually cost 5 lire, cost 100 for Bernhardt's opening night. The house was filled to the last seat when it had been more than half empty before. Above all, there was Sarah—Sarah with her retinue of secretaries, dressers, costumers, actors, her animals, trunks of costumes, hats, furs, jewels. Though her international status was recent, she already knew how to confirm it, how to carry Paris with her, how to lord in the best dressing rooms and over the finest managers. Duse, who knew no French, came and was impressed—more, it seems, with the ambiance of wealth and status than with the artistry of the performance. She felt that Sarah was striking a tremendous blow for the whole of the acting profession:

> And she came irradiated by her great aureole [she wrote later], her world wide fame. And, as if by magic the theatre was suddenly filled with movement and life, and began to glitter anew. To me it was as if with her approach all the old, ghostly shadows of tradition and of an enslaved art faded away to nothing. It was like an emancipation. She was there, she played, she triumphed, she took possession of us all, she went away . . . but like a great ship she left a wake behind her . . . and for a long time the atmosphere she had brought with her remained in the old theatre. *A woman had achieved all that!*

By the time Sarah left, Duse had made her decision. On February 26 she quietly took back her dressing room and performed in *L'Importuno e l'astratto*. But she also told Rossi that her old repertoire would not do any more. She wanted to do Dumas' *La Princesse de Bagdad*. Rossi was shocked. Dumas' play was in Sarah's line, though she had not performed it. It had also failed in Paris at the Comédie, with Croizette, a few months before. Duse insisted, and *La Princesse de Bagdad* was announced for March 18. The acquired momentum of Sarah's brief stay seems to have drawn a larger than usual, and rather curious audience to the Carignano. They applauded Duse's daring for reasons of local patriotism and stayed to applaud her for artistic reasons as well. For the first time Duse had a really attentive audience, which stayed attentive long enough in that lighted, noisy auditorium to recognize her great talent.

She did not stop here. She enlarged her repertoire at once to invite direct comparison: *La Femme de Claude, La Dame aux Camélias*. Within weeks Rossi had arranged a tour of the major cities of Italy for his company and its new star, whom he took to Venice, Milan, Pisa, Florence and Naples, and finally to the Teatro Valle in Rome.

In France, once Paris was conquered, the provinces followed suit. The situation was different in Italy because it had been divided into separate countries for centuries before 1860. Each major city was an independent cultural center and had to be conquered separately. But Duse's tour was a triumph everywhere. After the final performance at the Teatro Valle the mounted police had to be called out to keep the enthusiasm of the people from causing a riot. A torchlight procession that escorted her to her hotel left her, and many others, in tears.

When she finally returned to Turin on November 2 as Gilberte in *Frou-Frou*, she received wildly enthusiastic reviews of the kind that Bernhardt had received ten months before; they did not fail to mention the French actress and draw patriotically tinged comparisons. Dumas *fils* wrote to her and congratulated Rossi. Prince Napoleon was reminded of Rachel when he saw her.

During her first series of performances in Rome Joseph Schurmann, the manager of Bernhardt's Italian tour, offered Duse a contract for a tour of Europe. She refused, saying that she was only an unimportant Italian actress whom nobody would understand. In 1885, however, she agreed at Rossi's urging to a tour of South America, to follow up on Ristori's and Salvini's triumphs in that continent.

Everything went wrong from the beginning of the long sea voyage. Not long before their departure the news had come of Martino Cafiero's death; Duse was plunged into gloom and despair by it, while the tactful Checchi absented himself from home for a while. Now, on board ship, it became clear that the mourning for Cafiero had also been an indication of her feelings for Checchi. Duse was manifestly drawn towards her leading man, Flavio Andò, and the confinement of a ship made the triangle even more wearing than it would have been otherwise. This time Checchi could not be tactful any longer and his jealousy, Duse's nervousness, and Andò's lack of intelligence or tact left them exhausted before the performances even began.

Worse was to come upon arrival in Rio de Janeiro. The second lead, Diotti, who had fallen ill on board, died. The closely knit, small company was not only saddened but short one actor. The theater in Rio was far too large for the company, and in particular for Duse's style of acting; the sparse audience talked through the first performance, Sardou's *Fédora*. On the third night, Duse could finally report some sort of victory to Matilde Serao. It was only an artistic success, however, not a financial one, and as the tour went on financial difficulties were added to the personal ones of the star. In Buenos Aires Checchi finally decided to separate from his wife and the company, and to settle in Argentina, while the company dragged on to finish the tour.

In Italy she now had her own company, with Andò as her leading man. But she was a poor manager and Andò was not intelligent enough. The end of her love for him also came soon. *"Il était beau, mais il était bête,"* she said of him later. Beauty was no longer enough for her. She needed a man whose mind could respond to hers. She found that man in the composer Arrigo Boito with whom she had as harmonious a relationship as she was capable of. With him she spent much of the four years after her return from South America, a time when she hardly left Italy and concentrated on her acting and her intellectual development.

At first the relations between Boito and Duse were purely intellectual and platonic. Duse had hardly any formal education but she was, like Rachel and Bernhardt, an extremely intelligent woman, avid for knowledge and a coherent picture of the world. Under Boito's guidance she immersed herself in literature, particularly Shakespeare, whom Boito had translated into Italian. She learned French and began to read, especially in philosophy, a habit that never left her.

Her friendship with Boito gradually turned to love. Neither of them was free; Duse was married to Checchi, and Boito had an invalid wife. They remained lovers for several years, spending as much time together as they could. Boito translated *Antony and Cleopatra* for Duse, which she first performed with success in Milan on November 24, 1888. The summer of that year they had spent idyllically in a village near Bergamo, in preparation, in rehearsal, and in love.

Their collaboration in *Antony and Cleopatra* was the summit of their relationship. In the early 1890's Duse, now on her way to international stardom, had to absent herself increasingly from Italy, and though they continued to see each other, it was not the same any more.

As the foremost actress of Italy Duse was continually urged by managers, critics and friends to tour foreign countries. The failure of her South American tour in 1885 deterred her for several years from accepting any offers, but in 1891 she agreed finally to go to Russia, one of the countries that had been hospitable to foreign actors, especially Italian.

At the border between Austria and Russia—at that time the only real border in Europe where passports and official examinations were called for—a group of actors from the Burgtheater in Vienna saw the Italian troupe. The actress Jenny Gross pointed out to the Viennese playwright and critic Hermann Bahr a lady hidden in dark clothes: "There's some competition for us," she said. "Italians, also going to Petersburg. That lady was very ill during the night. Her name is Duse." The lady, shivering and sad, did not look much like competition to Bahr; he was traveling with Joseph Kainz and Friedrich Mitterwurzer, two of the most famous actors of the Burgtheater, the Comédie Française of the German language. He was barely curious.

Soon after their arrival in Petersburg, when they had a free evening the three men went to see the Italians because, as Kainz said, "I like Italian actors even if they are bad, better than the best Germans; one can always learn something even from the lowest of them." They saw *La Femme de Claude*. "Suddenly," Bahr wrote later, "Kainz grabs my arm and clings to me, and I hear Mitterwurzer draw his breath sharply; and I keep saying to myself: you must not burst out crying, you'll be ridiculous!

To encounter Duse unprepared, completely unforewarned, to be confronted with Duse when one merely expects some talented actress—to be face to face with Duse for the first time—that is simply beyond any power of description."

The short stay in Petersburg established a virtual pattern for Duse on her first European tour. On March 13, 1891, she gave her first performance in *La Dame aux Camélias*, before an empty house, in a small theater. The second evening was *Antony and Cleopatra*, and it was nearly sold out. Petersburg had fallen under her spell, so much so that she returned for a second series of performances in December of the same year.

Hermann Bahr wrote, he says, a rather confused article about his experience in the *Frankfurter Zeitung*. As a result he received a carefully tentative enquiry from a theatrical agent in Vienna asking if such a paragon of acting really existed. Bahr's reply prompted the impresario Tänczer to bring Duse to the Austrian capital.

The situation repeated itself. She was booked into one of the second string of Viennese theaters, the Carltheater. For the first performance, *La Dame aux Camélias* on February 19, 1892, all but the gallery was empty, and the box office sale, 800 crowns, made Tänczer feel foolhardy and very sorry for himself. Then came the performance. By the end of the evening Tänczer, himself in tears, knew that he had one of the greatest artists of the world on his hands. By the following afternoon the Viennese knew that something unusual was taking place at the Carltheater. The sale at the box office rose from 800 to 9000 crowns per performance. The second performance was *Fédora*, and one of the most conservative audiences in Europe came for the sake of curiosity and stayed completely taken aback by their own enthusiasm. On the third night Duse made a daring experiment. She performed *A Doll's House* by Ibsen, the most controversial contemporary playwright, who had hardly been performed in Vienna before. Here, too, she won.

Duse returned to Vienna twice more in that same year: In May for the International Drama Exhibition, and in the fall for

a third series of performances with Flavio Andò. She was celebrated and loved in the Austrian capital in a way in which
Rachel, Ristori or Bernhardt had never been. Thirty years later,
in the shabby impoverished postwar Vienna of 1923 she gave
her last performance in Europe before departing on the final
tour of her career, to America, and found the love of the Viennese unchanged.

Meanwhile she went on to triumphs in Berlin, Budapest, London, and found that she had become an actress of international
stature.

She not only aroused the enthusiasm of large general audiences, but of some of the most perceptive artists of her time.
Writers like Shaw, Hofmannsthal and Rilke became her enthusiastic followers. The greatest directors of her and the following generation, Stanislavski and Reinhardt, were inspired by
her. Stanislavski produced his first plays in Moscow in the year
in which Duse came to Petersburg for the first time. Until then
the chief influence on his thinking had been the Meininger Company, mainly because they had developed ensemble acting in
contrast to the current star system, and because their costumes
and settings were accurate and very realistic. He did not, however, like their declamatory style and their conventional modes
of acting. He found the style he wanted in Duse.

The great new effect that she brought to the international
stage in the early 1890's was a unique method of acting that
gave the impression of being unpremeditated and yet carefully
thought out, spontaneous and yet clearly a momentous, conscious achievement. It was a supremely economical method devoid of great gestures. It seemed completely natural and true to
life. Yet, at the great climactic moments, a throb of passion
would break out of Duse that would sweep the audience along
irresistibly. In that she resembled Rachel rather than the amply
built Ristori with her ample gestures. Rachel, until the moment
she "electrified" her audience, had the supreme elegance and
self-possession which her contemporaries described as resembling
a classical statue. Duse achieved her initial effects through a natu-

ralness that transcended anything done before her time—until she, too, gripped the audience with her display of *émotion forte*.

Duse knew the dramatic devices of her time, of course, and would use them occasionally. She knew the importance of pauses and silent acting. If the gallery cried or sniffed and coughed with too much emotional stress in *La Dame aux Camélias*, a pause would quiet them, or stronger acting would urge them on. Also, William Archer reports that as late as 1893 she accepted a recall in the middle of Act II of Sardou's *Divorçons*, reacting to applause in the manner of an operatic prima donna. In *Fédora*, towards the end of the play, she could hold her audience enthralled as she tried to get the stopper out of her vial of poison. Would she succeed before Ipanoff's arrival? Would she die?

In most instances, however, these were not the effects she used or sought. On the contrary. At times she seemed to go to extraordinary lengths to avoid "points." Her strength, her interest, her appeal lay in a psychological interpretation of character. That in itself was not new; Rachel had searched for the character of Phèdre, for example, and Bernhardt was still searching for it. Duse did the same, but her result was different. For Bernhardt a character was still all of one piece, an end result of intelligent, resourceful deliberation. For Duse it was a mosaic, its components often seemingly unrelated until they somehow produced a unified result. She would contravene all rules, turn her back to the audience, whisper, seem awkward, if any of these contributed to the desired result. Hugo von Hofmannsthal, who saw her in Vienna in 1891, put it perhaps most succinctly: "She acts the transitions; she fills the gaps of motivation; she reconstructs the psychological novel in the drama. With a pursing of the lips, a movement of a shoulder she portrays the maturing of a decision, the passing of a thought through the mind, the whole psycho-physiological experience which precedes verbal expression."

It was inevitable after her European successes that she would be urged to make a tour of the United States. South America

had been a failure in 1885. Now, eight years later, she went to
North America with similarly poor results. She had a harrowing
crossing, first of all, at the end of 1892, and arrived unprepared
for what she found. Unlike Sarah, she had no easily discernible
eccentricities, no stunning fashions, and no real talent for self-
advertisement. Her managers, Theodore and Carl Rosenfeld,
managed to miss her when her liner docked in New York, and
while they were chasing all over town, she drove alone to the
Murray Hill Hotel. She became known as "The hermit of Murray Hill." Except for a few personal acquaintances, especially
Mrs. Helena Gilder, whose husband was the editor of the *Century Magazine*, she saw few people. Worse, she refused to see the
members of the press, one by one, for the usual series of inane
interviews about breakfast habits and views of America.

The *New York World* of January 24, 1893, noted with approval that she was no "wily theatrical falsifier," had originality,
and dared to be natural. It also found Duse's Italian, though a
foreign language to most of the audience, infinitely more intelli-
gible than English as most native actresses spoke it. On the whole,
however, the reaction of the press was one of bafflement at
Duse's combination of extreme naturalness, even a kind of un-
awareness of the audience, and her tremendous climaxes, the
émotion forte of the big scenes in Dumas and Sardou. Some of
the early praise turned to antagonism when it became clear that
her fireworks on stage were unlike those to which critics and
public were accustomed; not only that, but at times she avoided
the fireworks altogether and left the audience cheated, so it felt,
of its emotional experience. The press criticized her mannerisms
on stage and her unwillingness to provide it with news off stage.
And it referred to Bernhardt—there is hardly a review that does
not mention Bernhardt. Often the mention is flattering to Duse:
"The Duse showed us the natural distress of a woman, as opposed to the theatrical anguish of even a Bernhardt . . ." "Mme.
Duse has been called Italy's Bernhardt. This is an injustice to
her . . ." Often, however, it was not flattering: "The Italian's
tones, though firm, full, and perfectly controlled lack the smooth

harmony that make the voice of Bernhardt as high above rivalry as is her genius . . ." which reads as if the two ladies were sopranos, not actresses.

The *Herald* advised: "Every artist on and off the stage ought to see her [Duse] and realize what great things may be achieved with apparently insignificant means." But the general public wanted to see great things achieved by great means, and the New York season with its expensive tickets ended in empty houses.

It was worse on tour. Duse was continually shocked at the garishness of the publicity, the distances to be traveled, at the bustle of the great cities, at the whole loud circus atmosphere. She was shocked at the reviews which condemned her plays as a collection of pornography, and took her to task for performing them. Boston was pleasant, the ticket sales lively (though the prices were criticized as too high) and public and reviewers were urbane. But Chicago—the Columbian Exposition was in progress and Duse found herself overwhelmed by that competition. She enjoyed the exposition itself, but the empty houses and the strictures of the *Tribune* about Sardou's plays sent her to bed with a searing headache.

From the beginning in New York she had postponed and canceled performances, as she usually did when she felt distressed or uncomfortable. Her distress increased as the tour went on. She could not bear all these criticisms of her work in the name of public morality, and all those attempts to invent an air of notoriety to surround her. Sarah had been through all of that and had enjoyed it. Duse, however, did not have Sarah's sense of humor, or her appreciation of the virtue of being talked about. The tour became an oppressive burden to her, and through her to the whole company.

The depressing progression of the half-empty theaters and wearisome journeys to the accompaniment of moral preachment lasted three months. At the end of April Duse sailed from New York, glad to be rid of that continent.

In May and June she performed in London. *La Dame aux Camélias* was first, as usual, on May 24, followed by *Fédora*, *Cavalleria* and the rest. She also added a contemporary English play to her repertoire, in translation: *The Second Mrs. Tanqueray* by Pinero, another play about a fallen woman. London was a balm after America. It had some of the best critics in the 1890's—William Archer and Bernard Shaw—and a far more advanced and sophisticated audience than New York.

William Archer was most enthusiastic, finding her "the most absorbingly interesting actress I ever saw." But, he, too, could not keep that other woman out of his mind. "I must admit," he wrote, "that Duse gives me far more pleasure than Sarah has given me for years past, simply because her art is delicate, noble and unobtrusive, while Sarah's art has overlaid her native talent until we are too often conscious of nothing but her tricks and processes." While Sarah had declined into "an exquisitely contrived automaton," one has with Duse "a sensation of passing out into the fresh air from an alcove redolent with patchouli."

Duse did not recross the Atlantic until 1896, but came to London again in the following year. As so often, she had been ill part of the winer and then taken some time, never quite enough, to recuperate. When she resumed her travels in 1894, she had a new manager, Joseph Schurmann, with whom she had signed an eight-year contract. He was her best manager, or at least the one who could manage her best. His ability to make money for her surmounted her habits of erratic cancellations and postponements of performances; her way of being indisposed because it rained or snowed, because a city looked dirty or a hotel room seemed poor; her occasional disappearance to a country other than the one she was to play in.

By the middle of the 1890's Duse was applauded rapturously everywhere. And there was the rub. She was not inclined to accept success as a desirable end in itself, or even as desirable. People applauded her in old and new interpretations, in performances she thought inferior, in roles she hated. The public did not

see her as she would be seen. To them she was the greatest ex-
ponent of *émotion forte*, the greater because she managed to
convey overwhelming emotion with complete naturalness and
abandon. The critic Alfred Kerr remarked on her rendering of
passion in particular: "She screams without regard for middle
class proprieties—she lies there and screams" and the sound
seemed to come from the soul and penetrate to the souls of the
spectators. To Hermann Bahr she was in those years someone
"who does not pay any attention to herself any more, who can
no longer control herself, who, cast loose from her own personality, overwhelmed by her inner drive, spews forth the forces
boiling within her, forces which frighten her to death . . ."

To her these were not stage effects; they were moments
brought on naturally by the extreme stress of the wild emotions
demanded in her roles. She was more concerned with nature
than anything else, and acted according to whatever she considered were its dictates. At times, in moments of great passion,
she disregarded the convention which prescribed that actors
should raise their voices when under great emotional stress, and
whispered. Her audience might then accuse her of lack of feeling, and be disappointed in the suffering she displayed before
them. While stars usually strove to make as spectacular an entrance as possible, Duse generally tried to slip on stage unnoticed
and to gain her prominence in a tour de force with her first
word and gesture.

Duse did not look like a prima donna, and was rarely recognized off stage. She also did not behave like a prima donna, except in self-defense. On April 9, 1895, during a performance of
Cavalleria Rusticana at the Teatro Valle in Rome, Queen Margherita requested her to visit the royal box. Duse declined re-
spectfully with thanks, "but her Majesty will understand that
it is humiliating for an actress to walk in costume through the
corridor." The queen understood and invited Duse to the
Quirinale Palace.

Her reticence about her profession went even further. She

did not tell her daughter Enrichetta that she was an actress. Enrichetta, placed in a German boarding-school, found out by
accident, and even after that Duse did not permit her to attend
her performances.

Willa Cather, one of her fervent admirers in the 1890's, characterized her attitude very well:

> The love of admiration, of homage, of publicity, the warm
> fellow feeling for others of the same profession, the genuine
> affection for the very outside of a theatre which are the almost
> inevitable accompaniments of an actress' life, seem never to have
> touched her. She has moved through the crowd of babbling
> Thespians without seeing or hearing them, she has worn the
> motley as though it were a nun's hood, she has gone from
> theatre to theatre as though she were going from shrine to
> shrine to perform some religious worship.

She was the opposite of Sarah in this. There was an inner core
of life—her family, her summer holidays—which Sarah also kept
completely and successfully private. Duse, however, in trying to
keep everything private, actually managed only to whet the
appetites of the press and public and had less peace than Sarah
did when she really wanted it.

Duse's rise to the summit of stardom can best be seen when
one compares her first tour of the United States in 1893 with
her second tour in 1896. Now there could be no doubt any more
that she was the other great international actress, and though
she was still the same Duse, very simple, very natural, very emotional, whom New York had rejected in 1893, the public now
flocked to her performances. She arrived on February 6, with
her ten trunks of dresses, to perform a repertoire from which
her most unpopular French plays had been dropped. *La Dame
aux Camélias* was still done, and *La Locandiera* and *Cavalleria*
but only one performance of *La Femme de Claude* was given.

The tour opened not in New York, but in Washington, a
clever stroke of Schurmann's. The whole atmosphere was more

dignified, and the audience was filled with Members of Congress, Government officials and even Justices of the Supreme Court. *La Dame aux Camélias* opened the season on February 17, and was honored by the presence of President and Mrs. Cleveland. The Clevelands were enormously impressed, one likes to think, though they may merely have wished to show their cultural discernment. President Cleveland came to several performances, and sent a magnificent bouquet of white chrysanthemums to Duse's dressing room. On February 21, Mrs. Cleveland gave a tea at the White House in Duse's honor. Here was publicity of a kind that even Duse liked. And, most pleasurably perhaps, here was also a place and an occasion where Sarah for once had not preceded her. The rest of the tour included New York, Boston, and Philadelphia, but not Chicago. Duse had stipulated specifically that her contract exclude that odious city with its *Tribune*. Thomas Edison invited her to Menlo Park and recorded the last sighs of Marguerite Gautier on his phonograph. Duse was so elated with her tour that she did not cancel a single performance.

Triumph elated her for a time, but she always had a reaction to it later. Now that she was praised everywhere she turned with a vengeance on her profession and her repertoire.

> Acting [she wrote]—what an ugly word! If it were merely a question of acting I feel that I could never have done it, and could never do it again. But the poor women in the plays I have acted so got into my heart and mind that I had to think out the best way of making them understood by my audience, as if I were trying to comfort them. . . . But in the end it is generally they who comfort me. How and why and when this inexplicable reciprocity of feeling between these women and myself began; that story would be far too wearisome—and difficult as well—if I were to tell it fully. But this I can say: though everybody else may distrust women I understand them perfectly. I do not bother whether they have lied, betrayed, sinned, once I feel that they have wept and suffered while lying and sinning and betraying, I stand by them, I stand for them . . .

A very interesting passage. Duse believed (there are several who have recorded her sentiments) that life is cruel and that it forces you to hurt or to be hurt yourself—a *fin de siècle* extension, or reversal, of the positive Darwinian concept of the survival of the fittest. The idea of hurting and being hurt was particularly evident in her concern for women. Unlike Bernhardt she did not like to play men's roles *à travesti*. She had no sympathy with suffragettism or female emancipation as such, but was concerned with the independence of women. She wanted everyone to realize that she was working, and she liked working women and girls. "Work," she said; "don't ask support from any man but only love; then your life will have the meaning you are looking for."

". . . Though everybody may distrust women I understand them perfectly. I do not bother whether they have lied, betrayed, sinned . . ." Does she unconsciously mean herself? Most likely. For she was always afflicted with a sense of guilt, fanned by her mother's death in her absence; by her father's death while she was far away, acting in Russia; by her relations with her husband, her daughter.

Duse, who thought deeply about art, about human motivation, who read extensively in Italian and French literature and philosophy, had, on the positive side, the intellectual and histrionic capability as Hugo von Hofmannsthal put it, to portray "the whole psycho-physiological experience" of the characters she put on the stage. It was a fortunate coincidence for her that she came to it in an age when these characters, and the views of the audience, were so closely in line with her inclinations or her needs. For the Victorian age, on stage, was the age of the fallen woman, the women "who have lied, betrayed, sinned . . ." Marguerite Gautier, Carmen, Frou-Frou, Santuzza, Mrs. Tanqueray, Mrs. Clarkson, Claude's wife, Magda, Theodora, Tosca—the list is endless. She has been all these, or thinks she has; life is cruel, one gets hurt or one must hurt others—and that is all done in these plays on a level of emotion, on a plane of feeling that

opened up a vicarious release for the inhabitants of the strug-
gling middle-class world of the later nineteenth century. Duse
portrayed these women with subtlety, with insight, and with
the complete immersion of her guilty soul in their guilty con-
sciences. "The whole tremendous show piece should not be
called Theodora in her hand, or La Tosca or Marguerite
Gautier" wrote Hofmannsthal, "but it should be called the Lady
of 1890, Our Dear Lady of the Quivering Nerves."

Now, as Hofmannsthal added, Our Lady of the Quivering
Nerves was playing the French melodramas. "She plays Sardou
and Dumas with the psychology of Ibsen. How will she play
Ibsen himself?" Hofmannsthal had the clearest view among her
contemporaries of Duse as the actress of guilt and unconscious
motivation. He also saw in her the restless search for fulfillment,
a fulfillment that did not need merely the great role, like Bernhardt, but the right work of art as environment. She did turn
to Ibsen, but transferred from the north of Europe to its south, he
was not enough. Her constant search led her to a philosophical
play by Renan, *L'Abesse de Jouarre*, which failed in Rome. The
plot is in keeping with the concerns of the time: The Abbess is
condemned to death by a tribunal in the French Revolution. She
finds that her childhood sweetheart is condemned as well, and
gives herself to him on the night before their execution. In the
morning she finds that she is pardoned, but he is not. A fallen
woman *manquée*, unredeemable: a perfect setting for Duse. Unfortunately, the play was dull.

She hated her repertoire and ascribed to it, rather than to herself, her distaste with her profession.

"*La Dame aux Camélias* fortunately has a golden thread to
which the false pearls of that play are attached: the golden
thread of passion. But the rest! the rest! . . . I feel humiliated
in the costumes of parts I am forced to play . . . I have only one
desire: to set fire to the stage, to throw all the manuscripts of
these roles into it, and all the junk of my actress' baggage."
Fédora, as Maurice Baring puts it,

is an ingeniously contrived machine for eliciting certain electrical effects from Sarah Bernhardt, and when we witness that process we are convinced that that process is a thrilling one. But in order to elicit Madame Duse's effects the machine would have to be constructed on a different plan. Fedora is just what is *not* needed for Madame Duse. She tries to make Fedora a convincingly internal and real woman, and we are not convinced. The truth is, we don't want to be convinced that Fedora is a real person and that this wild and lurid sequence of improbabilities and absurdities is a page snatched out of life.

"I have tried, I have failed, I am condemned to play Sardou and Pinero," she said despairingly in the early 1890's. She was simply too much for those plays. In a sense she triumphed over Fedora and the Princesse Georges, rather than with them. She made the plays into something they were not, and submerged the fast-moving plot devices of melodrama in the creation of full-bodied, noble, characters. But the material would not let her succeed. Just as we were beginning to believe, to see the woman Fedora, the melodrama took over again and, in spite of Duse, Fedora was resubmerged in it. Or, as Symons worded it, her Mrs. Tanqueray was "a chalice for the wine of the imagination, but the chalice remains empty."

Her audiences were enthusiastic about whatever she did, but she needed passion, not merely action on stage. When she turned to Ibsen, she found that he could fulfill only part of her desires —the desire for three-dimensional, serious, believable characters. He was not, at least to that era and to her, a poet. Between the quivering but false passions of Fedora and the real but subdued passion of Nora she found the frustration of unfulfilled promises.

In 1895–1896 she believed that she had finally found what she needed: the plays that would give her great, true characters to represent on stage, and that would be great poems, great emotional experiences at the same time. What she really found was different, though it did fulfill her inner wish: the plays she found gave her satisfaction not because they were great art but because they demanded great sacrifices of her, humiliated her, by failing grandly time after time. In that way one can explain why her career turned, and why she allowed extended, cruel suffering to be imposed on her by her new poet, Gabriele D'Annunzio.

CHAPTER 10 / Collision Course

THE eighteen-nineties are a special decade. They evoke specific pictures: the summer palaces of the very rich at Newport, girls in net stockings on the stage of the *Moulin Rouge,* large numbers of corpulent bearded men dining sumptuously, wasp-waisted women with sunshades on the promenade at Atlantic City or at Brighton or at Monte Carlo. There is a kind of nostalgia for the nineties that affects even those who grew up long after that decade; and it seems the end, not only of a century, but of an era, a whole way of life. Behind it lies the age of the great industrial development; after it we have the steady slide towards the world wars.

The nineties are the turning point of the age of competition and free enterprise. Economic competition had inevitably led to the survival of those who were really the strongest and therefore managed to monopolize their particular fields: Rockefeller in oil, for example, or Carnegie in steel. The nineties also saw the turn to the first, tentative opposition to these cartels take shape: the Sherman Anti-Trust Act was passed in 1894. Imperial competition completed the division of the world outside Europe and North America into colonies and spheres of influence. It also in turn brought on the first wars in which the European regiments were no longer easily and automatically victorious: Italy was defeated in Abyssinia in 1896, and at the turn of the century Britain had to commit her resources to the Boer War in a way which had never been needed in India, China or Egypt.

Competition is not merely a means for making money; it is also a means of establishing a hierarchical ranking. The powerful drives in the fields of economics and politics caused competition to spread to areas which had, at most, felt the competitive twinge on a local level and which now became national and international arenas of combat. The idea of world champions in sports arose towards the end of the nineteenth century, and found its culmination in 1894, when the first Olympic Games since ancient times were held. In the following year, the *Biennale* in Venice, the first great, consciously international art exhibition took place. New awards established a hierarchic ranking which imitated in sports and in art what the international expositions or world's fairs had been doing for commerce and industry.

The philosophy of life that underlay this idea of struggle for the top found its fullest expression in the country that could afford to live up to it most fully, unhampered by traditional aristocracies and other kinds of carry-overs from the past: the United States. The Gospel of Wealth according to Andrew Carnegie and his contemporaries provided not only the justification for the struggle in which the fit survived and in which wealth was an accurate measuring stick of fitness. It provided in addition a basic idea, of Calvinist-Puritan origin, that the individual had within him, innately, the means to determine and to establish his fitness; that if he only believed and worked with complete faith in his strength—but let the age speak for itself: One of the most prolific and widely read inspirational authors of the era was one Orison Swett Marden (what appropriate given names: the first recalling prayer, the second, toil!). President McKinley, that nineties statesman *par excellence*, called Marsden's book *Pushing to the Front* "an inspiration to every boy or girl that reads it, and who is possessed of honorable and high ambition." In another of his books, *Getting On*, Marden enunciates his creed: "If you are made of the stuff that wins, nobody can hold you back. A determined, gritty youth cannot be kept from success. Put stumbling blocks in his way and he takes them for stepping stones." This concept of fitness becomes somewhat more mystical in his *Miracle of Right Thought:* "Our heart longings, our soul aspirations, are something more than mere vaporings of the imagination or idle dreams. They are prophecies, predictions, couriers, forerunners of things which can become realities." Ella Wheeler Wilcox put that idea in verses, then considered poetry:

> No joy for which thy hungering soul has panted
> No hope it cherishes through the waiting years,
> But, if thou dost deserve it, shall be granted;
> For with each passionate wish the blessing nears.

The wish had to be passionate, of course, otherwise it would not work. "Your whole thought current," Marsden says in *The Divinity of Desire*, "must be in the direction of your life purpose."

Singleminded earnestness entitled its holder to signal benefits, and if these benefits did not come, he could console himself, like the rain-dancers of the Zuni Indians, that he had not been sufficiently singleminded. If he were really earnest he could rise from rags to riches through hard work and honesty, like Ragged Dick, the bootblack. (And no one would notice that Ragged Dick's progenitor, Horatio Alger, hid himself for life in a newsboy's home because the world outside was too frightening for him.)

The careers of the great actresses exemplified spectacularly the rise to the top, and their stage lives presented, over and over, the struggle and the striving for survival and success. *Tout ou rien; quand-même; à l'outrance*—the mottoes of Rachel, Bernhardt and Croizette, for example, have a tone of truculent enterprise to them that ought to have pleased Orison Swett Marden, if he did not still consider them simply women of sin. Sarah Bernhardt was always the most articulate; into the Album of the *Comédie Française* she wrote: "The intelligent being makes a virtue of egoism; the fool makes a vice of it." She also told Huret once: "I never loved the theater, in short, but once I was in it I did not want to vegetate in it; I intended to be among the first."

The theater reflected the atmosphere of the time: a spectator sport, not merely an artistic enterprise, a game with few rules fought by highly trained athletes. Going to the theater in the 1890's was still like the experience of Charlotte Brontë in Brussels when she was confronted with Rachel for the first time. Pulses beat feverishly even before the curtain rose. A sensation of peril could be felt obscurely as if one were to face a panther leaping into the cage at the other side of the bars. The acting was a passionate, cajoling, demanding, constant competition of the kind which turned the auditorium into an arena. "London is becoming the Belgium of the theatrical world—its recognized duelling ground," William Archer wrote in 1896. "The leading actresses of Europe have contracted the agreeable habit of popping across the Channel every summer to exchange a few shots, and we lucky dogs of critics have the privilege of sitting by and seeing fair."

The international actresses were the lionesses of that circus. Because they were quite different from each other and because they had much the same repertoire, they were compared, constantly, relentlessly. Shaw noted in the summer of 1895 that London had just had four Fedoras to compare, and Duse and Sarah Bernhardt "playing *La Dame aux Camélias* and Sudermann's *Heimat* against each other at Daly's Theatre and at Drury Lane."

The comparisons were not only between present performances. The memory of the great actresses of the preceding generation was often invoked for purposes of evaluation. Matthew Arnold's comparison of Rachel and Bernhardt is perhaps the most succinct: "Temperament and quick intelligence, passion, nervous nobility, grace, smile, voice, charm, poetry—Mlle. Sarah Bernhardt has them all. One watches her with pleasure, with admiration, and yet not without a secret disquietude. Something is wanting, or, at least not present in sufficient force. . . . That something is high intellectual power. It was here that Rachel was so great. She began, one says to oneself, as one recalls her image, and dwells upon it—she began almost when Mlle. Sarah Bernhardt ends." At times of course such a comparison between the generations is merely an exercise in nostalgia, as when Wil-

liam Winter holds up the memory of Ristori to attack Bernhardt, or praises Charlotte Cushman for her "strong, definite,
bold and free" style, chiding Sarah Bernhardt for her long pauses
and fixed stares, and Duse for turning her back to the audience
and whispering to the scenery. Ristori herself, the only one of
the four international actresses who saw all the others, quite ex-
pectedly did not like the second generation. She deprecated
Bernhardt and her kind as "modern tendencies, based on neurosis
and verily *à tout prix*," though she finds that Sarah "has great
talent and great artistic perspicacity." "Duse has talent," she says
in the same letter of October 1, 1893, "and is unique after Bernhardt in *fin de siècle* methods. She is more human, however. Her
facial nobility and absence of artificiality are gifts, yet art like
hers will die."

Bernhardt was extensively compared with only one contemporary other than Duse: Réjane. J. T. Grein, writing on Réjane as
Sappho, calls her the greatest actress of the time and puts Bernhardt below her because she does not have the ability to confront an audience with the unexpected. More often, however,
they are not considered comparable. One, Réjane, is naturalistic,
often vulgar; the other, Bernhardt, is graceful and lyrical. Duse
was generally considered more like Réjane than like Bernhardt.
Sarah herself, in her autobiography, compared Duse to Réjane,
with a purpose; she spoke of "the very great actress Réjane, the
rival of Duse, another great artist to whom she was much superior," thereby firmly assigning them both their proper places
below Sarah Bernhardt, who of course had no rival.

There were naturally as many different comparative evaluations as there were critics. On June 15, 1895, *The Saturday
Review* of London printed the most extended and interesting
comparison of the two, by its regular critic, Bernard Shaw. "The
week began," he writes, "with the relapse of Sarah Bernhardt
into her old profession of serious actress." From the first that
establishes his comparative point of view. The contrast between
Duse and Bernhardt, he continues, "is as extreme as any contrast
could possibly be between artists who have finished their twenty

years' apprenticeship to the same profession under closely similar conditions." Then follows a dazzling description of Sarah's dazzling appearance on stage, as contrasted to Duse's naturalness, without make-up, completely credible. "The truth is that in the art of being beautiful, Madame Bernhardt is a child beside her."

One of Shaw's complaints is that Bernhardt, in contrast to Duse, is always herself, not the character she portrays. Desmond McCarthy, in comparing them, reached the opposite conclusion; in his view Sarah always managed to be her part as well as herself, while Duse's personality sometimes got in the way of her role. Hofmannsthal was on Shaw's side, Ristori was on Mc-Carthy's, Max Beerbohm thought that both were unnatural, and several other critics simply said that they wanted Sarah (or Duse) to be herself no matter what the role was to be.

The newspapers often took permanent sides. In 1896, for example, when both performed in New York, the *Times* and the *Tribune* were for Sarah, while the *Sun* and the *Mirror* supported Duse for the crown. In her memoirs Ellen Terry, a friend of both actresses, hardly ever mentions the one without a reference to the other, so deeply engrained was their competitive relationship in her mind. Willa Cather, in writing of Duse, also could not keep Bernhardt out of her pages. Her comparison—"[Duse's] acting has been done in marble just as Bernhardt's has been done in color" may be too pat but does inadvertently make the rather valid point that Duse was artistically Rachel's successor while Bernhardt can quite fairly be assigned to Ristori.

Not only the critics, but the audiences became involved in the competition, took sides and tried vicariously to become part of the great struggle on stage. In this emotional atmosphere the individual could dream of being lifted out of the crowd—not so much to love the great star but to defeat his peers in competition, to reach the top of virility and masculine dominance by conquering the woman after whom thousands panted night after night. In 1892, Arthur Symons, then a youth in his twenties, wrote a poem that expressed the whole explosive situation. It was called "To a Great Actress" and addressed Sarah Bernhardt:

She has taken my heart, though she knows not,
    would care not
It thrills at her voice like a reed in the wind;
I would taste all her agonies, have her to spare not,
Sin deep as she sinned.

To be tossed by the storm of her love, as the ocean
Rocks vessels to wreck—to be hers, though the cost
Were the loss of all else; for that moment's emotion
Content to be lost!

To be, for a moment, the man of all men to her,
All the world, for one measureless moment complete;
To possess, be possessed! To be mockery then to her,
Then to die at her feet.

The greatest story of competition is, like most great stories about actors, apocryphal: Marie Colombier, then still a friend of Bernhardt's, gave a great party in London or Paris (the versions conflict), for actresses only. All who mattered had come: Old Fanny Kemble, Helen Faucit, Ristori, Janauschek, Modjeska, Bernhardt, Ellen Terry.

Marie Colombier proposed as the climax of the evening that the ones who were most illustrious in the public eye each perform a scene from *La Dame aux Camélias*—naked. Ristori, Janauschek and Terry were the judges, and all the others performed. The prize went to Helena Modjeska.

Such were the amusements of the Victorian mind.

Duse performed in London for the first time in May and June of 1893. It was one of the few years when Sarah Bernhardt missed the high season in the British capital, but her two and a half year world tour was taking her through Latin America at that time. In 1894 she was back, however, and the first glancing blows were struck. Schurmann's new policy for Duse was to schedule her to play in the major centers at the most favorable times irrespective of competition. That meant London in the late spring, which in turn meant Sarah Bernhardt. "No matter where you go," he said, "you run into Sarah." From now on Duse would not avoid her. The series of encounters which had its climax in Paris in 1897, really began in London in 1894.

London welcomed Duse in 1894 as it had in 1893; she seemed as impressive, though the novelty had worn off. "We feel an intimate, restful assurance of her perfect art, even while we are thrilling to her inimitable, irresistible touches of nature," wrote Archer. On May 18 she was invited to perform before the Queen at Windsor Castle and amused her with *La Locandiera*, almost the only play in her repertoire that was unlikely to offend the old lady. She gave twenty-three performances between May 7 and June 14, and Archer noted that Bernhardt generally gave the same number of performances in half the time. Duse's ability to resist her illnesses and her impulses was not great.

Bernhardt's performances were getting under way when Duse ended hers. Archer tells that on June 14, "Duse is reported to have surpassed herself in her final performance of Marguerite Gautier and to have swept the audience into a whirlwind of emotion and enthusiasm. She may have been stimulated by the presence of Sarah Bernhardt, who then saw her for the first time." Unfortunately nobody reported Bernhardt's reaction.

After their engagements had taken them to distant parts again for nearly eleven months, the two combatants met once more in the same season and in the same place in 1895. One of Sarah's new plays for London in 1895 was *Magda*, a translation of Hermann Sudermann's *Heimat* (1893), which she had first performed in February, and which Duse had also recently added to her repertoire.

The London critics in 1895, Shaw, Agate, and Archer among them, had a chance to see the two interpretations side by side, with yet another one, in the original German, added to this mêlée of competitive enterprise. The English audience could therefore see *Heimat* in German, French and Italian that season, but not in English. The French production was well presented, and the Italian was a miserable show, redeemed only by Duse.

Sarah Bernhardt was at Daly's, where she performed *Magda* on June 10 and on four later occasions. Duse acted it at the Drury Lane on June 12, and at the Savoy on June 27 as well as four times in July.

"It is no figure of speech," Archer wrote, "but literal truth, when I say that she has wiped the very remembrance of Sarah Bernhardt out of my mind. Yet I enjoyed to see Sarah in a human character instead of a mere Parisian confection, and thought her very good in her way." Shaw and Agate also thought Duse incomparably superior to Bernhardt, and Shaw's "intense professional curiosity" was aroused by Duse's blush—could she really blush to order?

To the author, Sudermann, who considered her the best interpreter of his play, Duse had written a few months earlier: "Your Magda has worked for ten years. She who writes has worked for twenty years. Magda spent sixteen years at home. She who writes never had a home." With her attitude toward work and toward acting it was natural that she could make Magda her own, while Bernhardt was never too happy in the role.

Magda was an interesting case rather than an interesting play. It was the story of a girl who had left home after having been seduced and made pregnant. She entered a theatrical career, and when, on a whim, she returned to her home town and her father's house, she was much like the international actresses who portrayed her. The play takes place on that return visit. There are many stormy emotional scenes and violent encounters, in the usual Dumas-Sardou manner, in which the father attempts to force the daughter to marry her erstwhile seducer, to set things right. She even goes so far as to meet the man, but when she sees through him and his vile petty character, she throws him out. In essence the play confronts small-town conventional morality with some large moral issues concerning good and evil, and for once conventional morality does not win in the end with the obligatory repentance and death of the heroine.

Bernhardt was at her best portraying the fantastic, exuberant side of the actress. But her Magda was so much Sarah that her presence in that small-town setting became completely implausible, and the idea on the part of her father and some others that she might settle down to a righteous provincial existence seemed ludicrous.

Duse's Magda was more humble, more natural in a way that made the return to the town into a trip home, not the result of a momentary whim. Though she lacked Sarah's flamboyance as the actress, she made the plot of the play seem more plausible.

In *La Femme de Claude* Sarah was clearly Duse's superior, but the play was becoming dated. *La Dame aux Camélias* was still the touchstone, and here the two performances, excitingly different, found ready partisans on both sides. Sarah's strength lay in her ability to present a Parisian cocotte, something Duse was basically not able to do. By displaying Marguerite's original state, Sarah made memorable the transition from pleasure-seeking courtesan to loving mistress to lonely dying invalid. Duse's Lady of the Camellias, as the German critic Harden put it "certainly never went out to supper with lecherous counts or giggled with common hussies, [and] remained just the same in the villa as in the *cabaret de luxe*." Her strength lay in underacting the role.

> In La Dame aux Camélias [Shaw wrote], it is easy for an intense actress to harrow us with her sorrows and paroxysms of phthisis, leaving us with a liberal pennyworth of sensation, not fundamentally distinguishable from that offered by a public execution, or any other evil in which we still take a hideous delight. As different from this as light from darkness is the method of the actress who shows us how human sorrow can express itself only in its appeal for the sympathy it needs. . . . That is the charm of Duse's interpretation of the stage poem of Marguerite Gautier. It is unspeakably touching because it is exquisitely considerate: that is, exquisitely sympathetic. No physical charm is noble as well as beautiful unless it is the expression of a moral charm; and it is because Duse's range includes these moral high notes, if I may so express myself, that

her compass, extending from the depths of a mere predatory creature like Claude's wife up to Marguerite Gautier at her kindest or Magda at her bravest, so immeasurably dwarfs the poor little octave and a half on which Sarah Bernhardt plays such pretty canzonets and marches.

For both actresses, as for all the others who played the role at the time, the individuality, naturalness and appropriations of the byplay, the "business," made or broke the performance. Sarah's byplay, startlingly inventive and natural, was yet more manifest, more theatrical than Duse's. So, for example, in Act I, when Marguerite dances, the weakness caused by the early stages of tuberculosis makes itself felt. Most actresses demonstrated that debility with a violent gesture, hand to the heart or throat, the body shaken with spasms. Sarah managed it with a few, small gestures; Duse merely stops and looks nervous. (She is right here, but one should remember that there was likely not one person in the audience any more in the 1890's who did not know that Marguerite was tubercular. The merest reminder therefore sufficed.)

Sarah also had an excellent scene in Act I, one of sheer business. After her encounter with Armand, at the party, she goes to the table, opens a casket, takes out a mirror and a powder-puff, shakes the puff, and powders herself. In her gestures, in her humming a song, are mirrored her life and her disbelief in the fervent declaration of love she had just received.

Duse also had an uncanny ability to make objects act for her and with her. The critic Hermann Bang describes how

a rose, a handkerchief, a chain came to life under her hands, and while she herself remains silent and almost motionless, these inanimate things act for her . . . One remembers, for instance, the flower she held in the scene with Armand's father. At first, while Marguerite's happiness seems secure, the flower stands proudly on its stalk, its petals stretched toward the light; but when doubt enters her mind, then fear, and finally, when her last hope vanishes, the flower begins to droop; as though touched by frost the petals shrivel, the stem grows limp, and the flower withers; by an imperceptible movement of her hands, Duse caused the flower to die of Marguerite's grief. It was an extraordinary effect—impossible to describe in words.

Or the opening of the final act, when Marguerite, on her deathbed, rereads the letter she received from Armand's father announcing his forgiveness and his promise to send Armand to her. Sarah read it aloud, softly, in that penetrating murmur of hers that could miraculously be heard in the last row of the gallery, then stops, and continues to recite the letter by heart. At the end she put it back in its envelope, ties a little ribbon around it, and puts it by her side, tears streaming down her face. Duse, who could not cry at will, made the scene less harrowing, without ribbon and recitation, but as moving in its simplicity.

The intense competition and the detailed comparisons could no longer obscure the fact that the Dumas-Sardou repertoire was wearing thin and that Sudermann was no more than a slightly updated Dumas. Bernhardt and Duse were looking for a new kind of play that would both be modern and suitable for their talents. The Free Theater movement, the most important theatrical development of the nineties, did not draw their attention. Antoine had founded the *Théâtre Libre* in 1887, and in 1890 introduced Ibsen to the French audience, following it with Hauptmann, Tolstoi, Verga, Bjornson, Becque, Porto-Riche and others. Brahm in Berlin, Grein in London and finally Nemirowitch-Danchenko and Stanislavski in Moscow founded companies to perform the new drama of Ibsen and his contemporaries. Duse managed to adapt some of the new drama to her purposes, and performed some Ibsen, at times in slightly bowdlerized versions, especially *A Doll's House* and *Lady from the Sea*. Bernhardt disliked the whole new movement and correctly found it unsuited to her talents.

Sarah was past fifty when Arthur Symons, that overcharged romantic, saw her in London at the Grattan Gallery in 1895:

Her fingers were covered with rings, her long and slender fingers; the nails were dyed with red henna—which I saw after-

wards in the East. . . . She seemed to me a vision, a heathen idol
one ought to worship—she had the evil eyes of a Thessalian
witch; she could enchant with her slow, subtle and cruel spell
men's souls out of their bodies. There was in this tall and thin
actress such fire and passion as I have rarely seen in any woman;
together with her luxuriousness, languor, indifference, haughti-
ness and hate. She seemed to me the Incarnation of the Orient.

A Thessalian witch could not play Ibsen or Hauptmann. In
1895, finally, it seemed as if the poet for Sarah had arrived. On
April 5 the Renaissance gave *La Princesse Lointaine* by Edmond
Rostand, with Sarah, Edouard de Max, and Jean Coquelin.
Rostand, only twenty-seven years old, had risen to prominence
the year before when the Comédie Française gave his play *Les
Romanesques*. William Archer, who saw Sarah perform *La
Princesse Lointaine* in London that summer, wrote: "Madame
Bernhardt chanted, or rather crooned, the part of Melissinde to
perfection. She was, in fact, playing her own character, for what
is she but the Princess in a fairy tale? An ordinary human being
she no longer is or can be, but just such a creature of exquisite
artifice as this Lady of Tripoli, clothed in jewels and exhaling
rhymes."

Duse redoubled the search for her poet when she became
aware of Sarah's success with Rostand's play. In 1895 she
thought she had found him in the new national poet of Italy,
Gabriele D'Annunzio.

D'Annunzio and Duse had met early in their careers. Duse
told Romain Rolland much later that she had met him when he
first came to Rome. He scared and outraged her by immediately
proposing to make love to her. She was then in her early twenties, a rising star, and he was still in his teens, which would put
it at about 1882. In 1886, she is supposed to have passed by him
backstage at the Teatro Valle in Rome when he apostrophized
her "O grande Amatrice." She was a great star by then and did
not acknowledge his calculated tribute. No records exist of
further meetings for some years. In April of 1894, Duse asked
Boito to send her a copy of D'Annunzio's novel *Triunfo della*

Morte which was having a considerable success in France at that time, more so than in Italy. In the early fall—his notebooks record the event for September 26—they met again, in Venice, just before the opening of the first *Biennale* exhibition. Whether they met in the early morning hours—she being up early after sleeping little, he returning late from his usual amorous pursuits—we do not know. One legend has it that they took a gondola together and traveled long through the city in the rising day. Another version says that Duse had spent the night alone in a gondola thinking about D'Annunzio, whom she had just seen, and that, when she landed in the morning, there he was. It is certain that they could not have had more than a week to renew acquaintance on that occasion because their engagements took them elsewhere by the first days of October.

The meeting was useful to both. Duse was searching not merely for new plays, but for the expression of enduring values, for something to which she could give, not her ability only, but her self. D'Annunzio, as he saw himself, was a genius who had slowed down. Though he preferred tall, statuesque women, there was some ardor about Duse, and a great talent that attracted him. The fact that she was older than he, by five years, may have been inducement rather than hindrance; the Princess Maria Gravina, his most recent main mistress, was older than he. Further, he had tried his hand at a few plays, but had not succeeded in breaking into the theater. Like Arthur Symons he also knew clearly the kind of appeal the great actresses presented in his time: ". . . the more the thing a man possessses awakens envy and cupidity in other men, the more that man enjoys it—herein lies the fascination of the ladies of the stage." For D'Annunzio love and art were one: the control of both objects—the woman and the work of art—had to go hand in hand. With Duse as his love he would be inspired. He would write the great Italian poetic plays, and she would perform them.

D'Annunzio is one of the few writers who make it really difficult to resist the temptation to substitute moral for artistic judgments. It is fortunate, therefore, that time has greatly dimmed his luster as a poet. His own age already recognized his lack of talent as a dramatist.

D'Annunzio leapt into prominence very young, with his imaginative poetry and, later, his novels. They fitted perfectly the inclinations of his time. Highly florid and sadistic, they are full of the most unnatural passions of the senses, and of the most amazing language to depict them, marvelously inventive and at the same time *schwülstig*—one must use that German word, for the German writers, especially of that time, knew how to write that way, with a kind of sensual, exotic, syrupy effusiveness—a word that, like the style it depicts, is untranslatable into English, for even Swinburne does not come close to its peculiar density. D'Annunzio looked back longingly to ancient Rome, but with a narrow Italian nationalism of imperialistic greed rather than any view whatever of Rome's meaning for civilization. In his novel *Le Vergini delle Rocce*, he created a Mediterranean superman, Claudio Cantelmo, the first of a series of supernaturally powered, attractive, talented men formed in the image of Gabriele D'Annunzio. The perfervid materials for his novels he derived from his love affairs, exploiting his women both for sex and for art. His mistress, Elvira Leoni, for example, had the crushing experience one day of coming upon some of the notebooks in which he collected ideas and passages for his work, and finding in them a dispassionate, clinical record of their most intimate relations and effusions. His motto was "Gloria, Amore, Voluttà" (glory, love, voluptuousness)—and he was fulfilling all three, but to his age he seemed much more than simply an Eau-de-Coty-scented sadist. Romain Rolland, who called him "a beast of prey," was yet charmed and entertained by him, and even found him a devoted friend—to men. Isadora Duncan, who should be able to judge, described later the effect D'Annunzio had on women—through his attention, his caramel-smooth voice, his fervor and charm. The American painter Romaine Brooks, a short-term love because she was too American to stay on when she saw his mode of operation, left a portrait of him done after the event, during the First World War. It shows something of what he must have seemed like to a woman—in contrast to his photographs which show an undersized man, short-legged, prematurely bald, with bulging eyes.

The years from 1895 to 1897 were very busy ones for Duse, and she was absent from Italy much more than she wanted to be. D'Annunzio harbored some resentment because she was not there sufficiently to inspire his muse. Moreover, her friend Giulietta Gordigiani had declined to proceed further with him than love of the soul, and that was not enough. His notebooks for a new novel, *Il Fuoco*, were growing too slowly for his taste; his other set of notebooks, the ones on his intimacies with Duse, were growing at an even slower rate. Finally, in 1897, he interrupted his work on the novel, and in six weeks wrote *La Città Morta*, a play based on a voyage he had made to Greece eighteen months earlier. As soon as he had finished he sent it off—to Sarah Bernhardt.

Sarah cannot have read it carefully, for she cabled almost at once to the poet "Admirable! Admirable! Admirable!," accepting it for performance. Her joy at obtaining *La Città Morta* was hardly artistic: Not only was D'Annunzio Duse's poet, but Duse was soon to be Sarah's honored guest at the Théâtre de la Renaissance in Paris. Duse was struck a double blow: she not only lost D'Annunzio's play which she had expected to take to Paris as her one new offering of the season; she lost that play to her gracious hostess-to-be.

After the London season in 1895, the two actresses parted again for their rounds of performances at home and abroad. In January 1896, Duse embarked on her second, highly successful tour of the United States. After a week in Washington, she opened her New York engagement on February 23 at the Fifth Avenue Theatre. Sarah Bernhardt, who had opened in New York on January 20, closed her first series of performances on February 24. The third skirmish was therefore of brief duration. The duel, by now something of an annual attraction of the London season, began again late that spring, but early in the following year it reached a new dimension when it was announced that Duse would perform in Paris. The French press, and several of Sarah's biographers, assert that Bernhardt "invited" and "persuaded" Duse to come and that she happily placed her theater at the visitor's disposal, rent-free. Schurmann, Duse's manager, categorically denies this. "Sarah . . . never asked her to come to Paris," he writes. "It was only after my star had indicated her willingness that I rented the Renaissance which Sarah Bernhardt let me have on exorbitant terms."

Sarah knew that Schurmann was determined to bring Duse, and that Duse now at last was willing. Schurmann was taking the Lamb into the Lion's Den, and so the Chief Lioness herself offered him her theater, mainly, of course, to prevent Duse from going to another manager who might, God forbid, be less kindly disposed toward the honored guest. Sarah wanted to make certain from the beginning that Rachel's mistakes with respect to Ristori were not to be repeated. Duse's appearances were to be welcomed and monitored and, if necessary, hampered. According to some of Duse's biographers, she, on the other hand, floated angelically on clouds of art above all these tactical considerations, admiring Bernhardt, blissfully unaware of all her devilish machinations. Neither Schurmann nor Lugné-Poe, her manager in later years, would have any truck with such a soft-minded view of Duse. Lugné-Poe in his book on the actress refers to the whole series of events of June, 1897, naturally and consistently, as a "campaign." Duse did not exactly come from a background in which the mixture of high artistry and high intrigue were unknown. She admired Bernhardt in many ways; she may not have anticipated all the stratagems that were to be employed against her. But she also knew that she was not yet forty while Sarah was well past fifty.

In the view of both Duse and Bernhardt New York and London had been alien territory, inveterately and indiscriminately kind to foreign actors. Now she would challenge Bernhardt in her own home, the cultural capital of the world, for the decisive duel.

Duse had hesitated for a long time before taking this step, and

Schurmann had to work hard to persuade her to go. Dumas *fils* had urged her to come several years before, just as his father had aided Ristori's first season in Paris more than forty years earlier. He had assumed that she would perfect her French and perform his plays in Paris in that language. Her decision not to do so, like Ristori's decision, was a sound one, the only one she could have made. She had hesitated particularly because her repertoire, unlike Ristori's, consisted largely of French plays. It was impossible to predict whether that would be an asset or not, whether it would help her because the plays were familiar to the audience, or hinder her because audiences would find it presumptuous of an actress to expect them to listen to Dumas in Italian.

Failure in Paris would be much more dangerous than failure in London, for the world still took its artistic measure from Paris, the city of the international actress par excellence. Duse was too famous not to be considered a challenger, and to be evaluated as that. Without the precedent of Ristori it would have been less risky.

Initially Duse may have believed in Sarah's invitation, but in view of later events it is hardly likely that she retained that belief, though she assured Huret, one of Sarah's biographers, of that fact. She was less disingenuous than that. She really came, "desiring the consecration of the capital of France, as Ristori had."

Duse's choice of repertoire was in itself a challenge. She could have concentrated on plays not in Sarah's repertoire: the Italian plays, Ibsen, and such works as Sardou's *Divorçons* or Dumas' *Denise*. Instead she chose to perform several roles done by Sarah, most notably *La Dame aux Camélias*, *La Femme de Claude*, and *Magda*, in addition to *Cavalleria Rusticana* and *La Locandiera*. One must add that the plays Duse and Sarah had in common were among their most successful plays, and if Duse had wanted to avoid direct comparsion, she would have deprived herself of some of the most effective portions of her repertoire.

There was not one new play in Duse's repertoire. She needed

a new work, and needed it desperately. D'Annunzio was of course her choice to write it, partly because of the well-publicized setback she had suffered with *La Città Morta*, partly because she really believed in his talent. Count Primoli, a friend of both and a man of culture in Rome, engineered a reconciliation.

The time was late, only a few weeks remained. D'Annunzio wanted her to go, Schurmann had completed the negotiations, but Duse refused unless she got a play by D'Annunzio to take with her. He said no at first, but then he promised to try, in one week of seclusion and feverish labor. Ten days after the reconciliation in his house, Count Primoli called on her at the Hotel Bristol in Rome. "She was just coming down the stairs to go out. When she saw me she waved a manuscript in a superb binding of ancient embroidery with bands of green moiré. 'I've got it,' she cried triumphantly. 'What?' 'Gabriele D'Annunzio's manuscript!'" He had written a one-act for her, *Sogno di un Mattino di Primavera* [Dream of a Spring Morning], and she was going to take her company into the country to rehearse it in a properly rustic setting.

Duse now had her play, and her theater, but Sarah had scored in the first round. She had come forward as the champion of the distinguished visitor, had offered her her own theater and her magnanimous support, and the Paris press lauded her for it extensively. Duse therefore arrived in Paris as Bernhardt's protégée, not her challenger.

Before her departure from Italy Duse had written to Count Robert de Montesquiou-Fésenzac, a mutual acquaintance, and asked him to effect an introduction of the host and the guest. Montesquiou, very aristocratic, very rich, very aesthetic and literary, was, it seems, amused and intrigued by the idea, though it turned into something of an ordeal for him.

Sarah was in Brussels when Duse arrived in Paris. Montesquiou managed to arrange a visit to Sarah's studio on the morning of her return from Belgium. The two guests somehow arrived before Sarah's return—maybe by accident, maybe by Sarah's design—and had to wait. Then Sarah came. "I was present therefore," Montesquiou reports, "at the initial impact ["*choc*" is the word he uses] of these two women who embraced each other so violently that the event seems to me to be a flattening collision rather than a token of affection." Pronier, Sarah's biographer, sententiously paraphrased a famous line from Racine for the occasion:

> J'embrasse ma rivale, mais c'est pour l'étouffer! [I embrace my rival, but only to strangle her.]

That evening Sarah was to perform in *La Samaritaine*. The center box at the Renaissance had been reserved for Duse and decorated with orchids. Duse came and, through the entire performance, she remained standing, supposedly as a sign of admiration for the great Sarah. Sarah is likely to have construed it differently for Duse to remain thus in full view of an otherwise seated audience. Seated, all except one—the innocent sufferer of the evening was Montesquiou, who escorted Duse to the theater and therefore also felt obliged to stand through the entire performance.

The evening was hot, the audience small and lethargic. Sarah's first question upon her return that day had been about Duse's box office; she had been told that almost all the seats for her entire stay were sold, and that scalpers were getting as much as 500 francs for a seat for the first night. That round went therefore to Duse, and Sarah, possibly with petulance rather than calculation, closed up her magnificent dressing room suite, assigning Duse a simple room far from the stage.

The next round, however, was definitely Sarah's. Duse had intended to open with *Magda*, a play that both performed, but in which her success had been greater than Sarah's. Sarah told her in her most sisterly manner that a German play performed in Italian was surely not an auspicious beginning, and that the French would feel much more complimented if Duse performed a French play. The choice fell on *La Dame aux Camélias*, perhaps the right choice under similar circumstances in New York or in London. In Paris, however, it was Sarah's property, nobody else would perform it there in direct competition with her, and the public, with some admixture of patriotism, considered that choice an affront to the gracious hostess.

On June 1, then, it was *La Dame aux Camélias*. The house was occupied to the last seat. Réjane and Bartet were there, after Sarah the two most important French actresses; and Prince and Princesses, Dukes and Duchesses, writers, composers, men of the theater, and of course the critics. Eugenie Doche was there, Dumas' first Marguerite Gautier in 1852, a very old lady now, invited, cleverly, to give the feeling of a festive commemorative occasion to the proceedings, and evidently quite content to see someone other than Sarah perform her old role.

In the center box was Sarah, "crowned with roses like Iphigenia led to her sacrifice," according to Montesquiou. She sat down, at any rate, and followed the performance with rapturous interest, taking care to make her rapture audible at pianissimo passages, and to applaud at the most inappropriate moments possible.

Duse came on stage very well and carefully groomed and costumed for once, but very pale and nervous. There is a little applause, it swells gradually, dies away. Her movements are tentative, her performance is below par—not at all like the performance of Bernhardt in her box at intermission, when she with her penetrating golden voice, and vivid pantomime, showered praise on her guest for the benefit of the throngs of visitors come to see her. In view of Duse's first act this was obviously a deed of endearing magnanimity, nothing else. The second act was not much different, the third act worse; at its end only the Italian contingent applauded, and even the great scene with Armand's father seemed tedious. Duse's Marguerite was a sad and sympathetic woman, not at all the great, gay lady of the *demi-monde* whom Parisians knew.

In the fourth act Flavio Andò's impassioned acting in Armand's denunciation of Marguerite earned him a considerable burst of applause that left Duse even more in the shadow. (Andò, who had not acted with Duse in some time, had been engaged especially for the performances in Paris. After this performance in *La Dame aux Camélias* he was replaced by Rosaspina and sent home.) In the final act, Duse, exhausted, gave a beautiful performance of the exhausted Marguerite, and was applauded. But it was too late. Sarah had been right, and the challenger had gone down in defeat. Sarah was too experienced a critic, however, not to have seen the writing on the wall even in this performance. "She seemed nervous to me," said Montesquiou, "at the end of the performance, and a quick parody of the slightly jerky style of the famous Eleonora, which she risked to show to a few of us, was not a good omen."

The reviews were cool, affable, correct, even cordial. Duse's gestures and manner were minutely described and criticized. There were no extensive comparisons to Bernhardt, or to Réjane and Bartet. They were not necessary; any idea that Duse could be measured against them seemed superfluous.

Sarcey, his claws almost completely drawn in, gave a detailed description of the illogicalities of Duse's interpretation. He found her surprisingly plain, but was, even on that wretched evening, impressed by the way her face could transform and animate itself. (Quite possibly he had not been more perceptive than the other critics; he had simply seen her before, in Vienna, in better days, and was using his knowledge, expecting greater things of her later.) Her Marguerite Gautier he found completely misconceived. Mme. Doche's had been the heedless, impertinent, spendthrift courtesan of Dumas' original conception; Sarah Bernhardt's was also a courtesan but a more versatile one, capable of tenderness and kindness. Duse's suggests a good little person, a courtesan—if one—of an entirely different order—sweet, a grisette rather than a cocotte, who could not possibly be cruel and who could only be conceived of ruining her lovers by making them buy her macaroni.

Jules Huret, on the other hand, was impressed with her acting, for "she managed to make it convey the epitome of human distress." Jules Lemaître found her grief and despair much too reserved. Emile Faguet said that she was an actress of melodrama "above the first rank" and warned her in all earnestness not to attempt tragedy, by which he meant French tragedy, a thing Duse had no intention of doing. Félix Duquesnel summed up the initial reaction several years later: "The first impression was complex, strange I might almost say. . . . One looked in vain for the traditional ideal. . . . One had to grow accustomed to it."

June 1 was a Saturday. For the following week Duse had announced *Magda*, *La Femme de Claude*, and *Cavalleria Rusticana*. She managed to do *Magda* before she fell ill and had to retire from the scene for more than a week.

Magda was not a play to appeal to a French audience, but Duse managed to make a much better impression than before. This time Sarcey did enter into a detailed comparison of Duse and Bernhardt and their basic conceptions of the role, finding that Duse's, though much less spectacular and impressive, was more valid and in the end therefore more convincing.

Somehow the visitor had not been put down after all; in fact, she had gone on to success in her second performance; now she was ill, which caused much sympathy to be extended to her. Rumors were flying moreover, in the usual manner of Paris. One said that Sarah, on the pretext of complimenting her, had kept Duse standing in a draughty corridor backstage for one whole intermission of *Magda*, and had therefore been the cause of her illness. Even more remarkably it was rumored that the piece of stage property "that had fallen dangerously near Duse had not done so wholly by accident." Sarah had reason to be worried, more maybe about her enemies than about Duse.

She had an opportunity at hand to put her enemies to rest once and for all. Dumas had died some eighteen months before, and a committee had been organized to solicit subscriptions for the erection of a monument to him. Now Bernhardt offered her aid: She would give a gala benefit, putting her theater at the disposal of the committee free of charge. She would ask Duse to participate, and they would do *La Dame aux Camélias*. Duse would do Acts II and III, and Sarah Acts IV and V.

Here Sarah made her first tactical mistake: She overplayed

her hand. To reserve for herself the two most impressive acts, including the death scene, and to give Duse Act III, in which she had failed most signally, made the connoisseurs smile at Sarah rather than Duse. In any case Duse refused, though she could not decline to participate. She offered instead to do an act from *La Femme de Claude*, and that had to be accepted.

The Dumas gala of Friday, June 14, realized the sum of thirty-six thousand francs, unheard of in the French theater until that time. It was an evening of Wagnerian proportions, the greatest theatrical event of many seasons. It opened with a one-act play, *L'Aveu*, by—Bernhardt, not Dumas, a piece of modesty into which the very reluctant Bernhardt had been forced by Sardou. Then came two operatic pieces sung by famous stars: A duet from *Il Trovatore* sung by Tamagno and Héglon, and an aria from *Lucia di Lammermoor* sung by Emma Nevada. Fourth on the program was Yvette Guilbert, the greatest *chanteuse* of the time, in a monologue. Then, finally, Duse in Act II of *La Femme de Claude* and then, finally, finally, Sarah in Acts IV and V of *La Dame aux Camélias*. That was by no means all. After an intermission Coquelin *aîné* recited a poem by Rostand, Nevada sang an aria from *La Traviata*, Tamagno gave a song, Héglon sang something from *Samson et Dalila* and then came the *pièce de résistance: Hommage à Alexandre Dumas*.

No matter how she tried, Duse could not overcome Sarah that night. For her act of *La Femme de Claude* she is recalled four times, and cheered. During the intermission Victorien Sardou, president of the monument committee, goes to her dressing room with a deputation of members, to congratulate and thank her. Duse is moved to tears, stammers and holds out her hands to Sardou.

"But," as *Le Gaulois* said, "after enthusiasm comes ecstasy."

Bernhardt renders her incomparable death scene incomparably, splendidly supported by Lucien Guitry. She is also recalled four times, but the audience calls for more. Sardou, with the committee, visits her, too, to thank her. And when they meet, they fall into each other's arms. At that moment, *Le*

Gaulois reports, Duse appeared as well and threw herself into Sarah's arms, "with all her force."

The *coup de grâce* came in the final scene, the homage to Dumas. The curtain rose, to disclose Carpeaux' bust of Dumas in the center of the stage. Grouped about it, upstage well towards the back, were the artists who had given their services that evening—all except one. She was in front, face to face with the statue, and then turns to recite a new poem.

Rostand had become party to the enterprise and written "L'Hommage de Marguerite Gautier à la Alexandre Dumas." Sarah now recited it, clearly the one and only incarnation of Marguerite Gautier this side of heaven.

> She recites these exquisite verses with a charm of tenderness, an intensity of feeling, that arouse new transports of enthusiasm. The whole audience is on its feet, quivering, with arms outstretched toward the prodigious artist, who makes an effort to bow, but is overcome by the force of her emotion. The curtain rises and falls an incalculable number of times, disclosing the great tragedienne in her gracious attitude of homage to the great dramatist. And then, with a movement of touching spontaneity, Sarah goes to La Duse, seizes her hand, and both incline before the bust of the master. The spectacle is one that will never be forgotten.

Even without the purple prose of *Le Gaulois*, it must have been a great moment, especially for Sarah, and for Duse the experience of being so spontaneously rescued from the obscurity of the *hoi palloi* at the back of the stage must have been a moment of intense emotion as well.

The emotion was sufficiently intense to keep Duse in health for the rest of her stay. Another contributing factor was the presence of D'Annunzio, come to see the opening of *Sogno*. With his usual kindness towards the female sex he told Duse: "You were insane even to dream of competing with that miraculous woman."

The miraculous woman had left for London on the day after

the Dumas performance, sure to have settled all matters satisfactorily. There she performed at the Adelphi from June 17 to
July 14 her usual repertoire including *Magda* and *La Dame aux
Camélias*. There, however, she ran into another competitor,
Réjane. On successive days both of them undertook Gilberte in
Frou-Frou, and William Archer found that in that role Réjane
now had the edge on Sarah, even though she did not have Sarah's
talent in general. Decidedly a trying season for the miraculous
woman.

Meanwhile, back at the Renaissance, Duse was finally coming
into her own. She had gathered her courage, and she was for
once really angry. The Paris season was almost over, the theaters
were one by one closing down for the customary summer recess,
but Duse was striking out as quickly as possible. *Sogno di un
Mattino di Primavera*, it is true, failed, with its story of Isabella
who goes mad after inadvertently holding her murdered lover
in her arms all night. "The theme is childish," Sarcey wrote.
"On the stage the play, if we can call by such a name this in-
fantile and pretentious poem, is an insufferable bore." After that
failure Sarah, still not satisfied, quickly announced from London
that she, too, would perform it, to redeem it supposedly, and
Sarcey wrote, by now angry at the whole campaign: "What fly
is biting her? . . . If she wishes to engage in a duel . . . she should
take refuge rather in those inaccessible regions which it would
seem Duse could never penetrate, and act *Phèdre* . . ."

La Femme de Claude, when given in full, was a success, and
so were *La Locandiera* and *Cavalleria Rusticana*. Not triumphs
by any means, but successes. And now at last, when Sarah left
matters in peace, an understanding was building up of what
Duse was really doing and what she had really set out to accomplish. Significantly it was the leader of the *avant garde*, Antoine,
the man who had introduced the new realistic drama to France,
who was most explicit in his evaluation. On June 19 he wrote a
review, speaking somewhat optimistically of her "colossal success," and calling her "a very great artist": He refused to "put
her in opposition to Sarah Bernhardt," and objected to those

who now were "delighted to flay her who has for so many years been the glory of the French stage." When he compares the two actresses in the role of Marguerite Gautier, he finds Duse magnificent in it and believes that she plays the scene with Duval *père* in Act III in perhaps a more moving manner than her rival. Over-all, however, he gives the palm to Sarah. Duse remains herself in the role, a creature of marvelous sensitivity and delicateness, but no courtesan. Sarah's personality does not get in her way, and she is a courtesan from head to foot. In the fifth act the death scene, played by Duse with the most intense realism, gives one less the feeling of tuberculosis and death than Sarah's with whom it remains a lyrical scene.

Towards the end of her stay, several other critics had also come to view her with much more praise. Léon Bernar-Derosne felt that in the second act of *La Femme de Claude* she made everything come to life in a way no one had ever expected. "And I wasn't exactly a child when I saw Ristori and even Rachel."

The chorus swelled to such an extent that Sarcey wrote rather petulantly: "There is no one but Duse now, Duse for ever! No more Desclée, no Réjane, no Bartet, no Sarah! La Duse, only La Duse! We are a funny people." Sarcey, however, also asserted his position on the foremost critic of his time in another, more sensible way. Under his pseudonym Sganarelle he wrote a letter in *Le Temps* suggesting that Duse give a special matinee for the actors and artists of Paris. Her methods, he said, had opened up new horizons, but her stay was short, and most artists had not had the opportunity to see her and learn from her.

Here, at last, was success. The press took up the appeal, and suddenly everyone seemed on her side. In *Le Figaro*, Gustave Larroumet wrote a leading article in which he assured Duse that Paris had given her the consecration of her glory. Before her coming Paris had the genius of three women: Bernhardt, Bartet and Réjane, representing, in turn, poetry, charm, and intelligence. Now a fourth Muse had to be added: truth. Even Jules Lemaître, Sarah's friend, joined the chorus, though he forbore to compare her to Sarah. His main point was that Duse was above all a realistic actress, but that she was, somewhat to his surprise, not brutal in the manner in which realism had come to be equated with a certain coarseness. On the contrary, she had charm, sweetness and tenderness.

The date for the special artists' matinee was fixed for July 6, and a telegram sent to Sarah in London asking her to extend Duse's lease beyond July 1 for that purpose. Sarah replied at once, putting the theater at Duse's disposal free of charge and asking merely that the invitations for the event should bear her name and Duse's side by side. That Duse refused. The matter went back and forth, the project was in danger of being abandoned because of Sarah's sudden insistence that repairs had to be made at the theater at once, until Schurmann cut through the Gordian knot and announced that there was such a demand for tickets that the Renaissance would be too small. The performance would therefore be held at the Porte-Saint-Martin. The story of Bernhardt's maneuver was leaked to the press and aroused further sympathy for Duse.

The event was Duse's apotheosis, a much more natural one than Bernhardt's in front of Dumas' statue three weeks before. The demand for tickets was immense and could not be nearly satisfied. The tickets were given away free, except for one hundred that were sold to the rich and noble to cover expenses.

Sarcey wrote: "It was one of the most beautiful houses I have ever seen . . . I could not do better than compare it with a violin whose strings are tightened and ready to vibrate under the bow. There was electricity in the air . . ." These were not the people who usually attended such performances; these were *gens de métier*, experts, men of taste, expecting something new and superior. They received it. Duse most likely never had another such audience. The most expert and sensitive members of the most cultured public in the world—Sarah had never had it, nor any other.

Jules Huret wrote the apotheosis of it in *Le Figaro*, and lifted it high above the apotheosis of the Dumas gala.

"I am afraid as I take up my pen, yes, afraid of my incompetence to describe, in a few rapid moments, the powerful, profound emotion of these three hours when an entire audience composed of the flower of French actors, of famous writers, great painters and celebrated sculptors, honored a foreign artist with the most resounding, the most enthusiastic, the most poignant demonstration that it is possible to witness."

There is a fever of expectation in the audience. Some have seen her, some have heard about her only. Will it be a struggle? Will it be a glorification? The decision comes soon. *Cavalleria Rusticana* is the first play, and it unrolls with masterful precision. "It is finished; I feel that the battle is already won—too soon for my combative tendencies, but just in time to make this unique audience complete and pure." Its unanimous enthusiasm was more than the praise of experts. "It was the unconscious and impulsive translation of their love of their art, the homage they paid . . . to their art thus ennobled before them, which added to their own feelings of pride."

One wonders if Duse remembered how Sarah had once so decisively added to her own feelings of pride—that had been long ago, fifteen years. Likely she had no time to remember. She played to mounting and mounting enthusiasm, played better than ever before, the last act of *La Dame aux Camélias*, the second act of *La Femme de Claude*. After that, Duse had a standing ovation from the entire audience through ten curtain calls. Handkerchiefs and hats waved, flowers flew, "Au revoir! Au revoir! Au revoir!"

The next morning the Comédie Française entertained her at breakfast in the Bois de Boulogne. Then she left. She had been scheduled to play ten times in eleven days, and had played ten times in thirty. She left, so Montesquiou complained, without a note or greeting to Sarah. He did not realize, one supposes, that noblesse obliges less in high artistic circles than in those of the high nobility.

Her apotheosis did not hide the fact that for Paris she was an artist's artist. Sarah was still the popular heroine. If Duse's success had been as universal as some of her biographers assert, then D'Annunzio would likely have reneged on his commitment to Bernhardt of *La Città Morta*. As he did not, he showed that he still believed her to be the better bet.

Duse, exhausted, returned to her apartment in the Palazzo Volkov in Venice only to leave it again and to rent a house at Settignano, near Florence. There she could be close to D'Annunzio and watch him write.

Sarah, to confirm her hospitality to strangers, rented her theater in the next year to the Italian Ermete Novelli and to a Spanish company. Neither were noticed much. She also brought an action in court against Schurmann for having maligned her, but had to withdraw it and was fined as a result of Schurmann's counter-action.

The result? The two actresses had, deliberately and methodically, embarked on a collision course that spring. They had collided and separated again. They had both survived the collision, which speaks for their power of resilience. That Duse survived and came away with her reputation unimpaired or even enhanced may give her the edge in the final count. The direct combat was never renewed.

CHAPTER 11 / An Institution

The parting shot of the encounter of 1897 was fired six months later. On January 21, 1898, Sarah gave the first performance of D'Annunzio's play *La Città Morta* in Paris. That evening Count Primoli gave a party for Duse at his mansion in Rome. It seemed more like a wake; Duse spent most of the evening lying on a couch, her hair disheveled and a hot water bottle on her stomach. Her host received a stream of telegrams sent during the performance to indicate its progress. Duse talked quietly about the play and Sarah; when others attacked the French actress she calmly defended her and her talent. Finally the news comes that the play has failed completely. By now Duse is feverish, laughs cruelly, and paces up and down. Suddenly she overcomes her jealousy, and breaks into a hymn of praise for D'Annunzio, the great poet, which leaves her so exhausted that she can barely bring herself to leave and go home.

La Città Morta, not a useful revenge, lasted for thirteen performances. It was Sarah's last new play at the Renaissance. In the same year she bought the dilapidated Théâtre des Nations, remodeled it sumptuously, and opened it on January 21, 1899, as the Théâtre Sarah Bernhardt, with a revival of *La Tosca.* The new theater was magnificent, and all Bernhardt. The foyer contained ten life-size murals of Sarah in her greatest roles, painted by Louise Abbéma, Georges Clairin and others. Sarah's dressing room was really a five-room suite near the stage, in which she could entertain for dinner or supper. Sunday dinners in large company soon became a custom.

The adventures at the Renaissance had cost her several hun-

dred thousand francs. Now, she hoped, her losses could be re-
couped at the new house with its 1700 seats as compared to
the 900 at the Renaissance. However, the management of the
new house was scarcely less chaotic than that of the old, and her
hopes were never realized. Much of the money she earned
abroad, especially in America, continued to meet the deficits of
disasters at home, and *La Dame aux Camélias,* as well as the
Sardou plays, were called upon time and again to redress the
balance. Sarah seems to have preferred the theater to lose money
when she herself was on tour, as if to reassure herself of her in-
dispensability, and the theater rarely failed to oblige.

Also, the house, being larger, placed the audience at a greater
distance from the stage. Sarah was, after all, fifty-five years old.

One of her first plays in the Théâtre Sarah Bernhardt was a
prose translation of *Hamlet* with herself in the title role. Paris
liked the play and Sarah inserted it in her repertoire on tour.
She made the mistake of bringing it to England, where it aroused
a fair amount of hilarity. Max Beerbohm, in a review entitled
"Hamlet, Princess of Denmark," said that the only compliment
one could conscientiously pay Sarah was that her Hamlet was
très grande dame. In her black tunic and tights, her head enveloped in an enormous yellow wig, and a long cloak dangling
from her right shoulder, she reminded one reviewer of a mos-
quito seen under a microscope. Another described the climax
of the play-within-a-play scene: an open fire is going on stage,
which darkens as the climax approaches. When King Claudius
rises convulsively and calls for lights, Sarah snatches up a flam-
ing torch, bounds to him, and with one grand, sweeping gesture
illuminates his fear-paroxyzed face; then she pursues him off the
stage shrieking vengeance and waving the torch. It was truly
Shakespeare by flashes of lightning, as Coleridge once described
Kean's performances.

Sarah Bernhardt had a considerable liking for roles *à travesti,*
male parts. She once explained her predilection, in part, by saying: "As a matter of fact, it is not male parts, but male brains
that I prefer."

Her first success, Zanetto in *Le Passant*, was a male role, as was her great success, the Duke of Reichstadt in Rostand's *L'Aiglon*. There were many others: Lorenzaccio in Musset's play on the Medicis, Pelleas (in Maeterlinck's play, once performed with Mrs. Patrick Campbell as Melisande), and others. In the nineteenth century male roles were not infrequently assumed by women. The only survival of that practice are the male parts for soprano in nineteenth-century operas; in the theater the practice is now mostly restricted to *Charley's Aunt*.

Edmond Rostand's *L'Aiglon*, first given on March 15, 1900, was the greatest triumph of Sarah's later career. Rostand himself was at the zenith, since the appearance of *Cyrano de Bergerac*, with Coquelin, in 1897, undoubtedly the most successful and popular play since Sardou in the eighties. Now he had written a *Cyrano* for Sarah, a play in which the fifty-six-year-old actress played a boy who never reached the age of twenty-one. The eaglet of the title was the son of the Emperor Napoleon and the Empress Marie Louise, Archduchess of Austria. At birth he became the King of Rome; during the action of the play, however, he is the Duke of Reichstadt, coughing out his lungs at the court of his grandfather, the Austrian Emperor Francis. In six acts and thirty monologues the play revived the whole Napoleonic past. Emile Faguet was furiously bored by it all, and the other critics were very divided, but the public roared its approval of the play and of Sarah on March 15, through thirty curtain calls. It ran for two hundred and thirty-seven performances and earned more than two and a half million francs, or 11,300 per performance, which indicates that the house was sold out nearly every night. It was still sold out at the last performance, when Sarah took the play to New York.

For the American tour of 1900–1901 Sarah had persuaded Coquelin to join her, and to perform Cyrano; she really wanted him for a role in *L'Aiglon* which he considered too small, but in New York she persuaded him to do it, by performing Roxane to his Cyrano, an equally minor role.

L'Aiglon opened on November 26, 1900, at the Garden

Theatre in New York, one month after Maude Adams had first performed it in English at the Knickerbocker. On December 10 came *Cyrano*, on the 17th *La Tosca* (with Coquelin as Scarpia), on the 18th *La Dame aux Camélias* (in which he was Armand's father) and on the 25th *Hamlet* (in which the second character, after Hamlet, listed on the program was the First Gravedigger: Coquelin). These five plays made up that whole sixth tour, but the success was, perhaps, greater than any Sarah had ever had in the United States. Sarah was no longer an actress only. She was now an institution. "Mme. Bernhardt," William Winter admitted sourly, "has attracted large audiences in many parts of the country, and has received from the press in general such adulation and advocacy as have seldom been awarded to even the authentic benefactors of human society." Edmond Haraucourt said that the five continents considered themselves sufficiently learned when they knew two words of French, and two names of French history: Napoleon and Sarah Bernhardt.

L'Aiglon was Sarah's last great, genuine achievement in a new role. Though the play has not stood the test of time nearly as well as *Cyrano de Bergerac*, it was a golden, not a gilt opportunity for Sarah, and she used it fully and yet with that economy of means that, at her best, made her an unrivaled actress. Her heroics, sword in hand, her monologues vividly conjuring up the Napoleonic era, and her twenty minutes' dying were in the tradition of her repertoire and yet seem to have struck the audience as fresh and poignantly original and individual. She did not strain or shout, she just moved and talked Rostand's facile, skillful verse swiftly and skillfully.

". . . I admired Rostand's skill," Symons wrote, "as I saw how skillfully it was written to be acted; scrutinize the first act and you will see that it was composed like a piece of music, to be played by one performer, Sarah Bernhardt. To her, acting was a performance on a musical instrument. One seemed to see the expression marks: piano, pianissimo, allargando, and just when the tempo rubato comes in. She never forgot that art is not nature, and that, when one is speaking verse one is not talking prose."

Analogies to music seemed natural to drama critics of that time; the connection between music and the theater, particularly pervasive in the nineteenth century, served the international actresses to great advantage.

The nineteenth century, first of all, produced much of the greatest music of Western man, and very little of his greatest drama. It was the century of grand opera. Many of the stage stars began as singers or had training in singing, Rachel and Ristori among them. Auber, the Director of the Conservatoire in Bernhardt's time, was an operatic composer. The famous playwrights were also librettists, often primarily so. Eugène Scribe, for example, was one of the most important librettists of his day; Verdi's operas *Un Ballo in Maschera* and *I Vespri Siciliani* are based on his work, and he wrote all the libretti for the French operas of Meyerbeer, the most popular of Parisian opera composers, from *Robert Le Diable* (1831) to *L'Africaine* (1865).

Verdi, Puccini and the French and Italian composers fell back on the popular dramatists of their day for their libretti, and that meant mostly the French. The most famous composer set to music the most famous play: *La Dame aux Camélias* became *La Traviata* in 1853. Verdi also made operas of Hugo's *Hernani* (*Ernani*) and *Le Roi s'Amuse* (*Rigoletto*), apart from the Scribe plays. Ponchielli used Hugo's *Angelo*, Rachel's play, for *La Gioconda*, Mascagni made Verga's *Cavalleria Rusticana* into an opera, Cilea used Scribe and Legouvé's play for his *Adriana Lecouvreur*, Giordano composed *Fédora, Mme. Sans-Gêne* and *La Cena delle Beffe* (a play Bernhardt performed), and Puccini adapted Sardou's *La Tosca*. All this in addition to the operas of the French composers, Massenet, Halévy, etc., many of which were based on the same repertoire.

In the second half of the nineteenth century it was as important to the playwright to have his work made into an opera as it was to be made into a film in the nineteen-thirties and forties.

The house of Ricordi in Milan was the Metro-Goldwyn-Mayer of its time.

The term prima donna, applied to the principal singer, was also applied to the principal actress. Singers and actresses did not distinguish between themselves as they did later. Jenny Lind, the soprano, for example, was greatly impressed with Rachel when she visited Paris in 1841. She compared her own strengths and weaknesses on stage with those of Rachel, clearly believing that they both worked in the same medium.

Fifty years later, in 1894, William Archer reported that he saw two performances of *Cavalleria Rusticana* within a few days of each other, and wrote a detailed comparative study of Emma Calvé as Santuzza in the opera, and Duse in the play.

For the prima donna, the one who sang and the one who, more or less, spoke, one came back time after time, not because of the work in which she appeared but because of the performance she gave. Sarcey said of Rachel that one went to see her as one went to hear Patti. Prince Georg von Hohenzollern wrote a pamphlet about Rachel in which he plots her voice range (two octaves, from F below middle C to F in alt), and gives her rendering of certain famous lines in musical notation. Grein used such terms as *staccato, capriccioso* and *fortissimo* in referring to Sarah's vocal inflection and speech. Arthur Symons called her voice a musical instrument and found that she played upon it as a conductor plays upon an orchestra.

Yvette Guilbert said almost the same of Duse: ". . . the miracle in her was her voice. Majors, minors, rising, dropping, chromatic." In *Magda*, when she returns to the small town, the scene with the lover who had deserted her began "in arpeggios, and ended rhythmically . . . in syncopes, pauses, and the final chord." Duse said that she drew from certain repetitive passages in Wagner some ideas for her Marguerite Gautier.

Sarcey took Duse to task for one of her interpretations in Act IV of *La Dame aux Camélias:* At its climax Armand hurls the money he won at the gaming table at Marguerite's feet and, in a long tirade, accuses her of faithlessness and evil. Dumas has her stand there, silent, desperately keeping her promise to Armand's father not to let the son know how she really feels. "But that" Sarcey says, "did not suit La Duse. Since it is she that people come to see and hear in her tours, it is necessary for her to dominate the scene . . ." To accomplish this, Duse, in the midst of these insults, as if she wished to stop Armand, keeps uttering *"Armando! Armando! Armando!"* in a crescendo of pathos. Actually Duse's cry was a virtuoso performance, passing with each "Armando!" from incredulity to fright to hurt to heartbreak.

Count Primoli, Duse's friend, recounts that Verdi once saw Duse perform the role of Marguerite. After seeing that particular scene he said: "That little Duse! If I had heard her before writing my opera, what a splendid finale [of Act III] could I possibly have made of this *crescendo di Armandi* which she invented!"

For Sarcey, the critic of drama, Duse had, to his disgust, made a fine dramatic scene into an operatic finale. For the great audience, however, to whom that distinction meant little, that "Armando!" was the equivalent of a thrilling *cabaletta* in a Verdi opera. To them Bernhardt's tirade in *Adrienne Lecouvreur* and Patti's rendition of *Una Voce Poco Fà* were comparable experiences. They came to see Bernhardt drop her handkerchief in *La Dame*, or for Duse's cry, as they came for Melba's high C.

The operatic attitude towards actresses assumed ludicrous proportions. Helena Modjeska, the Polish actress, tells a story that explains that temper: In 1878 she opened her first major New York engagement with *Frou-Frou*, acting, of course, in English. One scene in the play calls for great speed in speech, and she got into such difficulties "that I could scarcely understand myself, not to speak of the audience. To my great amusement, a young critic, Mr. Steinberg, of the *New York Herald*, said quite seriously in his notice about 'Frou-Frou' that my rapid speeches were like Wagner's music to him—the less he understood, the better he liked them. He added, further, that this rushing cataract of sounds was most impressive."

Better perhaps than any other aspect, that emphasis on music, ludicrous or not, explains the phenomenon of the international actresses. The great operative divas became international stars in the generation before Rachel. Rachel's achievement remains unique, though even in her case the newer plays (*Adrienne Lecouvreur* by Scribe and Legouvé, Soumet's *Jeanne d'Arc*, Schiller's *Mary Stuart*, Hugo's *Angelo*) were at least as important on tours abroad as the prestige plays by Racine. Ristori's repertoire, and that of Bernhardt and Duse, needed enormous stage-presence, great adeptness at "business," movement and gesture, and great vocal or declamatory ability. It needed little understanding of character, or of what was being said on stage. It was, in short, operatic. Opera is often performed in a language with which the audience is not familiar. In the Anglo-Saxon countries the rare performance of an Italian opera in English still arouses protests from the public. Bilingual performances are frequent. In the nineteenth century they also occurred in the spoken drama. The Italians on the international route indulged in bilingual performances, like the one Ristori gave of *Mary Stuart* in New York, with a German supporting cast; or Salvini's Othello in Italian to Booth's Iago and an English supporting cast. In neither case did the star know the language of the rest of the company, and the performance must have seemed like some operatic evening for which the singers are assembled from all over the place and are nevertheless able to go through the performance simply because the stage business of *La Traviata* or *La Gioconda* is much the same at the Scala in Milan and the Metropolitan in New York. On June 2, 1897, after her first performance of *La Dame aux Camélias* in Paris, Duse spoke with President Félix Faure of France. He congratulated her warmly and she replied confessing her fear that the audience would find her performance unrewarding because she acted in Italian. "What? You acted in Italian?" replied Faure. "Your art is so full of passion and truth that I did not even notice that you did not act in French."

Obviously President Faure was being polite, and the story is among Duse's apocrypha in any case, but that it could be is symptomatic of the whole situation. A certain amount of snob appeal was of course involved. James Agate spoke of "the ecstasy of the highbrows who understood Italian, and the even greater extravagance of those who did not."

Max Beerbohm was almost the only major critic who dared to cry "humbug." In his essay "An Hypocrisy in Playgoing" he took up the case of Duse:

> Eecostoetchiayoomahniacevahrachellopestibahntamahnta-fahnta . . . Shall I go on? No? You do not catch my meaning when I write thus? I am to express myself, please, in plain English? If I wrote the whole of my article as I have written the beginning of it, you would, actually, refuse to read it? I am astonished. The chances are that you do not speak Italian, do not understand Italian when it is spoken. The chances are that Italian spoken from the stage of a theatre produces for you no more than the empty, though rather pretty, effect which it produces for me, and which I have tried to suggest phonetically in print. And yet the chances are also that you were in the large British audience which I saw, last Wednesday afternoon, in the Adelphi Theatre—that large, patient, respectful audience, which sat out the performance of "Hedda Gabler." Surely, you are a trifle inconsistent? . . . why not confess your boredom? Better still, why go to be bored?

Perhaps, he says, these people who flock to Duse's performance really feel that they are taking a means to edification. "We needs must praise the highest," they say—and "Duse is (we are assured) the highest; therefore we must needs see her, for our own edification, and go into rhapsodies."

This atmosphere of culture or snob appeal through language explains in part why the international actresses were much more appreciated abroad than at home. Once they were established nothing could shake their reputation. Sarah's mistakes that would make Sarcey's or Lemaître's blood curdle passed unnoticed in Moscow or Milwaukee. The beauty of voice, the electrification through gesture sufficed. The results were that an actress at times began to stress sound and action at the expense of sense.

Lemaître, for example, said testily after Bernhardt's *Léna* in 1889: "She recites her lines like a schoolgirl intoning her prayers at night before her first communion. Is this because she has got used to performing before audiences that do not understand French? I am rather inclined to believe that she has become so accustomed to scenes of violence and torture, which are so generously dispensed in the sanguinary dramas of Victorien Sardou, that she had gradually lost the faculty of expressing the ordinary sentiments of everyday life." After one of her revivals of *Théodora* he once said that her voice survived its daily "singing" and remained pure gold. "But have you noticed the bizarreness of her diction?"

What would the Paris critics have said if they had heard Sarah on tour in foreign countries, when she at times substituted for a tirade of Césarine's, let us say, her own impromptu tirade on the deficiencies of the local hotel or the stupidity of the audience —and then witnessed the applause?

L'Aiglon was the last occasion when a playwright could give Sarah the kind of new play that supported the strong points of her acting, and that at the same time had some literary, or at least theatrical merit. Sardou's last play for her, *La Sorcière*, caused riots in Montreal because it puts the Catholic priesthood in a bad light. On her way to the station she needed to be protected by the police, and de Max, her partner, had to take refuge in a tobacco shop. Sir Wilfrid Laurier, the Canadian Prince Minister, telegraphed his regrets.

La Sorcière, and some revivals of Sardou and Dumas were atoned for by further revivals of *Phèdre* and of Racine's religious play *Esther*, which, like its original performance at a girl's school was done by women only, including Sarah as Assuérus with a blond beard. But on the whole Sarah's repertoire in these years was the same, costume play after costume play, by Sardou and his imitators. The Théâtre Sarah Bernhardt was becoming the last bastion of the romantic play in a historical setting—even

La Dame aux Camélias now had a historical setting—while the rest of the theatrical world had moved on to the work of Ibsen and the Free Theater movement. Increasingly she retreated to the past, revived the plays in which she had been successful, more and more the verse plays, and almost always costume. Eventually *L'Aiglon* surpassed one thousand performances.

She continued to tour. In 1902 she went to the one country in Europe which she had consciously avoided. She had never forgotten the war of 1870, and her dislike of Germany, partly formed by the persistent accusation of German origin, had never abated. Her granddaughter Lysiane says that Sarah was requested to tour the German Empire by the French foreign minister, as part of a diplomatic rapprochement. The tour was a diplomatic rather than artistic occasion, at least in her eyes. She received a bouquet of camellias from the Empress—a very small bouquet, she reports—and the Kaiser Wilhelm II saw two of her performances in Berlin, when she opened with *Fédora* on October 16, 1902.

Sarah liked to recall later, especially after the First World War, that she had gone only for the sake of Alsace-Lorraine, that Berlin had been openly hostile towards her in the beginning, that mounted police were there to protect her from the initial wrath of the enemy, and that she had conquered in the end. The truth seems to be that she was received very quietly, and that she was listened to politely. The Germans had heard a lot about her, and many had seen her. They, as self-conscious victors, bore her no personal grudge. But the acquired momentum of London and New York, where nostalgia began to play an increasing role with each tour, was not there. Sarah was now nearing sixty. She had come to Germany too late. Yet she was applauded and returned on later occasions, in 1904 and 1905, as well as in 1908 when she was no longer able to repeat her success, and the critics turned unkind.

In one other respect times had changed since Rachel's day. The anti-Semitism of the later nineteenth century had its effect on her. Rachel had been revered by a Czar and his grand-dukes.

Bernhardt's carriage was stoned in the Czar's city of Odessa and there were anti-Semitic demonstrations in Petersburg and Moscow for which the grand dukes hardly atoned by giving Sarah enough sables for a coat and muff. Worse still, anti-Semitism had risen in her own country. The Dreyfus affair split France into bitterly opposed camps. The drama critic Lemaître founded a "patriotic" organization of anti-Dreyfusards, which was joined, among others, by Coppée, one of Sarah's playwrights. Sardou was pro-Dreyfus, as was the playwright Octave Mirabeau. Maurice Bernhardt believed in Dreyfus' guilt. His mother courageously made her feelings known that Dreyfus was innocent in her eyes and supported Émile Zola throughout his campaign.

At the time Dreyfus was finally exonerated, in 1906, Sarah was as usual on tour.

The United States tour of 1905–1906 was different from the Coquelin tour of 1900–1901; it exhibited Sarah at her stubborn best. She began it in South America, her last time on that continent; in Rio she seems to have aggravated her knee injury which eventually led to a complete loss of movement in one of her legs.

The theaters of the United States were, in 1905–1906, at the mercy of the Klaw-Erlanger syndicate, which dictated policy and performances. Sarah was under contract to the brothers Shubert, who were trying to break the monopoly. Sarah refused to buckle under, and was therefore excluded from virtually all legitimate theaters across the country. A lesser performer would have been stopped by that. Sarah, however, was too well publicized and too powerful. In Chicago, Columbus, and some other cities she performed in tents. In Los Angeles she performed at "Venice in America," a pier built over the ocean. She finally had a triumphal return to New York, where she did have a theater, the Lyric. The great publicity of her fight with the syndicate obscured the private fact that she was in pain almost all the time. Though she still managed to play tennis in the summer of that year at her estate at Belle-Isle, the pain and stiffness in her knee increasingly impeded her movements.

An American tour would yield Sarah between 500,000 and
750,000 francs, or 100,000 to 150,000 dollars. At times, especially
in London or New York, she would appear in a private house
and earn additional money; one such occasion was a joint appearance of Sarah Bernhardt and the soprano Nellie Melba at a
party of Lady George Cooper's, who paid them $2,500. The
main event was Murger's poem "La Ballade du Désespéré" with
music by Herman Bemberg, who accompanied the performance.
Melba sang Death, while Sarah recited the lines of the Poet.
Nevertheless Sarah was in almost continuous financial straits.
Part of the cause was simply a permanent state of chaos. She did
not believe in banks and made all financial transactions in cash.
Large amounts had to be transported about at all times, and
sometimes they were simply lacking. Once, in 1904 or 1905, Mrs.
Pat Campbell lent her one hundred pounds, and got them back
later, in full view of everyone in the green room, in a little silver
casket. Sarah, who powdered and rouged herself in public, did
not mind either who knew about her financial difficulties.

Her caprices were part of her legend. Interviewers dutifully
recorded all she said, and so the public assumed that her seemingly eternal youth was due to the consumption of lemons in
large amounts, that she would omit a scene in a production if she
did not really feel it; and so on. She enjoyed all that hoodwink-
ing, and played along with it for fifty years. Her friends at times
felt the necessity to defend her against the change of publicistic
cupidity. Zola, for example, said correctly: "It is not she, but
you who make the publicity; you, the Public, that can never
hear enough about a favorite singer, and you, the Press, who
are not ashamed to sate such a longing for tittle-tattle." If Sarah
herself minded the publicity, she never confessed it.

She had aristocratic tastes and ways of behavior, liked osten-
tation, and had a strong authoritarian streak in her. She was
wrapped in chinchilla up to her nose until July. She liked her
dignity, and refused to have anything to do with anyone—prince
or magnate—who lacked respect for her. She hated crowds, waiting rooms, or meeting lots of people. Her house on the Boule-

vard Pereire, which Maurice Rostand found fairly awful, did
not contain tame pumas any more, but it still was full of lesser
animals, and the number of knick-knacks was great even for a
late Victorian mansion. "Heavy stuffs hanging over the ceiling,"
Melba found on her first visit, "drooping down and catching
the dust, skins of animals on the floor, heads of animals on the
walls, horns of animals on the mantelpiece—stuffed tigers, stuffed
bears, even a stuffed snake." There were also busts of Sarah,
tapestries, easels, plants, and a goldfish bowl. In that environment she held court.

> The antechamber, where visitors lingered in waiting; the
> quaint noise next door as of *frou-frou*-ing gowns and shuffling
> feet; then folding doors flung apart as by magic; a figure in
> white on a gilded fauteuil; around her, in semi-circle, her sec-
> retaries, intimates, devotees; the confusion of the visitor, dazzled
> by this unexpected *mise-en-scène;* her graceful smile, her suavity
> of address, her witchery to make one feel as if a great queen
> were bestowing favours; her sublime acceptance of words of
> homage and her sudden bow to the next worshipper. It was
> very solemn at the moment, like so many things which Sarah
> did *pour la galérie . . .*

The Sarah who was not playing to the gallery was delightful,
cordial, vivacious, a bit unpredictable but generally kind. The
summers of her later years she spent at Belle-Isle, a rather inaccessible island on the coast of Brittany, where she built a simple
house into a complex of houses, some of them permanently inhabited each summer by old friends like Georges Clairin. There
she relaxed and recovered, had luxurious picnics and fishing ex-
peditions, played parlor games and tennis, and talked. The only
game she did not participate in was charades. In all games she
was a poor loser; in tennis especially, after her injury, her partners were hard put to arrange for her to win.

For the rest of the year she acted, in Paris or elsewhere, every
night, and sometimes in the afternoon as well. In January of 1906,
in Boston, after forty-four years on the stage, she acted between

8:30 P.M. on a Friday, and 10:30 P.M. on a Saturday, Fedora, Phèdre and Césarine. Her endurance was fabulous. She could, like Coquelin and Talma, sleep whenever she wanted to, and awaken refreshed after an hour. Léon Brémont, one of her leading men of the 1890's, reports that to prepare him for a role she rehearsed portions of *Lorenzaccio* with him every night from midnight to five A.M., after the evening's performance of *La Dame aux Camélias*, and that at 9 A.M. she was at the theater again every day to talk to set designers, costumers and dozens of other people, for most of the day.

Duse had gone to her apartment in the Palazzo Volkov in Venice after the month in Paris 1897. From there she soon went to her house near Florence for a continuation of her own private Calvary. After a pilgrimage to Assisi D'Annunzio had rented a house near hers. Soon he was protesting his love for her, begging her in tears to stay, while also taking the most meticulous notes about her and her love.

They were living side by side in adjoining houses in Settignano outside Florence, he at La Capponcina, which he rented from the Marchese Giacinto Viviani della Robbia, and she at a much more modest place that they renamed La Porziuncola. The difference between the houses showed the difference between the characters. Her house was in dark colors, mostly deep reds and greens. Her studio held engravings of Shakespeare and his house in Stratford. Books and roses were almost the only decor. The bedchamber was bare, almost cloisterlike. Above the bed she had a portrait of Keats and his epitaph: "Here lies one whose name was writ in water." D'Annunzio's house was different. Though he was 70,000 lire in debt he at once began an immense development to remodel the entire house, until it "combined the luxury of a Medicaean prince and the hodge podge of a curio shop." Romain Rolland called it "a real bazaar." He was particularly impressed with the sumptuous renaissance bed, with its vase of olive branches at the foot and twig of laurel at the head. The home corresponded to the style of the man—the phony cathedral atmosphere in which every item was in turn decorated with another item, like the similes that he loved to pile on similes, magnificent, ostentatious, exhibitionistic. There he worked for hours at his medieval writing desk, with tremendous energy and concentration. "I get up at seven o'clock, take a bath, fence, a gallop on my horse. I go in for exercise. Not until ten o'clock do I sit down at my table. And I don't budge from it till nine in the evening. I eat at my writing table. . . . All I need is 20,000 sheets of my special paper made for me by Miliano Di Fabriano, plenty of ink, the sight of 500 quills which have been specially collected for me from geese stripped alive. All this gives me an extraordinary desire to write." He actually wrote with these quills, using as many as thirty a day. When he worked he worked very hard, and when he did not—"When I have finished a novel or a play, I allow myself every form of relaxation. . . . [Then] during the day, after a rest, I allow my body to live on its own, abandon itself to all its ardor, its violence. Above all, I don't allow myself to think of the work I am preparing, so as to leave the brain at rest and receive impressions during the night when the gods descend . . ."

D'Annunzio's heavy, lush style and fervid imagery were in step with much of the writing of his time, and with the other arts. The painting of Gustave Moreau and Odilon Redon, in its links between sensuality and morbidity, its preoccupation with snakes, for example, and their relation to human beings and human shapes, bears on the same point. Scenes in Bernhardt's *Théodora* had the quality of a Redon painting, and the sex-related, somber aspects of mythology and the Bible, which these artists selected, fit in well with the preoccupations of D'Annunzio. The predilections of the age—not of art—are clear when one compares their selections from mythology and history with those of David or Delacroix. Moreau's "Galatea," with its dark masculine head brooding over a seductive female, seems to come out of a D'Annunzio novel. His "Salome Dancing before Herod" looks like the setting for a Sardou play. The artist, the novelist, and the actress mix in a description by the critic Walkley of

Sarah, the new type, and "her embodiment of Oriental exotism: the strange, chimaeric, idol-woman: a compound of Baudelaire's Vierge du Mal, Swinburne's Our Lady of Pain, Gustave Moreau's Salome, Leonardo's enigmatic Mona Lisa." One would have liked to salvage Leonardo from that company.

Sarah, the Thessalian witch, fitted D'Annunzio's style, but Duse fitted the man. Her passion for suffering and jealous reproaches complemented D'Annunzio's passion for sadism, and stealthy affairs. Romain Rolland and his wife were staying at the Hotel Baur-au-Lac in Zurich in 1899, while Duse was performing and D'Annunzio came. In the next few days the Rollands found that they had no life of their own, enveloped, almost choked as they were by the problems of their two friends, their bitter quarrels and their inability to separate. They clung to the Rollands, confided in them, and though Rolland found D'Annunzio alone pleasant, cordial and easy, D'Annunzio with a woman was impossible, and with Duse, worse. She is wildly worried one evening because Gabriele threatened suicide, and the Rollands must watch over him. Another time D'Annunzio violently denies to Rolland that he ever deceived Duse or had anything but disgust for prostitutes, and Rolland is offended at the abuse of his intelligence. She is desperate on another occasion that he might leave her—"What have I left then?"

D'Annunzio's threat of suicide, Rolland found out later, was connected with his novel which was reaching completion, *Il Fuoco* (The Fire). He used his threat to try to convince Duse that she was not a character in the novel, and even read her some passages from it.

Il Fuoco had been in preparation since 1897. He cannot have doubted the effect the book would have on Duse; she and he are the main characters in it. It was, of course not his first novel about his own love affairs, nor was he the first writer to use such materials. But it is doubtful that any woman had ever been used so viciously as Duse in *Il Fuoco*. From the beginning, he had been taking notes on her, each day, after having left her, and set down with feverishly sensual crudity all the recollections of the hours of love.

Schurmann, Duse's manager, saw the manuscript of the novel and went to her at once; he asked her permission to let him do everything he could to prevent publication. She said she knew the novel, and stalled. When he reached his hotel, he received a note from her: "I did not tell you the truth a little while ago. I know all about the novel, and have agreed to its publication, for all my sufferings, great though they may be, do not count when it is a question of adding one more masterpiece to Italian literature. And then—I am forty years old—and in love."

Duse may have thought she knew the whole novel, but she did not, and she was deeply shocked when it came out. The book was an immediate *succès de scandale*, but many strong voices were raised in indignation. Arthur Symons, D'Annunzio's translator into English, hesitated to touch the book and turned to Duse for counsel. He found in it "luxury, horror, beauty, obscenity" but "no actual vision—that is beyond the vision of the voluptuary." Henry James found in it a great description of Venice, and beyond that the basic theme of "the physical destruction into which the man drags the woman by way of retribution for the fury of physical surrender into which she had beguiled him." He continues: "The temporarily united pair devour each other throughout a series of exotic convulsions and nervous reactions that are made interesting—interesting to us— almost exclusively by the special wealth of their consciousness."

Il Fuoco deals with the poet Stelio Effrena and the actress Foscarina. Foscarina is twenty years older than Stelio, a whore of whores, insatiable and possessive, yet wildly abject before the god Stelio. He hates her for making him love her. He observes her critically, notes her sagging chin, the crow's feet and black lines around her eyes. He realizes that she draws him because of her age, and is fascinated by the thought of the lovers she had before him—how many, who were they, and above all, could they satisfy her as well as he can?

Beyond that, the fact that she was an actress attracted him,

and at one point of the novel he states the attraction of the actress
—of the adulation that the concept conjured up in him, and still
and all, in his age—and the element of competition for the scalp
to be gained. Here Stelio speaks in Arthur Symons' translation:

> Regret stung him for never having possessed the actress after
> some theatrical triumph, still warm with the breath of the
> crowd, covered with sweat, pale and panting, still wearing the
> traces of the tragic soul that had wept and cried out in her, with
> the tears of that intruding soul still damp on her convulsed face.
> For the space of a lightning flash he saw her outstretched, full
> of the power that had drawn a howl from the monster, throb-
> bing like a Maenad after the dance, parched and tired, yet need-
> ing to be taken, to be shaken, to feel herself contracting in a
> last spasm, to receive some violent germ, in order to quiet down
> at last to a lethargy without dreams. How many men had come
> forth from the crowd to clasp her after having panted for her
> lost in the unanimous mass? Their desire had been made of the
> desire of thousands, their vigour multiplied . . .

The reaction was as stark as the novel. Sarah wrote that she
would never again play the work of a poet who had stooped to
such uncleanness. A veritable campaign against D'Annunzio got
under way in Paris, and he, always more popular in France than
in Italy, became alarmed. He turned to Rolland with the request
to explain to the public that Duse was, of course, nowhere in
the book, but Rolland declined to defend him.

While they loved and quarreled, Duse performed his plays.
On January 11, 1898, a few days before Bernhardt's first performance of *La Città Morta*, Duse had given *Sogno di un mattino di primavera* its Italian premiere at the Teatro Valle in
Rome. She looked magnificent, and acted well, but only the
presence of Queen Margherita prevented a riot. The final curtain fell on complete silence. When it rose again after the intermission on Goldoni's *La Locandiera*, the house broke into a
tumultuous "Evviva Goldoni." D'Annunzio, impeccably elegant
in evening dress, smiled and talked to everyone as if everything
had gone well.

That winter Duse had her heart set on forming a company with Ermete Zacconi to perform D'Annunzio's plays. Schurmann, who dreaded the prospect, was much relieved when the money could not be found, and Duse had to embark on an ordinary, profitable tour of Portugal, Spain and the south of France. During a brief stay in Paris, Duse refused Bernhardt's request for her permission to perform *La Città Morta* in Italy, where Duse held the rights to the play. Her refusal was only partly caused by the wish to curb Sarah. She really intended to perform D'Annunzio, believing that he would be one of the greatest playwrights when she, her name writ in water, would be forgotten. She had bought D'Annunzio's dramatic output for her sole performance from his agent, for a very large sum; as most of his plays were yet to come, and what was on paper of doubtful theatrical value, the agent had been pleased.

The tour of 1898 was a tremendous success, of course. Thirty-six curtain calls in Lisbon after *La Dame aux Camélias*, ovations everywhere. In the winter of 1898–1899 she went to the other side of the Mediterranean—Cairo, Alexandria, Athens—and triumphed there. Yet, her letters from that tour are reports of ennui and discouragement; she has no work, she writes, she does nothing of value, she will die soon.

But the tour finally gave her the money for her project, and Schurmann could not prevent her any longer from performing the works of the master. On April 15, 1899, Duse and Ermete Zacconi opened with *La Gioconda* at the Teatro Bellini in Palermo. The prices of seats were extraordinarily high for that rather poor city. Old sets had to be used as the complicated new scenery did not arrive in time. All that may have annoyed the public. The presence of the Duke of Orléans, and all of Duse's struggle did not avail. There was a noisy riot at the opening performance.

La Gioconda was dedicated to "Eleonora Duse delle belle mani." The play opens with Silvia Settala (Duse) in an agony of doubt, having just saved her husband Lucio, a sculptor, from suicide over his model Gioconda Dianti. He still loves Gioconda.

In the third act the two rivals confront each other and Silvia lies to Gioconda, telling her that her husband has dismissed her. Gioconda thereupon wants to destroy an unfinished statue for which she served Lucio as a model, but Silvia saves it—at the expense of her hands which are crushed beneath it. Silvia is left handless, alone, by the Sea, justly punished for denying Gioconda her realm, the studio; deserted by her husband, and agonized, in the last scene, by her child Beata's request to be held in her mother's arms. Even without the specific reference of the dedication—"to Eleonora Duse of the beautiful hands"—the play is more sadistic than *Titus Andronicus*.

Duse refused to be daunted by the theater riot caused in Naples by *La Gloria*, another of D'Annunzio's obsessions with blood and sadism under the guise of artistry that is beyond good and evil. Duse went on, dragging his plays through failure after failure in Italy—and feeling at the same time that she was failing him. Her exaltation knew no bounds in these years; her theater was a temple to her, and D'Annunzio its new high priest, beyond good and evil in his priesthood. She refused to see that there was no idea in D'Annunzio's drama, only gore cloaked, at times, in very effective sensuous poetry. Schurmann implored her not to ruin herself, not to alienate the public, but she stood her ground.

Il Fuoco was published in March of 1900. On April 13, Duse, with what feelings we know not, gave a gala performance of *La Gioconda* at the Burgtheater in Vienna and received the highest decoration possible for her position in life—one only two Austrian actresses had received before her. D'Annunzio came, too, and, for once, the play was applauded. She took the play on to Berlin, gay and happy now, and her relationship with the poet proceeded as if nothing had happened, while all summer long her supporters in Paris and elsewhere protested against D'Annunzio's inhumanity towards her.

In 1901 Duse performed *La Città Morta* for the first time, without much success, and on December 9, 1901, she did his *Francesca da Rimini* at the Teatro Costanzi in Rome, in a production that cost 400,000 lire, probably the largest sum ever spent in Italy on the production of a play.

The lavishness of the production would have done credit to Daly or Belasco, though neither of them would have been anywhere near as clumsy. At the premiere a genuine bombardment by catapults on stage nearly knocked out one wall of the theater. Thick smoke, to simulate gunpowder-smoke, blinded and nearly asphyxiated actors and audience. Not only the smoke, but the audience, escaped from the theater hissing.

Pirandello, not yet a famous dramatist, witnessed the performance and wrote later: "I do not think that I ever suffered as much in a theater as during the first performance of D'Annunzio's *Francesca da Rimini* at the Teatro Costanzi in Rome. The art of the great actress seemed constrained, distorted and even shattered by D'Annunzio's overdrawn heroine, just as the action itself was constrained, distorted and shattered by the immense stream of D'Annunzio's rhetoric." He believed that Duse received permanent harm from acting in the poet's plays, from subjugating herself to all these masks without humanity. Her art, he felt, was the opposite of D'Annunzio's.

In 1902 Italy celebrated the eightieth birthday of Adelaide Ristori, with festive performances all over the country, and, of course, many articles and interviews. Ristori, who had once referred to Duse as her "younger sister," still liked her very much. The *Sketch* in London published an interview with her on January 29, 1902, in which she said: "I admire her immensely. She has an individuality which resembles that of no other actress, and, with her mobility of feature, exercises a fascination which no one escapes and which concentrates the whole attention upon her. . . . It is a pity that her repertoire is not somewhat more diverse, that one might judge better her versatility." But she was more outspoken on D'Annunzio himself. "Let us not speak of 'Gioconda,' a wound to good sense. I do not deny D'Annunzio's talent, but he must stop writing for the theater. Duse has great talent, but she is ill, neurotic, like our century."

Duse eventually wrote a thirteen-page reply—obviously

ghosted by her poet. By now she was having fits of fury at
the audience reception of D'Annunzio's plays in Italy, and proceeded to force his plays on foreign managers. She had triumphs
in Trieste and Gorizia and was pleased, completely ignoring the
fact that absolutely anything from Italy would be well received
there, in the Italian-speaking portions of the Austrian Empire.

On October 8, 1902, Duse embarked at Cherbourg for her
third tour of the United States. Originally she had planned, or
pretended to plan, a large repertoire including Goldoni, Dumas
and Sardou. But before the actual preparations were under way
she had changed her mind. It was to be D'Annunzio, and nothing but. Now came the bitter reverse of the past. In the early
1890's, in Petersburg or Vienna or Berlin, the theaters had been
empty the first night of her appearance and full the rest. Now
they were full the first night and empty the rest. The tour
opened in Boston where tickets had been auctioned off at high
prices for the first performance. It went to Philadelphia and
New York, and Duse even permitted the inclusion of Chicago
in her tour, so great was her sense of mission. The Chicago *Daily
News* called her "the greatest dramatic genius of the century"
but found *Francesca* a horrible play. The New York *Daily
Tribune* had only one word for her repertoire: odiferous. And
the Washington *Evening Star* said angrily: "Why D'Annunzio
should write a play such as *La Città Morta* is a question for that
foreigner alone to answer. But why Duse should do it and expect
Americans to accept it is a question the audience asked itself."
This reaction was not the same as the traditional moral strictures
about Dumas and Sardou. The protest indicated that the plays
were not only immoral, but poor and dull. Only James Huneker
rose in their defense: "*La Gioconda, La Città Morta*, are really
lyric masterpieces in little, though many will wince at the
themes, at their bold development and treatment. When floated
on the wings of Richard Wagner's mighty music in *Die Walküre*,
the incestuous loves of Siegmund and Sieglinde are applauded;
prose, be it as polished and as sonorous as D'Annunzio's, has not
the same privilege as music . . ." On January 14, 1903, Duse gave

Magda, her only non-D'Annunzio performance, and left to the accompaniment of the final judgment by the *Tribune:* "The distinguished Italian actress has had a season of variable fortune, making known some of the worst plays that have ever been seen."

Duse was impoverished and ill when she returned to Rome in the autumn. The Berlin banker Robert Mendelssohn, who had married her friend Giulietta Gordigiani, came to her and offered her a loan of one million lire to straighten out her finances and to give her time to rest and recover. She accepted only 300,000 lire and returned them within a year. One good result was that she entrusted her money to Mendelssohn and was personally provided for through his careful and efficient administration of her funds.

Other friends turned to help in other ways but could not save her from D'Annunzio. The break could come only in one way, in the theater, and in the end it did come.

In 1904, Duse, though ill, was persuaded by her poet to join a young company, one in which her age stood out, which was one of her poet's special pleasures in the whole relationship. It was the Talli-Gramatica-Calabresi Company. Irma Gramatica was the leading lady, and obviously D'Annunzio's relations to her were as usual prompted by his art. The great new play was *La Figlia di Jorio*, in which Duse was to act Mila Di Codra. Gramatica had agreed to wait and to take over from her only when the play went on tour in Italy. Duse was ill in Genoa during the early stages of the rehearsal, recovered, and fell ill again. Finally the poet decided that he would not wait even a few days for her recovery, and that Gramatica was to have the role from the start. It was the crowning injury, but Duse agreed though she had the right to say no. She even forced herself to send her costume for the role to Gramatica. The premiere was in Milan, on March 3, 1904, in the presence of the eighty-two-year-old Ristori. Duse, feverish in her bed in a hotel room in Genoa, that evening enacted the most pitiful scene in her relations to D'Annunzio, watched only by her faithful friend Matilde Serao. As the hour of the opening approached she became more and more excited and began to recite some of her lines from the play, in the end acting out all her lines and most of the rest, giving, according to Serao, one of the most ineffable performances of her life. After that, she sank back, exhausted but also somehow relieved and purged.

La Figlia di Jorio was D'Annunzio's one, definite success in the theater. The play had dramatic validity, its peasant setting echoed the *verismo* of Verga, and the poet was for once hailed by an audience. The irony was that his one success should be without Duse.

She stayed in Settignano for the rest of that year, in time to have another terrible scene or two with D'Annunzio, who by then had another major, not casual, mistress, the Marchesa Alexandra Carlotta di Rudinì. Duse lowered herself so far as to write to her and offer to share the poet, but Rudinì knew that Duse had no bargaining position left. Finally, Duse had a violent fit on a visit to the Capponcina, cried that she wanted to burn it down, and had to be restrained by servants. It was over. She fled across Europe and from an obscure hotel in Paris she wrote to Romain Rolland, in the depths of rejection: "Perhaps you have forgotten my name. Nevertheless I venture to recall my memory to you. I would like so much to see you again . . ."

Duse's neurasthenia and asthma may have been psychosomatic. Her figure was rather squat and inclined to stoutness, but her face, pale, intense and delicate, dominated her appearance. It had pathos in it and a certain mournfulness that could disappear fast when her interest was aroused. She was musical, loved Beethoven especially, and had a passion for the Russians. Once, at a luncheon given her by the actors of the Comédie Française, she was asked where she thought the best theater could be found. Without hesitation she replied: there is only one theater in Europe—the Russian. She was not invited back.

She read a great number of books, mostly philosophy, religion and history, and very few works related to the theater except for plays under consideration. She wanted and needed solitude, disliked the general public, ignored the audience as much as possible, and hated particularly the reporters and interviewers that pestered her continuously.

Duse wore simple clothes, often expensive, and hardly any jewelry. She was the exact opposite of Bernhardt, with her rings, spangles, bracelets, pins, and her very clear and obvious though well-chosen elegance. Duse's dresses, her lack of makeup and her whole simplicity stood out on social occasions, enhanced as they were by her natural movement and gait, those of a born aristocrat or at least the general image of aristocracy. At home she wore white, loosely fitting gowns. Her costumes were simple, too, but their rich fabric and color made up for the lack of adornment—dark red for Césarine, heavy black for Fedora, combinations of yellow and white, and gold and silver for Marguerite Gautier.

Lugné-Poe says that her rooms had to be overheated and always arranged in the same way. The bed had to be with its back to the light, and certain photographs of famous paintings by Rembrandt and Velásquez had to be there. She also had a death mask of Beethoven, and generally there was a phrase of Machiavelli's or Nietzsche's tacked up on the wall.

Her social life was small and continued mostly under duress, but she had a large, impressionistic correspondence, often conducted by means of long telegrams. During and after performances she was especially intractable. The King of Württemberg once sent his chamberlain to her dressing room, and when she declined to receive him, came himself during the following intermission. First he knocked, then almost pounded on her door, explaining who he was. No avail. The king had to leave angry. Under similar circumstances she refused to visit the Queen of Belgium in her box. After a performance she could be exalted, and completely depressed the next day. "At Monte Carlo," a friend reports, "we stayed at the Victoria, the dullest, if most aristocratic hotel in the place. But Duse has a taste for the dismal and the melancholy. She is very sad—the saddest woman I have ever known. She cannot even bear people's voices. After the strain of her performance she drives home quite alone, and sits down to her supper in solitude and silence."

After a very successful performance of *La Dame aux Camélias* in Rostow she told Princess Bajatiski the reason for her unhappiness: "Because they see only the one who is on stage. What do they know about me?"

Yvette Guilbert, who admired her greatly, said: "No one has loved suffering like Duse. She understood, better and deeper than all other great actresses, all the chants of suffering. It was the divine hymn of her life. Joy made her poorer, suffering enriched her."

The plays of D'Annunzio caused a change in her acting, which became apparent when she finally left D'Annunzio and returned to the proper sphere of drama. In the 1890's, her work had been *émotion forte*. Bahr wrote of her old form: "One did not feel at all that one saw an artificially created character, but a fearfully suffering woman, borne down and torn apart by pain, a woman under torture who uttered yells of fury and crying need, which otherwise are muffled by some reticence even in the final stages of wild abandon." The public, he knew, wanted to be shaken and moved with the utmost violence. She was, as Agate put it, "The actress for all unhappy women."

Émotion forte was impossible in the D'Annunzio plays, which combined horror and disgust with languorous verse, and with endlessly static situations full of endless speeches. It seems that Duse did learn something in playing D'Annunzio, for he could not be done like Sardou or Dumas, with quick movements, small pieces of equipment held in the hand, with "business." She had to recite, use her expressive face, and move, perhaps in the manner of Rachel—statuesque, perfectly controlled in voice and pose —rather than in the manner of Bernhardt—feline, with large strides, sudden moves and electrifying outbursts.

More than any actor or actress Duse absorbed the attention of the younger generation of continental writers—Rolland, D'Annunzio, Pirandello, Hofmannsthal and most notably Rainer

Maria Rilke. In him she evoked several philosophical and psychological considerations of the idea of appearance and reality, and the whole concept of the artistic ordering of experience that is inherent in the drama. He dedicated his early dramatic poem *Die Weisse Fürstin* (The White Princess) (1899; 1904) to her, but was afraid to bring it to her. He captured her sadness and its value to her as an actress in a poem, "Bildnis," maybe the best poem characterizing any of the four actresses. He wrote of her in the *Notebooks of Malte Laurids Brigge*.

Both he and Hofmannsthal saw something religious in her acting, something that evoked the Passion Play rather than merely the passions—the play on words is present, it seems unconsciously, in Hofmannsthal, to whom "the living artists are like the miraculous dead bodies of the saints whose touch aroused the dead and cured the blind. The living artists go through this darkening, senseless existence, and whatever they touch glows and lives."

The senseless existence—the whole generation of Housman, Hofmannsthal and Rilke could see itself reflected in that woman's restless search for meaning in life, which one can see mirrored even in her photographs, restlessly striving to be more than they are, to present an image that is more than a picture, instead of a picture that is the image of conscious artistry like the photographs of Sarah Bernhardt.

Lugné-Poe, who became her manager in 1905 after Schurmann had given up, knew and estimated her well. He was a man of considerable taste, knowledge and experience in the theater, he admired her more than any other artist, and he suffered greatly from her ways and means. Basically, he says, "once she had sown sorrow around her, she appeared serene and better tempered for the whole day." He knew also, for example, that there would be trouble before a performance of *La Femme de Claude*, but not before *La Locandiera*. No wonder the audience felt she lived the part, if, before acting Césarine, she would be a thorn in the flesh of the people around her all day.

Duse had enthralled Lugné-Poe as an actress when he first saw her in Holland in 1896. A former actor of the Théâtre Libre under Antoine, he developed his own experimental stage, le Théâtre de l'Oeuvre, which exerted a wide influence for more than thirty years and introduced many major contemporary playwrights and plays to Paris audiences. The beginning of the relationship was typical. Lugné-Poe wanted to meet Duse because his wife Suzanne Desprès was to act *La Gioconda* in Paris. Duse received them both, and talked to them, fascinated them, encouraged them to go ahead—and then played *La Gioconda* at the Vaudeville just before Desprès was to act it at the Porte-Saint-Martin.

From then on, however, Lugné-Poe was deluged with telegrams; he had evidently been chosen, and it was in the nature of Duse's power that the chosen one rarely managed to escape. Lugné-Poe insisted successfully that she drop all her D'Annunzio repertoire. She took up a few plays from the Ancient Greek, Ibsen, Gorky's *Lower Depths* and Maeterlinck's *Monna Vanna*.

In her five years with Lugné-Poe Duse's performances were not announced more than 80 to 100 times a year, and many fewer were given. That needs to be compared to Bernhardt's more than 250 performances per year. Duse was horrified at the idea of acting in the same play night after night, and always performed in repertoire only. Lugné-Poe had to dance attendance on her at the oddest hours and occasions. One time, in 1904, she called him urgently to Munich from Paris in order to tell him that she would be in Paris in ten days' time. Two days later, on hearing that Suzanne Desprès was to do *La Gioconda* in Brussels, she wrote one of her characteristic letters:

Well.
So be it.
I envy you. There's a truth.
You and Suzanne, I envy you.
You have *good work*, a good play!
A *Latin* play.

You are going to Brussels.
(And I adore Brussels.)
You do not sleep, you do not eat to find one thing.
Which *perhaps* call itself:
Art.
Perhaps *Life.*
Perhaps *love.*
Perhaps the only reality.
Perhaps . . . just the opposite.
Well,
And I detest both of you when you write to me:
"*Continue* to stay in Germany," really?

The phrase "I detest" was very frequent with Duse. She came to hate her friends because they wanted to curb her constant impatience and restlessness. She hated to be alone, yet she regretted that the actor, unlike the painter or sculptor, could not isolate himself from people. She was both intense and selfish, and did whatever she felt like doing, without regard for the consequences, or the inconveniences she caused. To combat her restlessness, she took long hot baths and often did not get out of bed for weeks. She drank bottles of Valerian for her nerves. She often changed hotels, and even more often rooms within a hotel. Lugné-Poe remembers that during one short stay at the Continental in Paris she had five different rooms.

Her day began at seven as a rule, though Lugné-Poe and Suzanne Després were often called at five or six. At seven she received her secretary, Spinelli, who had to wear a dinner jacket for the occasion. He brought her newspaper; theater gossip interested her especially. Then she dictated telegrams to friends in various places, all female, all high society. At 8:30 or so came her lady's maid and, so Lugné asserts, by that time Duse had already decided if she would play that evening. But the actual declaration did not come until 5:00 P.M. She canceled the performance if the telegrams and messages she received troubled her, or if her feeling about the public did not seem just right.

All day long she was able to absorb completely the energy of all those around her. She seemed to draw strength from exhausting them. If those she needed at the moment were not there, she sent them telegrams: "come, I am at the end of my strength! ..." Often Lugné-Poe found a friend he did not know at her bedside, just come from Russia or Scotland, and already in tears. Yet he said that anyone who thought he was Duse's real confidant was naïve.

In 1905 or 1906, at the Savoy in London, Duse called Lugné and Suzanne to come from Paris in order to straighten out some affairs with a local theater manager. Duse, though ill, kept an eye on the situation, driving the two relentlessly. When they had finally done the work, the two of them, exhausted, decided to flee from London. Just as they were about to leave the Charing Cross Hotel, where they had spent their few hours not occupied by Duse, Duse—whom they had left prostrate at the Savoy—appeared. She had sensed the impending escape and reestablished the bondage once more. On another occasion, so Edouard Schneider tells, Duse sent a telegram to a friend in Florence from a different city in Italy: "Come tomorrow, I must speak with you." The friend came on the next train, and immediately went to Duse, who said quite naturally: "I am on my way to Florence. You come with me, but you may of course have lunch before we leave." In Lugné-Poe's biography of her one can sense the tremendous love-hate that Duse managed to build up in those on whom she had any hold.

Duse was paid fabulous sums, but she spent them, largely because she kept her company all year, even when she performed no more than once a week on the average. She was kind to her artists, but distant, and neither traveled with them nor stayed in the same hotel.

Duse hated rehearsals, and had as few as possible. These rehearsals were generally held at the hotel, in her drawing room. She prepared for them with great care—she arrived at the minute fixed by her for the event. Though it was her drawing room, she

wore a hat and gloves "to make my Italians behave." She rarely
spoke her own text; the prompter gave her lines aloud. She directed, placed the actors, showed what she wanted; slowly she
elicited the reactions and lines from her cast and shaped the production until the dramatic great scene came up. Then she would
pick up the text, forget the prompter and, spectacles on her
nose, she would take hold of the scene, identify with it and carry
it through with all the strength of the public performance.

Carlo Galvani, who participated in such a rehearsal in 1905,
of *Hedda Gabler*, was told by Duse: "You don't know misfortune! If you don't, you must find it. Tell yourself that you are
unfortunate and you will see how your acting improves. I do it
well because I carry bitterness within me." With that she beat
her breast once and tears came into her eyes. Then she controlled herself and the rehearsal continued. Sara Teasdale wrote
her *Sonnets to Duse* at about that time, and the first one begins:

> Oh beauty that is filled so full of tears,
> Where every passing anguish left its trace . . .

Because she believed that she was an unfortunate being in a
necessarily cruel world, she was good and generous to a fault.
She gave without asking questions and was often the victim of
schemers. She was extremely kind and considerate of the unfortunate, the sick and poor, and equally inconsiderate of everyone else. She liked to be pitied and said many things intended to
elicit sympathy, about her health, her appearance, her loves, her
losses, etc.

As an example of her kindness, in London she heard once that
old Rossi, her director in Turin, was in straitened circumstances.
She wrote him a perfectly charming letter of reminiscence in
which she explained that she wanted to show her esteem for him
both privately and publicly. She had long considered how that
could be done. She was to take an extended holiday in the following year that she would like to interrupt once. "I thought
to give myself a pleasure and have an evening in your honor, in
Rome, for example, next year, in which I ask the favor of being

permitted to participate." That is—if the idea appealed to him at all, if he would be so kind.

In London, in the spring of 1904, Suze Rueff was in Sarah Bernhardt's dressing room during *La Dame aux Camélias*. Duse had come quietly and unobtrusively, to see the death scene, and found no empty seat in the house. The two embraced and, while Sarah sent someone to arrange for a place for her guest, they conversed, or tried to. Rueff noted the strain and slipped out of the room.

Sarah still managed to damn her with great praise. In 1905, when she found that Duse was planning another season in Paris, she once more offered her her theater. That time Duse declined, in one of her short-sentence, emotional letters in which she thanked her, but also said "Your hospitality—never have I forgotten it, never shall I forget it"; and added that she could not forget Sarah's frequently expressed opinions of her (Duse's) art.

In Paris in that autumn of 1905, Lugné-Poe produced Gorky's *Lower Depths* in his theater at her suggestion. The critics applauded, but the public stayed away. So Duse acted in it for one evening—in Italian, with the French cast—to bring in the public, and succeeded brilliantly. She effaced herself, put Suzanne Després in the foreground, and insisted on a salary of 10 francs, the lowest in the cast.

Lugné-Poe arranged tours to South America, to Scandinavia, and throughout Europe. She was in Vienna almost every year, as much of a favorite there as Sarah was in London. After D'Annunzio Duse gave hardly any performances in Italy but had more and more extended tours, and more and more frequent cancellations. From those trying years Lugné-Poe remembers her acts of kindness, for he loved her in spite of his finding her a terrible trial. After seeing Suzanne Després in *Doll's House*, Duse sent her her own costumes as Nora, to have and to keep. Després was Nora incarnate, she said, and she herself would not act it again. In 1906 Duse came to London from Florence specifically to participate in the Ellen Terry Jubilee. She herself declined any such celebration for herself.

Her love for Ibsen's plays prompted her to tour Scandinavia once more in 1905–1906, but the main object of the tour was not achieved. She came too late to see Ibsen himself, who was near death by then, and the knowledge of her failure sent her to her sickbed at once, from which the good nature and musicianship of Dr. Egeberg, rather than his skill as a physician, rescued her in the end. It was small consolation to have Edvard Grieg attend her performance of *Rosmersholm* and applaud through eleven curtain calls.

Duse's illnesses had recurred with increasing frequency during her travels. In 1905 she had tried to retire, and returned to the stage after a few weeks in spite of doctor's orders. In 1909 it became imperative to stop. Lugné-Poe simply declined to be responsible for her further appearances. After a performance of *Rosmersholm* in Vienna Duse suddenly announced her retirement.

CHAPTER 12 / A Legend

IN 1914, the President of the French Republic awarded the Cross of the Legion of Honor to Sarah Bernhardt. The Legion of Honor is not a very rare decoration, but it was a rare occasion nevertheless: no actress, in her capacity of actress, had ever received it, and even now the citation tried to pass lightly over that embarrassing fact. Sarah could have had the award much sooner if she had been willing to accept it as director of her theater, as professor at the Conservatoire—anything. But she had stubbornly insisted, and now she had won, providing another milestone in the transformation of the actor from the servant to whom a nobleman might throw a large coin, to the member in good standing of high society.

In part the change was an unconscious recognition of an industry—it came to be called that in the twentieth century—that was rapidly growing in size and affluence. In 1880 the United States and Canada, for example, had 3,500 cities in which performances took place in a total of 5,000 theaters. There were 250 traveling companies apart from the much larger number of resident organizations. In 1912 there were 6,000 theater towns with a total of 8,000 houses in the two countries.

Sarah Bernhardt's position in the first decade of the twentieth century was one no other actress had ever enjoyed. When she was in the United States the newspapers chronicled whose dinner invitations she accepted; the Boston *Traveler* complained in 1910, during her stay in the city, that "stage women" used to accept the invitations of society with great eagerness, but "today they are almost as difficult as royalty to approach." At that pinnacle in society Sarah resided, not as the wife of a tycoon, but as a tycoon in her own right.

No tycoon, however, was adulated like her. "After a performance of *Phèdre* or *La Dame aux Camélias*, sometimes after *Tosca*, I have seen great ladies kneel before her and kiss the hem of her gown, produce a small pair of scissors from their bag or pocket and, with great dexterity snip a bit as a souvenir." Suze Rueff attributes that to her acting, but there is more involved here, quite clearly, and not necessarily anything that Sarah or the worshiper consciously understood. Reynaldo Hahn, too, remarked on "the applause of the English matinees, the frenzied applause of women and girls," even after a perfunctory performance of *La Dame aux Camélias*. He also describes Miss L., "a romantic old maid," who "has made of her sitting room an altar sacred to Sarah, loaded with photographs—with trifles she has worn and even touched—a pair of gloves, a garter, some artificial violets, a hairpin. And this altar is eternally renewed, dressed with flowers, lit up." She visits Sarah, is too shy to look up, merely says "Oui, Madame chérie; non, Madame chérie," and asks Sarah's permission to attend her performances as if they were a religious rite.

Suze Rueff also remembers from her childhood the time Sarah invited her to lunch. The headmistress of her school would not let her go alone and Miss Seeley, the English mistress, therefore had to accompany her. When Sarah received them "to my amazement Miss Seeley knelt down before Madame Sarah and kissed the hem of her gown. I was somewhat taken aback, for I had never seen this done before, though I was to see it many times afterwards." Sarah once expressed the romance of her appeal by saying: "Avant ma mort je suis entrée dans la légende."

Schurmann, Duse's manager, had a more practical view of the power of the great actress. "A feminine success," he said, "in the best sense of the word, is the most lasting of all, since an enthusiastic woman generally carries along her husband, her husband's friends and all her relatives to the box office." Sarah knew this aspect, too, of course. The advance program of her tour of

the United States in 1896 is consciously and deliberately addressed to women only. In it Sarah is quoted abundantly on the
subject of the cultural rise of American womanhood: "Yes, I
adore this country, in which woman reigns, and reigns so absolutely. She comes and goes. She orders, wills, exacts, instructs,
spends money recklessly and gives no thanks. This shocks some
people, but it only charms me." The tone is belligerent. Magda
was her most important new role that season, and the main
theme of that play, in the words of that curious feminist, Bernard Shaw, is "the revolt of the modern woman against that ideal
of home which exacts the sacrifice of her whole life to its care."

Sarah was conscious of the influence actresses could exert on
the position of all women because she knew that the theater was
one of the few professions in which women outshone men. She
knew that she embodied in her way of life and in her status the
aspirations of a whole new class of women. Her manner of life
encouraged freedom, her whole being stood for a kind of independence that was as far from submission to a male society and
to public opinion as any in the past. After 1890, when she was
reaching towards fifty and when the inclinations of women were
beginning to concentrate on the New Woman, the Twelve
Pound Look, and the Suffragette, Bernhardt, more than any
other, stood out as a symbol of the aspirations of her sex.

Sarah's role in female emancipation was clearest perhaps on
her United States tour of 1910–1911, because it came near the
height of the suffragette movement. Though not a suffragette,
she liked the movement and found it useful for her purposes. A
play on Joan of Arc was in her repertoire and the combination
of Sarah and Joan exercised a particularly strong influence. On
her arrival in New York on October 30 she was met by one
hundred women belonging to the Joan of Arc Suffrage League,
led by their president. Every woman carried a cane bearing a
yellow pennant on which the name of the League was inscribed.
A pennant embedded in a bouquet of chrysanthemums was presented to Sarah. Both sides seem to have been profited: the suf-

fragettes used Sarah's fame as much as she used them for her
publicity.

Amidst all the royal treatment, an occasional observation crept
into a review that season intimating that the redoubtable institution, The Divine Sarah, was no longer what it used to be.
Though the reviews praised her, and deprecated, for example,
the younger generation of actors and actresses, players such as
Maude Adams or Ethel Barrymore who "rose to fame despite
the fact that their modes of pantomimic expression might have
been counted on the fingers of one hand," they liked Sarah
mainly because she belonged "to the old-fashioned school of
Scribe and Sardou." Sarah did not like nostalgia and did not
want to be a relic, but it was becoming more and more difficult
not to stand still and let the world pass by.

Most of her time was now spent in revivals of old productions
—*L'Aiglon, La Tosca, La Dame aux Camélias, La Samaritaine.*
The only new play of 1909–1910 was *Le Procès de Jeanne d'Arc*
by Emile Moreau, in which she moved the audience deeply
when she answered the Bishop of Beauvais who asked her her
age. Sarah half turned to the audience and replied with utter
simplicity: "Seventeen years." Witness after witness reports that
she seemed it, too, at that moment. She was then sixty-five. *Le
Procès de Jeanne d'Arc,* however, had one other point in its
favor: As it dealt with a trial it permitted Sarah to sit most of
the time. Her knee had been worsening every year since 1905,
and movement was becoming increasingly difficult for her. In
the last years she had had to change the death scene of *Tosca:*
she no longer jumped off the parapet; she was now shot by the
soldiers.

If Sarah had been less completely indomitable, the decline
would have dismayed her. In the autumn of 1910, at the Coliseum in St. Martin's Lane in London, she appeared in a one-act
play. The Coliseum was not a regular theater, but a music hall
with trapeze artists, jugglers and trained animals. It may sound
worse now than it seemed at the time, for the music halls paid
extremely well and Sarah needed the money badly. She hesitated

because it aged her: Other aging actors and actresses of fame had used such circus means to support themselves. In fact while Sarah performed at the Coliseum, Réjane did Act II of *Madame Sans-Gêne* and Jane Hading Act IV of *La Femme X* at the London Hippodrome.

In October Bernhardt, now a great-grandmother, embarked for the United States once more. Her leading man was Lou Tellegen, twenty-seven years old, a large, robust man who had once been a model of Rodin's. She opened at the Studebaker Theatre in Chicago on October 31, with *L'Aiglon*, and performed across the United States for eight months, in her usual repertoire.

The seats at the Studebaker cost one, two and three dollars, no longer the fabulous prices of the 1880's. Otherwise the effect was tremendous. The efforts of the age of public relations seem small compared to the tide of newspaper publicity which swelled around Sarah. Page after page was devoted to her long before her arrival: "Divine Sarah on Way Here." "Bernhardt is Coming Here." "Sarah Bernhardt Sails for U.S." Once her performances had begun, the Waterbury *American*, for example, wrote, "At Sixty Six Bernhardt Bedevils Chicago," and gave it the sub-heading: "City Falls Down to Worship at her Shrine." Her publicity stretched to papers in towns where she would never be seen: the Wilkes-Barre, Pa., *Record;* the Jamestown, N.Y., *Journal;* the Watertown, N.Y., *News;* the Wichita *Eagle;* the Macon, Ga., *News,* and hundreds more.

The first American performance of *La Samaritaine*, in Chicago on November 10, was reviewed all over the country, and the commotion about putting Christ on stage was tremendous. A bill establishing censorship was introduced into the Pennsylvania legislature in an attempt to prevent her performance of that play in the state. Tempers rose so high that mounted police was used to escort Sarah from the Philadelphia railroad station to the Bellevue-Stratford Hotel, and the Director of Public Safety ordered the management to withdraw the play. Sarah was stubborn and performed anyway, and managed once more to be front-page news all over the country.

Sarah still played every evening and three matinees per week. The receipts were still fabulous: two weeks at the Studebaker in Chicago earned $54,000, of which $40,000, or eighty per cent, were for her and her company; she was seen by twenty-three thousand people. Apart from these statistics her timeless youth was the single thing mentioned most often. She enhanced it carefully in the interviews she gave. She predicted that she would die of a heart disease on stage, in full view of the public; she gave the recipe for eternal youth: "Eat lemons, work hard and say your prayers to the dear God," which was faithfully reproduced in hundreds of newspapers.

In Europe that winter she added something new to her repertoire: teaching. She undertook to give a master class in acting to a group of about twenty young girls, mostly English and American, for which the fee seems to have been very steep. The English actress May Agate and the American Elibabeth Mack left written records of the course, which illustrate better than anything the feeling of royalty that surrounded Sarah. The class was held on the stage of the Théâtre Sarah Bernhardt at 11 A.M.

> . . . outside the stage-door, in the Avenue Victoria, any morning of that winter, shortly before eleven o'clock, one would see a strip of red carpet unrolled, a group that would now be called "fans," but were then known as "admirers," would gather on the pavement, wet or fine, to await the descent from her car of Madame Sarah. Under a fur wrap she would be wearing some pale, clinging gown, high necked and low-waisted, flowing down to her delicately shod feet . . . Malmaison carnations sent daily from London would be pinned to her corsage, the wearer clutching a capacious-looking brocade bag. For in spite of thin shoes and strips of carpet, Madame Sarah was nothing if not practical-minded—and there were bunches of keys, numerous jewels and cash to be carried about!

The scene inside resembled a court of ladies-in-waiting drawn up around a throne, rather than a class. It was all very ceremonious and formal. Mme. Bernhardt was preceded by a maid who brought a small cushion of gold satin, as if a crown were resting on it, which was deposited on the throne where there were a number of pillows previously prepared. Everyone rose as Mme. Sarah entered and remained standing while she greeted her intimates, had pillows and lamp adjusted and finally received the class book from the maid. Then she noted that the girls were still standing, and, as if surprised, requested them to be seated. At that point, according to Elizabeth Mack, the hardiest of them sprang forward and dropped to her knees before the Queen, offering her a bouquet of orchids. When it had been accepted and exclaimed about, the other girls, one by one, stepped forward, with carnations, violets, roses, each devoutly kissing the Great Lady's hand. After the opening ceremony, Sarah listened patiently to the work prepared for recitation. She rarely got angry at any of them, and at times she recited for them, magnificently, some passage from *Phèdre* or *Andromaque*. Even here she gave her money's worth. May Agate, who became a major actress, declares that she learned much in her course.

Toward the end of the course, the classes had to be held at her house, however, because she was ill. When she sat there, all in white, under a life-size portrait of herself, also in white, Elizabeth Mack reflected that she had lost none of her grace and charm. She was nearing seventy, and still worked most of her usual day, as she had since 1880. She rose at 9:00, received some people while taking her bath, went to the theater at 10:30 to teach, lunched at noon and rehearsed usually from one to six. At seven she dressed for curtain time at eight. Sometimes she still listened to a new play after midnight.

The season of 1911–1912 had been a swan song of a sort. Sarah had undertaken her last full-length costume play, about Queen Elizabeth of England. The visit of the shy young Prince of Wales, later King Edward VIII, could only recall his grandfather and namesake of thirty years before. Even the great jubilee of October 23, 1912, could not hide the fact that her situation was not good. It contained, among other events, the "British

National Tribute to Sarah Bernhardt," consisting of one hundred thousand signatures collected all over the British Empire
to commemorate the fiftieth anniversary of her debut on stage.
For an old woman who had had more adulation perhaps than
any in history, it did not mean as much any more as it would
have before. She needed one hundred thousand dollars.

Robert Gross, the brother of the manager Maurice Gross,
wrote an article called "The Real Bernhardt" in *Theatre Magazine* at about that time, in which he reflected on her finances.
Managers, he said, always have to give her between fifteen and
twenty-five thousand dollars before each American tour, as an
advance for which she offers her life insurance as a security.
Where, he wondered, did the money go? It went into many
things. She had bought her estate at Belle-Isle for 20,000 francs,
but by the time the whole complex with its houses and cottages
was finished, she had spent four million. At one point some enter-
prising gentleman had built a hotel on the edge of her property,
for sightseers come to gape at the Great Lady. She bought it to
regain her privacy. The money also went into the failures at her
theaters, into the pockets of her son Maurice, and of lots of
others, into masses of flowers and the rest of the decor which
she had first needed for her status and which had become second
nature. Money was beginning to be harder to find, and she
needed it as much as ever.

Usually four or five years elapsed between Sarah's tours of the
United States. In 1912, however, after a mere eighteen months,
she returned, with a small company this time, doing one-act
plays under the management of Martin Beck, mostly in music
halls, "numbers" lasting for thirty to forty-five minutes.

The usual gossip said that she went because Paris refused to
accept Lou Tellegen as a star, but it is more likely that Paris
refused to yield the necessary money, now that she herself could
no longer perform as much as before. Sarah had been suspected
of liaisons with many men—with almost all the men who worked
with her at some point, from Victor Hugo, forty-two years her
senior, to Edmond Rostand, two years younger than her son

Maurice. Lou Tellegen at twenty-seven was much more than
two years younger than Maurice Bernhardt, and the fact that
the suspicion could arise attests, perhaps, Sarah's claim to eternal
youth, and the willingness of the public to grant it, more than
anything else.

Tellegen was not as completely without talent as his detractors
would wish. Sarah never, not even with Damala, tolerated a
completely hopeless case on stage. He left Sarah in 1913, stayed
in America to act in silent films after she went home to Paris in
May and subsequently married the singer Geraldine Farrar. We
have a visual record of Lou Tellegen, not only in America but
in France, for Sarah had undertaken yet another new task in
1912. She had made two films, one of her new play *Queen Elizabeth*, the other, of course, of *La Dame aux Camélias*. Both are
such sad caricatures of Sarah's work that one must give Tellegen
the benefit of a doubt, at least in the hope that he was better
than the dreadful pasteboard Essex of that production.

The film of *Queen Elizabeth* seems to have used the stage sets
of the play, and a great procession (which looks puny after
Griffiths and De Mille) forms its visual climax. Sarah looks amaz-
ingly young as the old Queen Elizabeth, and the film gives her
opportunities, in rapid succession, to act Love, Anger, Greatness, Queenliness, Remorse, Fury, and Death, the latter by falling
dramatically on a previously placed, enormous pillow. Sarah did
not believe in films and used this particular one as an attempt
to recoup some of the 200,000 francs she had lost in the production of the play itself.

The film of *La Dame aux Camélias* unrolls with lightning
speed. Here her limping is apparent—she moves from chair to
table, very deftly disguising that both are needed to hold her up
with less pain. She wears a tremendous fur-piece to leave Auteuil
after her interview with Armand's father, and in the scene near
the gambling table she has one momentary appealing gesture—
one second in which an attentive observer can get a glimpse of
what Sarah may have been. As for the rest, even the famous
dropping of the handkerchief in the final scene is nothing.

In the early 1900's Sarah could still bring a Paris audience to its feet—literally—with a line in *Andromaque* in a *matinée classique*. In 1913, she seemed no longer ageless. The Austrian critic Julius Bab saw her then in *La Dame aux Camélias*. He was horrified at her makeup and dress—a dressed-up corpse. But even then, when she began to act, one could see the great transformation: her voice, her facial expression at moments made her young.

On March 15, 1914, she undertook once more a revival of *La Dame aux Camélias* in Paris. It was to be her last. In May, during a performance in Charleroi in Belgium, she fell on stage and when she tried to rise she found that she could not move her right leg any more. It still was not her last performance. She was scheduled to perform once more, and she did, holding on to furniture and stopping to hold her breath when the pain was too great. Then she went to Belle-Isle. At the end of the following month the Archduke Francis Ferdinand was assassinated in Sarajevo, and in the general end her particular one was submerged.

Duse also became involved in films; it was the only acting she did in the decade of her retirement. The difference between her and Bernhardt emerges here, as everywhere. To Bernhardt the film was theater transferred to a technical process, and something to make money with. Beyond that it was of no interest to her. Duse, on the other hand, thought about it and reached a number of valid and interesting general conclusions, and also saw that she could do nothing about them.

To her the film was an entirely new field, and it was an error to put old wine into new bottles. She did, of course, not live to see talking pictures, only the silent film, and she thought that its great advantage was its silence and its consequent avoidance of the babble of languages and voices. It could avoid confusion, but it needed a new art. She regretted that she was not young enough any more to devote herself to it, or to see its full development.

She had proposals from all over the world for making films, including one from David Griffith, whom she admired greatly. She negotiated with many, but finally gave all film producers one generic designation—"monsters"—and stopped. She did make one film, however, which is preserved: *Cenere* (1916). Artistically, it is greatly superior to Sarah's films. It can be seen without embarrassment, even in the dramatic movements when, for example, Duse beats her head against the wall in anguish. It is not a play *manqué*, but a film with indoor and outdoor scenes that relate to each other; it is the story of a mother who delivers up her little son to his father, a soulless mill-owner, in the early scenes. Duse's face is not shown in them, only her movements and her back, because she would have seemed the grandmother rather than the mother of the child. Still a decade younger in 1916 than Bernhardt in 1912, she looks a decade older than her former rival.

In the second part of the film, the son returns, now a grown man, to see his mother, and here one can get glimpses of the greatness of Duse, of the amplitude and perfect proportion of her movement. The film, it is true, had progressed rapidly in the four years since Bernhardt had made her productions, but still the difference is greater than that span of time between the Keystone Cops at Queen Elizabeth's Court, and the old peasant woman's face lighting up as she sees her son, and the deep bow she gives him—her master, one feels at once, by virtue of class and education. When she finds that her son loves her, the change in her is slow and believable, and the end, her death, is moving. Apart from her performance the film is an ordinary tear jerker.

The years on either side of *Cenere* were restless and unhappy for Duse. Before her retirement, her tours with their constant movement and change of scene had appeased her restlessness. Now her travels became unnecessary and invested with a sense of futility and repetition.

A deepening sense of futility pervaded all her plans. In Florence, and even in the small town of Asolo where she lived later, she constantly kept hotel rooms as well as her permanent house.

At one point, Edouard Schneider writes, she had three apartments in Florence, two of which she never inhabited. Furniture was being moved about constantly. Once, later on, when her money had run out, a friend invited her to move into a carefully prepared apartment in Rome; she accepted with joy, but on the morning of departure from Florence to Rome she handed her friend a letter declining the invitation: "I do not work, I contribute nothing, and I cannot accept a deliverance of any kind which I have not earned." Truth, action, work, Schneider says, were three of her most frequently used words.

One catches glimpses of her in those years: at a castle in Touraine where a young Austrian girl, a poet, sees her, and deeply moved, gives her one of her poems; Duse's reply is bitter: "Heart, talent! That is too much, my dear. Mediocrity is the true gift of the Gods." At times she stays in Pirano, at a monastery. Then she is at Viareggio with Isadora Duncan. She is deeply grieved about the death of Isadora's two young children in an auto accident in France and finds it hard to accept Isadora's wish to surmount her grief and return to an active life: "Isadora, do not seek good fortune. You carry on your forehead the sign of the elect." The elect, that is Duse's theme, must suffer because they are the elect. That is her main consolation, but really her apology for her life's achievement as an artist.

Other glimpses of Duse—in 1911, in a theater in Ravenna, she is absorbed by the play and unconsciously leaves the rear of the box where she usually sits in the theater; she is recognized and cheered. She then decides to return to the stage, but changes her mind again. In 1912 she meets Yvette Guilbert in Italy; the two become animated by a plan for a joint tour of university towns in the United States; they would hold readings of literary and dramatic works. Again she drops the project. In the same year she turns down a proposal from Max Reinhardt, transmitted through the actor Alexander Moissi.

On occasion she sees Enrichetta, who hardly speaks Italian and eventually marries an Englishman, Edward Bullough, a professor at Cambridge. Duse, so her friend Olga Signorelli reports,

sent a telegram to Enrichetta every day of her adult life. On the
day of her wedding she sent none, and did not send any more.
Enrichetta, she rationalized, did not need her any more.

Her capacity for absorbing people's attention and for drain-
ing them emotionally had not disappeared. During the summer
of 1912 Duse and Rainer Maria Rilke were both in Venice, and
saw each other almost every day for several weeks. Rilke, sensitive and shy, is greatly moved by her. His letters of that summer,
mostly to the Princess Thurn und Taxis, are witness to this
gradually complete absorption by her concerns, fears and hurts.
He feels a kinship for her sadness and sensitivity and is drawn
into her net of sorrow and melancholy. He is appalled at the
waste and tragedy of her life and gradually, like so many, inches
towards the desperate attempt to help when no help is possible.
"I would give much," he writes, "if I could bring Duse to a
happy thought, to the beginning of hope . . ." Then he begins
to hope himself: can one find her a play, a theater, a reality
worthy of her, to allow her to work, to keep her from simply
disappearing? Here "at some unseen point tragedy flows from
a vessel that is after all merely toppled over and not broken."
He feels the imperative need in the end to have Duse perform,
even under the simplest conditions, for the sake of art and man,
not for her own sake as such. Much of his time in 1912 and 1913
is spent in trying to find the play and the occasion, and by the
summer of war, 1914, he is still trying.

In June 1920, Rilke came to Venice for the first time after
the war. Duse arrived shortly after, and the threat of a repetition of the summer of 1912 prompted him to pack his suitcases
at once and go to Switzerland. Though he was sorry later, he
knew that he could not bear her again.

In 1913 Duse participated in an international woman's congress in Rome. She was no suffragette, however, and did not
believe in male-female competition. In 1914 she founded a home
for young actresses in Rome, the *Casa delle Attrici* in the Via
Nomentana. She donated 10,000 lire to begin with, and interested the Queen and ladies of society in the project. The house

opened in May, 1914, a pleasant, airy, sunny place for talking and reading, stocked with many good books. But it was not a home for young actresses, only an anguished old woman's idea of what would have been good for her in her youth: a home, contact with other girls of her age, reading and self-improvement. But girls who want to become famous need clothes and men, and the Actress' Home would have collapsed of its own basic concepts if the war had not come.

Italy joined the First World War in 1915. Duse did not act at the front, perhaps because she felt too keenly the suffering of the soldiers in the trenches to be able to entertain them. She often stayed in Udine, however, which until the Italian defeat at Caporetto served as army headquarters. She wrote letters for soldiers whom she visited in hospitals, and did hundreds of obscure, unpublicized good deeds for individuals. In the great human disaster she finally could lose her sense of private disaster and give herself fully to others, asking nothing in return. Here she was at her best, displaying in the service of others that fine sensitivity to their feelings which, in supposedly happier days, she had used to draw the sensitive into her net. Toward the end of the war she rented a small house in Asolo, at the foot of the Alps and very close still to the front line. It was as much a home to her in her last years as she ever had.

D'Annunzio, who had fled his creditors to France before the war, really came into his own in 1914. A man so obsessed with gore and chauvinism needed a holocaust, and his first effort was to draw Italy into it. His inflammatory proclamations contributed to the strength of the war party. When he finally returned from France to Italy in 1915, he was welcomed as a national hero by many, and gave a speech which did much to force the not unwilling hands of the Italian government. Shortly afterwards it declared war against Austria-Hungary and Germany. One by-product of his intense patriotic fervor was that he became inviolable to his old creditors who were still awaiting his return; nobody would have dared to be so unpatriotic as to take the national hero into court. In spite of his age D'Annunzio managed to join in the fighting, and now he was in his element: women, luxury in a Venetian palazzo, and daring exploits that culminated in the first air raid of the war over Vienna. He had the makings of the renaissance condottiere in him, and the war gave him a full share of glory. It comes as a relief, almost, to realize that, given the opportunity, he could live up to his high standards of bravery and defiance of death.

Duse had no glory at all in the usual sense but immersed herself in obscure service. She was aware of D'Annunzio's exploits and bombing raids on Austrian naval bases, and sent him a series of letters and telegrams to warn him of dangers and to counsel him, signing herself mostly "Consolazione," their old pet name for herself.

Sarah Bernhardt also had glory, as typical for her character as that of Duse and D'Annunzio. She returned from Belle-Isle to Paris on July 28. Four days later France and Germany were at war and she was urged to leave the capital. In early September, as the Germans were approaching Paris for the second time in her life, she acquiesced; she took a last taxi ride down the Champs Elysées, remembering the last war, the one of 1870, and wondering, so Lysiane tells us, quietly, if she would ever return. Paris had always been a trial to her artistically, not like London or New York, but she loved it all the more, and she was a patriot. She went to Andernos, near Bordeaux where the French Government went soon after. This time, however, the enemy did not succeed in reaching Paris.

Dr. Pozzi, who had operated on Sarah's leg in 1898, put it in a plaster cast after her fall in Charleroi, to curb the constant pain. Now in the late autumn she had the cast removed to see if rest and immobility had led to any improvement. The pain returned almost immediately and it was finally decided that the last hope lay in amputating the leg. Sarah was advised against it because of her age, but the only alternative—a bed-ridden existence for the rest of her life—was worse. The operation took place on February 22, 1915. Sarah infused her friends, her doctors and her associates of many years with courage. She was the one who joked and reassured them—not the other way. Nine days after the operation she had her first crisis of uremia, but in April she was back in Andernos making plans for the future. In August she returned to Paris and on August 26 was present at the reopening of her theater. When she was carried into her box the entire audience rose for an endless ovation.

She quickly gave up any hope of using an artificial leg. A light sedan chair was constructed instead in which she would now be carried everywhere. In 1916 she was carried to the front, to perform before the soldiers less than a mile behind the front line trenches. With infinite patience and infinite patriotism, she went from post to post with her recitations. One does not know how the soldiers received her, and whether her presence had any meliorating effect on the men afflicted with the beastliness of trench warfare. She tried.

As soon as she could she performed in a short play that permitted her to remain seated in one place, *Les Cathédrales*, which she also gave at the Théâtre Sarah Bernhardt for two weeks, and then carried to England and America.

It was a patriotic piece that brought on stage some heroines of French history and legend, against the background of the great French cathedrals. Sarah impersonated the cathedral of Strasbourg, the city that had been in German hands since 1871.

By spring she was on tour. She left France not to escape the war, but forced by the imperative necessity to make money. She was also recognized as the cultural ambassador of France, her most famous citizen, to allied Britain and the neutral United States. In April she performed *L'Une D'Elles*, a one-act play by her granddaughter Lysiane, at the Coliseum in London. In one performance, May Agate reports, Sarah rose from her chair on stage—so strongly and so well that all expected she had forgotten her debility and would fall headlong on stage. The whole audience gasped, and Ellen Terry cried out loud. Sarah merely leaned across the table, happy with the effect achieved.

On September 30, 1916, she sailed for New York and her fourth and final American farewell tour. The tour was to take

almost two years, due to a long interruption by illness and another operation. She suffered most grievously perhaps from the
deficiencies of her repertoire though she was ingenious in her
choices: The fifth act of *La Dame aux Camélias*, the trial scene
from *The Merchant of Venice*, where she was sometimes Portia,
sometimes Shylock; *La Mort de Cleopâtre, Le Procès de Jeanne
d'Arc*; a small piece by her son Maurice; *Les Cathédrales*. She
could not do a real play, she could no longer create a full-size
character, she had a small, third-rate company—she was really
doing stunts, not acting. She could still enthuse the undergrad-
uates at Harvard, and bring the audience to fervent cheers when,
shortly before the entry of the United States into the War, she
would recite the *Marseillaise*. But she also knew that she was
described in her publicity as the Oldest Woman on Earth. True,
a man would have to be going on three score to remember her
first appearance in America in 1880. Once, after watching the
magician Houdini perform in Boston, she took him home in her
limousine and suddenly put her hand on his shoulder and said:
"Houdini, give me back my leg." She was serious. Uremia set
in again in March 1917, and an operation was necessary. The
entry of the United States into the war in the following month
did much for her morale and strengthened her to continue her
tour. On November 11, 1918, Armistice Day, her ship docked
in Bordeaux, and she learned the news.

After the joy came the anti-climax. She was deathly tired of
circuses and stunts. She had no play she could do, and for eighteen months she did not perform.

Her real heroism was quiet. In spite of all the millions she had
made she needed more, or believed she needed more, and could
not rest. The money was no longer for herself; she was nearing
eighty. It was for her son Maurice, who was now incurably ill
and could not have supported himself now even if he had ever
done so. He had paralysis agitans and by 1920 he could not eat
by himself any more. He survived his mother by five years.

Her return to the stage was dignified and in a way a triumph.
A cunningly devised production of Racine's *Athalie*, begun

during Holy Week in April 1920, carried through twenty-five performances, as long a series as that beautiful but static religious work has ever had. But one cannot continue a career with one very undramatic play. The summer of 1920 Sarah spent as usual at Belle-Isle, telling stories to her young friends, and never letting her personal anxiety about her future and that of her son dim the joy and tranquillity of others. Though she ate extremely little by now, and drank nothing except milk, which was almost her entire sustenance, she took great pains still to devise menus for her guests. She had at times dabbled in writing: a book about her experience in a balloon, three one-act plays, a new version of *Adrienne Lecouvreur*. Except for her autobiography none mattered much. Now, in her last three years, she produced two novels and a book about acting, intended to bring in some money.

In the autumn she finally had a new play. Louis Verneuil, the fiancé of her granddaughter Lysiane and a writer of light comedies, concocted a piece called *Daniel* in which she did not have to move, did not appear until the third act and died at the end of the fourth. Verneuil reports that when he read it to her in the spring of 1920 she was so moved that, with tears in her eyes, she could only murmur "thanks."

Maurice Rostand, the son of her poet, who also wrote a play for her in her final years, says in his book about her that she played a worthless play by the worthless husband of Lysiane, and that she said of it: "I know very well that it is junk, junk, junk." Verneuil, in turn, in his book about Sarah asserts modestly that he saved her career with the two plays he wrote for her, and that she also performed a rotten little play by Edmond Rostand's son. The truth is that the confines of what could be done for her and with her were so narrow that a good play would have been a miracle; and that in any case the quality of the play did not matter.

The editor of *Comoedia* appealed to critics and others who came to the first performance of *Daniel* on November 5 to bring at least one flower for Sarah. The flowers rained on her at the end, even from the critics who simply praised her for sixty years of greatness, not for that one event.

In 1921 she went the rounds once more, London in April, Madrid in May, always carried in her chair. In October came *La Gloire*, the play by Maurice Rostand, which was superior to Verneuil's melodrama but, on the other hand, a poem and an intellectual exercise more than a play. Yet it was an enormous success; the public was grateful to see Sarah once more, and in something more exalted than Verneuil's play. She came down with her third major attack of uremia at the time of its opening, but played on, with a strength that really did not seem human any more. In February and March 1922 she gave forty-eight performances in six weeks, in the French provinces. On April 20 she opened with the last play she ever performed, Verneuil's *Régine Armand*.

Arthur Mayer wanted to arrange a world-wide Sarah Bernhardt Benefit, to take place in every city she had ever played. She refused, saying that she wanted to have only the money she earned herself. She went on earning it, in 1922 and 1923. She could not, it is true, earn much, and she could not change her spending habits in her old age, but she tried. With *Régine Armand* she went to the Low Countries once more, to Switzerland, and through the French provinces, traveling in her special car whose large doors could accommodate her litter. In the autumn of 1922 she went to Italy. Near Marseilles she had an auto accident in which her car was smashed. Now she had to travel by train, being handed up and down the steep steps time after time, sitting up for hours in great discomfort. On top of that the Italian public was turning indifferent and the theaters were empty. It was a pitiful final journey which ended in Turin on November 30, with a performance of *Daniel*.

She returned to Paris, and took up yet another play, *Un Sujet de Roman* by Sacha Guitry, the son of her old partner Lucien, a much better role than any she had had since her return to the stage. She put her energy and enthusiasm into the rehearsals and looked forward to the public dress rehearsal (*répétition gén-*

érale) on December 23. One hour before the performance she fainted in her dressing room. Her fourth attack of uremia had come. And still she did not give up: She could not appear on stage any more, but she could make a film. As she could not go out, the studio came to her. "Bernhardt, Dying, Acts for Movies," was a headline in the Boston Sunday *Advertiser* for March 18. She acted in *La Voyante*, which was not completed.

Twelve days before her death she still insisted on attending the opening of a new play by Maurice Rostand. After the first act, a witness reports, almost the entire audience filed past her and each one kissed her hand. A few days later she asked the widow of Francisque Sarcey to come and see her. Mme. Sarcey expected to find her in bed. No, Sarah was up, make-up in place, in a rose satin robe, with a corsage of roses, enthroned in the library. She spoke kindly while a faint sweat of agony was visible on her forehead. Nellie Melba came to visit her, too, and found her ready for her great death scene, with rouge, lipstick and wig. "Ah, Melba," she said, "you still have your golden voice. My golden voice no longer needs me because I am dying." At the moment of farewell the pose disintegrated and Sarah clung sobbingly to her old friend.

Once, in 1936, riding through New York in a cab, Mrs. Patrick Campbell talked about Sarah to James Agate: "[Mrs. Pat] told me how she dined with Sarah three nights before she died. Sarah was wearing a dress of pink Venetian velvet with long sleeves, sent for the occasion by Sacha Guitry. Knowing she had not long to live, she sat there with a white face eating nothing and infinitely gracious. Her son, Maurice, was at the table, paralysed, and fed by his wife. At the end of the meal Sarah was carried upstairs in her chair; turning her head at the staircase, she kissed one finger and held it out. Both knew they would not meet again."

On March 23 her strength gave out completely and the film was interrupted. The crowds stayed day and night in front of the house on Boulevard Pereire. Sarah is supposed to have said of the newspaper men who had gathered: "They have tormented

me all my life, now I can plague them by keeping them waiting." She did not plague them long. Canon Loutil administered
extreme unction on March 25. At eight P.M. on March 26 Louis
Verneuil informed the press that Sarah Bernhardt had died a
few minutes earlier.

In the January 1921 issue of *Theatre Magazine* Alice Nielsen
published some personal reminiscences of Duse on the occasion
of the news that the actress was coming out of retirement. Nielsen had studied with Duse years ago and remembered that D'Annunzio once drove her to the station and said to her, in English:
"Why you study with Signora Duse? She can teach you nothing; she too old." Duse was then forty-two.

She was now sixty-two and she was old, older than her years,
worn by disease, nervousness, and the immense strain her roles
had always been for her. Her reasons for coming out of retirement were mostly mundane. Her fortune, so carefully administered by Mendelssohn in Berlin, had suffered with the war and
been wiped out after his death. She had been reduced to live on
an annuity much too small for anyone; she had been forced to
accept some invitations to live here and there, at the homes of
friends; she had come to the edge of poverty according to some
who knew her then. She told Schneider that she had enough
money to finish her days in quiet at Asolo; but she could not
stay anywhere quietly, and now, after the war, she needed something to live for. As she wrote to her friend Olga Signorelli:
"Believe me, Olga, it is not only the daily bread that makes me
go back [to the stage]. All tortures do not matter: only not to
be dead before one dies." Though she reached an agreement to
act with Ermete Zacconi in Turin she told Olga that she would
have preferred to start in a foreign country because one had
more freedom there. In the last moment, as her train was about
to leave Rome for Turin, she wanted to give up again; Olga
would not let her, and the plunge was made.

On May 5, the voice of Ellida Wrangel, that young, unfor-
gettable voice of the Lady from the Sea, was once more heard

off stage at the Teatro Balbo in Turin, and then she came, a gray-haired, frightened old lady, deadly pale, still without makeup, still with the same simple reserve. The entire audience, deeply moved, rose to its feet and applauded almost with solemnity rather than joy, for ten minutes. At the end of the performance the stage was covered with flowers, the horses of her carriage were unhitched and crowds of young men, and old, rolled it to the hotel. The crowd would not leave until, like a queen once more, she had shown herself on the balcony.

From Turin she went in solemn triumph across Italy, to Milan, Genoa and Rome. When she left Rome, Silvio D'Amico, the critic of the *Tribuna*, too young to have seen her before her retirement, brought her an enormous bouquet of white roses to the station. At Duse's request Olga took it and left it at a nearby church.

Her new success was with the young as much as with the old; it was not only nostalgia. But success frightened her, the new turmoil and applause upset her as much as the gathering silence had upset her. Her continuing tours really became continuing battles with herself and her health and nerves. In autumn, in Rome, she was plagued by asthma and neuralgia and had to postpone her performances in Naples. When she received a telegram from Zacconi telling her, in answer to her inquiry, that her newly hired manager was not to be trusted she at once ordered her bed made and lay ill for several days. In January 1922, in Florence, she felt feverish and cancelled twenty-three out of thirty-three performances. In one span of two weeks, with her company of course fully paid, she gave a total of four performances. Nielsen, in her recollections, had spoken of the disappointed audience of twenty years before when Duse cancelled as often as she had performed. Now it was worse. In Florence her deficit ran up to 100,000 lire. She was a trial to her friends and managers, obsessed at times with the idea that people around her were acting against her interests. Yet it was she who was spiting herself. In 1922, for example, during some work on *The Lady from the Sea*, she remembered an annotated edition of the play she had left in Asolo. She at once sent her secretary there to find it. When he could not locate it, she ordered him to crate and ship all her books. Soon she received fourteen crates and managed to find what she wanted. Zacconi said gently that she would never recoup her finances as long as she acted in that way.

But she could not help herself. She never could—why should she now that she was old and her illnesses so much worse? As the disastrous tour of 1921–1922 wore on her debts got larger instead of being paid. One day she would be well, the next day she could not lift herself off her bed. In the spring she disbanded her company and fled to Asolo, but not for long. Schneider saw her in Paris in July when she told him that D'Annunzio had written a very kind letter about her to the press. "He summoned up all I had done, all my past work, even the things I had forgotten. Things I would never have said to him. It was very nice of him to remember them and to say them. . . . The letter was lovely, very touching; but that was all. [He] is the same that he used to be. He thinks of a thing, he speaks of it, he writes it. And, no sooner has he given a form to his thought . . . than it is finished."

D'Annunzio was the great man of the hour, or perhaps only faintly great and faintly ridiculous. He had been upset by the betrayal, as he saw it, of the City of Fiume, adjacent to newly annexed Italian territory in the northeast. Fiume had been permitted to fall to an international administration and was likely to be lost to Italy. So, with a handful of men, he set out from Venice for Fiume, gathering support on the way. With this improvised "army" he took over the city in the face of an Allied Administration, and held it for almost a year and a half in one of the more fantastic episodes in the aftermath of the war. He established a state, proclaimed a constitution, *La Carta Del Carnero*, and held on to his realm until, to the infinite embarrassment of the Italian government, Italian army units had to be sent to force him out. He had actually gained Fiume for Italy, but he had also seriously undermined the Italian government and its democratic institutions, which in any case had always been a matter of indifference to him. He had thereby assisted and, at times at least, directly cooperated with a new man in the political arena who quickly imitated his Fiume Legionnaires with another pseudo-Roman concoction: The Fascisti. Mussolini visited D'Annunzio in Fiume and offered his help. The poet half accepted, and then recognized too late that he had merely been used by the younger man.

D'Annunzio sent Duse a large bouquet of red roses when she returned to the stage. In July 1922, she sent him a telegram asking his permission to perform *La Città Morta* again. "I beg immediate consolation and consent." *Consolazione*—the word was to remind him of his old name for her. Early in August the two met at the Hotel Cavour in Milan. There were no witnesses to this meeting and the conflicting accounts of it are without foundation. He returned to his house on Lake Garda, which he had filched earlier as confiscated enemy property and renamed "Vittoriale Degli Italiani"; soon he was to build magnificent structures there with money Mussolini spent wisely to buy his silence. Mussolini "marched" on Rome that autumn; D'Annunzio could possibly still have prevented his assumption of power at that point.

The situation was not much better for Duse in her second season, 1922–1923 than in the previous year. Her health was worse, her cancellations more frequent. By April she was confronted with imminent bankruptcy and the necessity to disband the company. A loan from an old admirer of her art saved the day. In Rome, where she went to recoup her finances at the large Teatro Costanzi, the manager committed suicide and ruined the prospect.

After that misfortune she received a visit from the new prime minister. Mussolini seems to have been genuinely anxious to help her, because she was, after all, one of the artistic glories of Italy. They had a long discussion about the Italian theater, at the end of which he asked her to draft a proposal for its regeneration. His request showed the administrator's lack of comprehension of the artist; Duse could act but not draft proposals, and nothing further was done. She did, however, refuse his offer of a pension. It is clear that she was not taken with him. She did not care for Fascism, it seems, because she did not care for warlike noises and did not want to be the standardbearer of Italy in Paris or elsewhere. Not only Mussolini, but the Commandant of Fiume, as she persisted in calling D'Annunzio, were now repugnant to her sure sense of humanity, sharpened by age and by war.

She had never taken charity. "As long as I can drag about, as long as I can stand, I must work, for it is right that I should live by my work alone." There, for once, Sarah Bernhardt and Eleonora Duse felt exactly the same.

In the end, before her American tour, Mussolini sent her 30,-000 lire, which she used for her company. He also proposed to take care of its members should she be unable to complete the tour.

Through the help of Katherine Onslow, Duse obtained a contract to perform in England and an advance to enable her to prepare adequately for it. Now at last she could go to a foreign country where she had wanted to start again in the first place. In her first performance at the New Oxford Theatre, in *The Lady from the Sea*, she used flowers on stage that Ellen Terry had brought her; the audience rose for a standing ovation after *Ghosts;* and *La Porta Chiusa*, and even Gallarati-Scotti's *Così Sia* (So be it), which had been booed in Rome, were well received. These four plays, two by Ibsen, two Italian, were her main repertoire for the last months, with an occasional addition of *La Città Morta*. All except the last were plays in which Duse played the role of a mother, one she had never really played in life to her own satisfaction. Now, on stage, it was the only role she wished to play, her one opportunity to fulfill herself in a make-believe world that she could still make magnificently and terrifyingly real. Now she could show herself, suffering and serving without recompense and hope. There were no more Marguerites or Magdas for her, or Césarines or Giocondas. She was drawn above all to Ellida Wrangel, the Lady from the Sea, because she is alone, because she seems mad to some and because she loves the sea for its solitude. James Agate saw her role in it clearly in 1923: "The play is a godsend to a great artist whose fate is not so much doing as suffering that which Fate has done to her. With Duse, speech is silver and silence is golden. It is not so much that she 'acts' when she is silent, as that your mind has leisure to take in the accumulated wealth of all that has been said with voice and face and hands." Eva Le Gallienne, who saw Duse often during her final American tour, observed: "One of the things that particularly impressed me was her bold use of silences—like rests in music."

In her moving frailty Duse could still *be* on stage—without words or "business" she could with her face and hands convey, without seeming to, the emotions for which others needed many more means. "And to me," Arthur Symons wrote, "whenever Duse had to return again and again after that immense applause which was given her by the entire audience, she seemed as frail as a ghost, somewhat shrunken in body, and at the same time so pathetic in the effort she had to make when she bowed slightly and with that wonderful grace she always had one felt literally terrified as to what might happen to her . . ." He probably knew that cylinders of oxygen were kept in her dressing room at the New Oxford Theatre to revive her, if needed.

Her last European performances were in Vienna, in September, where she played three times. Vienna was shabby now, no longer the Imperial capital but an impoverished over-large city in a small, defeated country to whose ruin the Italians had contributed much. But the love of the Viennese for Duse was unchanged. Even in that poor place there were thousands of flowers and tremendous crowds after the performance calling to her and asking her to come back. The contract for America had already been signed. At the old Imperial Hotel Olga Signorelli took farewell from her: "Pray to God," Duse said to her, "that I can give the first ten performances. I have a debt of honor, and I promised myself to pay it off at the rate of 5,000 lire per performance." The contract with Morris Guest specified twenty performances in the Eastern United States. She was to receive $2,500 per performance, most of which was intended to pay her debts in Italy and to support the company. Guest had taken the unprecedented step of insuring the entire tour with Lloyd's for $360,000.

She opened in New York with *Lady from the Sea*. The place was the Metropolitan Opera House, a ridiculous piece of commercialism, for she could hardly be seen and surely not be heard in the far reaches of that cavernous house. But the total income from the first performance was $30,000, most of which, of course, did not go to her. "It was," as Alexander Woollcott wrote in the New York *Herald* on October 30, "as a matter of fact, the largest taking for a single performance in the history of the American Theatre. This was paid to one who, when she first came here in the fullness of her youth and beauty, played to row on row of empty benches. But that was thirty years ago. Since then she had become a legend. Last night some of us knew why." Here, he said, was a major Ibsen play, a nondescript Italian company (though he liked Duse's new young leading man, Memo Benassi) and "a reunion, a tribute, and a legend come true."

"Her performance of Ellida Wrangel was among the few truly and exhilaratingly beautiful things which we have seen in our time. One who had to wait far into the twentieth century to see her whom the world called the greatest actress of the nineteenth left the Metropolitan with the feeling that he had never seen any human being of such luminous and transcendent beauty."

Heywood Broun's review in *The World* was more skeptical. He found that he was witnessing a beautiful performance, but had a "most unhappy time." To him Duse was merely "one of the most finished and expert stage technicians"; the physical conditions in the Metropolitan Opera House he found hard to accept, and he was particularly troubled by the language, a trouble he had not had with the visiting Russian company, the

Moscow Art Theatre. Of all the languages he did not know, he said, Italian was by far the hardest for him to understand.

The style of her performance seemed strange to him: " 'Conducting' is precisely the word we intend, for the performance . . . was all but operatic in its dependence upon a definite and visible beat. We felt that if for an instant the hands of Duse ceased to clasp, to rise, to fall, to soar or droop, she herself and everybody upon the stage would be struck mute. . . . Sometimes we watched amazing fireworks, but to us it seems that Duse and her companions, again like opera singers, and more particularly Italian ones, live for their arias." He was disappointed in Duse not because she was poor, but because he had been told that she was the one who had carried naturalism farthest. That he found utterly untrue. Her acting, in fact, seemed to him "of the florid school."

Now even Duse was out of date.

Duse managed to escape from the Met and continue her performances at the Century Theatre, performing the rest of her five-piece repertoire. "Across the gulf of those abominable theatres, Eleonora Duse became a kind of . . . legend of herself," wrote Kenneth Macgowan.

On November 13, Duse performed *Così Sia* in honor of the Moscow Art Theatre which was also performing in New York, and especially of Constantin Stanislavski and Olga Knipper, Chekhov's widow. In a speech after the performance, Stanislavski cited her abiding influence on the Moscow Art Theatre: not a day had gone by in the last twenty-five years without her being mentioned in a rehearsal. With her love for the Russian theater and its ways that was undoubtedly the best moment of her American tour.

It is wrong to blame Morris Guest for the misfortunes of Duse's tour. Her contract with him specified twenty performances, and when they were over, she could have returned to Italy. It was her own wish, however, to accede to the tempting offer of Fortune Gallo for an extension of the tour. She was to receive $3000, instead of the $2500 agreed to with Guest, and to go to Havana and California for the winter, and wind up the tour in the Middle West and East in the spring.

In Havana she was ill again, and felt reasonably well only in San Francisco in March. The journey across Arizona left her prostrate—she was affected by the heat and by the dust seeping into her railway carriage through closed windows. Then the weather changed and they returned to the cold of late winter in the Midwest. Detroit was torture. As usual she had to perform in the largest theater available. Indianapolis was no better. On her arrival in Pittsburgh the Hotel William Penn offended her and she moved to the Schenley.

Her biographers have often held her management responsible for her death. They, especially the European biographers who did not know the United States, asserted that the slave drivers forced Duse to leave San Francisco where she was reasonably well and to travel across the fiery furnace of Arizona into the bitter cold of the Midwest. Arizona is not a fiery furnace in March, and though it is hard to say anything favorable about midwestern weather in late winter and early spring, one can protect oneself against it. The truth is more likely to be found in Lugné-Poe's remark that all her friends, even her impresarios tried to protect her, and that she seemed to want to provoke them. An artist who refuses to move or to perform cannot be moved, as Duse had shown very often in earlier years, when she was in relatively better health. Now that she was near the end of her physical resources, she was indomitably going on to her doom, with an increase in impatience. That impatience, for example, sent her driver in San Francisco to the hospital after her departure; she had completely exhausted him.

Duse arrived in Pittsburgh on April 1, 1924, and spent some days in bed. On April 5, the day of her performance at the Syria Mosque, she insisted—so Eva Le Gallienne reports—on walking to the theater from the Schenley Hotel. There was a driving, sleety rain and Duse was drenched by the time she arrived.

The programs of *La Porta Chiusa* said, "Duse's acting is a tri-

umph of mind over matter." The performance was still that
triumph. She barely managed to get to the stage from her porta-
ble dressing room, which was always set up close by its side.
She sat through most of the performance, but somehow, with
her hands and her face and voice, she was still wonderful. Sobs
mingled with the applause at the end, when she had given her
final lines: "Sola! Sola!" Alone, alone. The words were sym-
bolic. She had always felt alone: To Lugné-Poe she had once
said, despairingly, "Je n'aime pas personne." (I love no one.)
She could not accept love or give it. Only on stage, in that distant relationship across the footlights, or in letters, could she
really give something of herself.

After the performance she broke down. "Basta, non posso
piu." She could do no more now. On April 15 she disappointed
her last audience when she did not give her performance in
Cleveland. She was not reported seriously ill until April 19,
when pneumonia had set in as a complication. On the next day,
Easter Sunday, she asked her actors to come and see her. They
had been pacing the streets and corridors, anxious and fearful.
When they came she was no longer capable of recognizing them.
Her devoted companions of the final years, Desirée von Wer-
theimstein and Maria Avogadro, were near her all the time. At
1:00 A.M. on Monday she stirred and asked if the baggage had
been packed for their return. She was insistent that they leave at
dawn. An hour later she raised herself once more and said, in
French, "We must get on with it. We must leave. Get to work."
And then, "Cover me up." She did not see the dawn any more.

That day her body was taken to Samson's Funeral Parlor, and
the tragic comedy of her final journey began. D'Annunzio, who
would not help the living, was aroused to national fervor by the
dead: "The tragic death of Eleonora Duse could not have been
accomplished more tragically," he telegraphed to Mussolini. "Far
from Italy the most Italian of hearts has died. I ask that the
adored body be returned to Italy at the government's expense.
I am certain that my pain is the pain of all Italy. Listen to my
prayer and answer." Mussolini answered with a telegram, printed

in all the Italian press, in which he tried to put himself into the best light: "The fate of Eleonora Duse, to whom a year ago I offered a pension so that our sublime actress would not need to leave Italy, grieves me profoundly." He acceded to D'Annunzio's request. Prince Gelasio Caetani, the Italian ambassador to the United States, was posthaste dispatched to Pittsburgh to take over.

Catherine Onslow and Duse's other friends and associates on the scene knew Duse's last wishes, which were nothing like the ideas of Mussolini, and there seems to have been a rather undignified scene at Samson's Funeral Parlor. The objections raised were sufficiently violent to keep the body from being moved for a whole week. Prince Caetani prevailed in the end, and the body was sent to New York on April 28, where it lay in state at the Church of St. Vincent Ferrer at Sixty-sixth and Lexington. Fifteen thousand people gathered outside the church, according to the New York *Times*, for High Mass on May 1. Giovanni Martinelli sang, high Italian officials were present, and the black shirts of Mussolini's fascists were in evidence. On May 2 the body was put on board the S.S. *Diulio*. According to some reports, the actors, who had been the chief objects of Duse's final solicitude, were almost left stranded after all, in spite of promises and commitments by Mussolini. They were finally permitted on board in order to avoid further scandal, and took turns, during the voyage, to pray at her bier.

In Italy, of course, Mussolini had it completely his way. There was a tremendous show in Naples when the *Diulio* docked on May 10, and in Rome the following day: Military honors, flags, speeches more befitting a dead general than a dead actress. And yet through all the panoply of the emergent fascist empire penetrated the real sorrow of a whole nation. Finally she was permitted her rest in Asolo.

Once Duse was dead, D'Annunzio elevated her almost to the level of his mother for whom he had set up a votive lamp. A bust of Duse was placed in his study, opposite his writing table. He was scandalized that Enrichetta destroyed his letters to her

mother, but on the last day of his life he was at work on a dedication to Duse. He outlived her by fourteen years. He became
a Prince and from his heavily gilded cage he watched the rise of
Mussolini, sardonically and impotently.

In September 1937, "wrinkled as an old turtle, trembling and
invalided" he went to Verona to meet Mussolini, who had just
returned from Berlin, to express his fears about Italy's future.
But Mussolini excused himself and left; he had already sold Italy
to Hitler. D'Annunzio died on March 1, 1938, and the news of
his death was quickly stilled, for ten days later Hitler collected
Austria as the first installment of the new pact with Italy. Perhaps it was lucky for Duse not to have reached the age of Ristori.

In Anouilh's *L'Alouette*, a play on Joan of Arc, as the play
draws toward a close with the burning of Joan at the stake, the
Squire Beaudricourt runs in and cries: "Stop! Stop! Stop!" He
finds it an injustice to end the whole play like that; it should end
with the coronation of the Dauphin at Rheims, Joan's finest
moment.

It may be unjust, too, to end this book with the death of the
last international actress. At Duse's funeral the new age was already howling around the corner. The blackshirts were there,
and violence was done to an international artist whose great and
sincere love of her country was never confounded with the political aberrations of its regimes. Duse's funeral characterized
the beginning of an era in which the international actresses could
have no part.

The end of their era, the real curtain call, was the funeral a
year before. If Duse's looked into a void forward, Bernhardt's
looked back over three generations of theater of free men and
free enterprise. One must end therefore with the funeral of
Sarah Bernhardt.

She lay in state for three days. People lined up for blocks from
the Porte d'Asnières to the Place Wagram and on to the Boulevard Pereire, and fifty thousand passed her bier. March 29 was
Thursday of Holy Week, and the weather was perfect. The

service was at the church of St. Francis de Sales. Sarah was carried in the famous rosewood casket which had been made for
her thirty years before. The procession moved down the Boulevard Malesherbes and the Rue Royale, turned into the Rue de
Rivoli and went through the Rue Saint Denis and the Avenue
Victoria to the City Hall for the official tribute. Then it turned
back to the Rue de Rivoli and went through the Rue Saint Antoine and the Place de La Bastille to the Théâtre Sarah Bernhardt. There it paused for thirty seconds. Then it finally took
the long road out to the Père Lachaise Cemetery. The city was
still between eleven and one that day. From early morning the
people of Paris had gathered along the route, until they lined it,
several hundred thousand of them, to mourn the passing of a
queen.

SELECTED BOOK LIST

THREE of the four actresses who are the subject of *The Gilded Stage* seem to have enduring fascination. On Ristori nothing of note has been written in this century, but Rachel, Bernhardt and Duse have sizable bibliographies to which several items were added in the last few years. If one then adds the more general background, one arrives at a list of hundreds of books even if articles are not taken into account. There are thousands of those—reviews, evaluations, reminiscences, interviews—and additional thousands of articles and news stories in the daily press.

The list included here therefore is selective and does not represent a complete record of works consulted. It includes the more important of these works, of course, as well as a list that hopefully will be of use to a reader who wants to pursue some of the subjects of *The Gilded Stage*. For that reason the list is classified and lightly annotated. The first part, "The General Background," is restricted to a few works of cultural history, and to some biographies of persons who are important to the background but have no particular connection with the theater. The second part, "The Theatrical Background," somewhat arbitrarily separated from the two parts devoted to the four international actresses which follow it, contains some general works on the drama and the theater, and works on other relevant actors and actresses. Finally, in the third and fourth parts, the list includes a selection of the biographical and critical works on the four.

When possible, books are given in English translation even when the present author used the original and translated it himself.

I. THE GENERAL BACKGROUND

Adams, Henry. *The Education of Henry Adams*. Boston, 1918.

Alger, Horatio, Jr. *Ragged Dick: Or, Street Life in New York with the Boot Blacks*. Boston, 1868. (Novel.)

Allen, Frederick Lewis. *The Great Pierpont Morgan*. New York, 1949.

Behrman, S. N. *Duveen*. New York, 1952.

Brogan, Denis W. *The French Nation 1814–1940*. New York, 1957.

Brooks, Van Wyck. *The Confident Years, 1885–1915*. New York, 1952.

Carnegie, Andrew. *Autobiography*. Boston, 1920.

Delacroix, Eugène. *Journal*. transl. by Walter Pach. New York, 1948.

Giraud, Raymond. *The Unheroic Hero*. New Brunswick, New Jersey, 1957.

Goncourt, Edmond and Jules. *Journal*. 9 vols. Paris, 1894–1911.

Holbrook, Stewart H. *The Age of the Moguls*. Garden City, New York, 1953.

Lynn, Kenneth S. *The Dream of Success*. New York, 1955.

Maigron, Louis. *Le romantisme et les moeurs*. Paris, 1910.

Marden, Orison Swett. *The Miracle of Right Thought*. New York, 1910.

———. *Pushing to the Front*. New York, 1894.

Marsan, Jules. *La bataille romantique*. Second series. Paris, 1924.

Northrop, Henry D. *The Life and Achievements of Jay Gould*. Philadelphia, 1892.

Smith, Denis Mack. *Italy: a Modern History*. Ann Arbor, Michigan, 1959.

Veblen, Thorstein. *The Theory of the Leisure Class*. New York, 1934.

II. THE THEATRICAL BACKGROUND

Agate, James E. *The English Dramatic Critics*. London, 1932.

Archer, William. *The Old Drama and the New*. Boston, 1923.

Arnold, Matthew. "The French Play in London," *Irish Essays, and Others*. London, 1882.

Arvin, Neil Cole. *Eugène Scribe and the French Theatre, 1815–1860.* Cambridge, Mass., 1924.

Baldick, Robert. *The Life and Times of Frédérick Lemaître.* London, 1959. (Among other things, a good introduction to the romantic style of acting.)

Bobbé, Dorothie. *Fanny Kemble.* New York, 1931.

Boston Theatrical Performances. 5 vols. Chicago, n.d. (Unpublished MS in the University of Chicago Libraries.)

Braun, Sidney D. *The "courtisane" in the French Theatre from Hugo to Becque.* London, 1947.

Brown, Thomas Allston. *A History of the New York Stage, 1732–1901.* 3 vols. New York, 1903.

Brunetière, Ferdinand. *Conférences de l'Odéon.* Paris, n.d.

Bulman, Joan. *Jenny Lind.* London, 1956.

Bulthaupt, Heinrich Alfred. *Dumas, Sardou und die jetzige Franzosenherrschaft auf der deutschen Bühne.* Berlin, 1888. (A typical condemnation on moral grounds.)

Campardon, Émile. *Les comédiens du roi de la troupe italienne pendant les deux derniers siècles.* Paris, 1880.

Campbell, Mrs. Patrick. *My Life and Some Letters.* London, 1922.

Cole, Toby and Chinoy, Helen Krich, eds. *Actors on Acting.* New York, 1954.

Collins, Mabel. *The Story of Helen Modjeska.* London, 1883.

Descotes, Maurice. *Le drame romantique et ses grands créateurs.* Paris, 1955.

Duchartre, Pierre Louis. *The Italian Comedy.* transl. by R. T. Weaver. London, 1929.

Elssler, Fanny. *The Letters and Journals of Fanny Ellsler* (sic) *Written Before and After her Operatic Campaign in the United States.* New York, 1845.

Gautier, Théophile. *Histoire de l'art dramatique.* 6 vols. Paris, 1858.

———. *Les maîtres du théâtre français.* Paris, 1929.

Got, Edmond. *Journal.* 2 vols. Paris, 1910.

Gronowicz, Antoni. *Modjeska, Her Life and Loves.* New York, 1956.

Guex, Jules. *Le théâtre et la societé française de 1815 à 1848.* Vervey, 1900.

Heine, Heinrich. "Über die französische Bühne," *Sämtliche Werke,* vol. 8. Leipzig, 1915.

Houssaye, Arsène. *Behind the Scenes at the Comédie Française.* London, 1889.

――――. *Life in Paris.* New York, 1881. (Both of Houssaye's books in English are translations of sections of *Les confessions; souvenirs d'un demi-siècle, 1830–1880.* 7 vols. Paris, 1885–1891.)

Ihrig, Grace Pauline. *Heroines in the French Drama of the Romantic Period.* New York, 1950.

James, Henry. "The Théâtre Français," *French Poets and Novelists.* London, 1878.

Janin, Jules G. *Histoire de la littérature dramatique.* 6 vols. Paris, 1853–1858.

Joannidès, A. *La Comédie Française de 1680 à 1920.* Paris, 1921. (Contains a statistical record of performances.)

Kennard, Joseph Spencer. *The Italian Theatre.* 2 vols. New York, 1932.

Knight, Joseph. *Theatrical Notes.* London, 1893.

Leathers, Victor. *British Entertainers in France.* Toronto, 1959.

Lelièvre, Renée. *Le théâtre dramatique italien en France, 1855–1940.* Paris, 1959.

Lewes, George Henry. *On Actors and the Art of Acting.* New York, 1878(?).

Lucas, Hippolyte J.-J. *Histoire philosophique et littéraire du théâtre français.* Paris, 1843.

Mantzius, Karl. *A History of Theatrical Art.* 6 vols. London, 1921.

Martersteig, Max. *Das deutsche Theater im neunzehnten Jahrhundert.* Leipzig, 1904.

Maurois, André. *The Titans.* New York, 1957. (On Dumas, father and son.)

Mirécourt, Eugène de. *Histoire contemporaine.* 140 vols. in three series. Paris, 1867–1870. (vol. 24: Jules Janin. vol. 110: Mlle. Georges.)

Modjeska, Helen. *Memoirs and Impressions: an Autobiography.* New York, 1910.

Moody, Richard. *The Astor Place Riot.* Bloomington, Ind., 1958. (A meticulous, detailed reconstruction which is also very readable.)

Moses, Montrose J. and Brown, John Mason. *The American Theatre as Seen by its Critics, 1752–1934.* New York, 1934.

Muret, Théodore. *L'histoire par le théâtre.* Paris, 1865.

Noël, E. and Stoullig, E. *Annales du théâtre et de la musique*. Paris, n.d.

Odell, George C. D. *Annals of the New York Stage*. 14 vols. New York, 1927–1949.

Petit de Juleville, Louis. *Le théâtre en France*. Paris, 1889.

Porel, Paul and Monval, Georges. *L'Odéon*. 2 vols. Paris, 1876–1882.

Schlenther, Paul. *Theater im neunzehnten Jahrhundert*. Berlin, 1930.

Salvini, Celso. *Tommaso Salvini*. Rocce San Casciano(?), 1955.

[Salvini, Tommaso.] *American Tour, 1882–1883*. New York, 188–

————. *Leaves from the Autobiography of Tommaso Salvini*. New York, 1893.

[————.] *Notes et souvenirs sur T. Salvini*. Paris, 1878.

Schultz, Gladys Denny. *Jenny Lind: The Swedish Nightingale*. Philadelphia, 1962.

Skinner, Otis. *Footlights and Spotlights*. Indianapolis, 1923.

Soubies, Albert. *La Comédie Française depuis l'époque romantique*. Paris, 1895. (Includes a table of performances, 1825–1894.)

Szwarc, Herc. *Un précurseur du romantisme: Pierre Lebrun*. Paris, 1928.

Terry, Ellen. *Memoirs*. New York, 1932.

Vitu, Auguste. *Les mille et une nuits de Paris*. Paris, 1884. (Reviews from *Le Figaro*.)

Weiss, J.-J. *Le théâtre et les moeurs*. Paris, 1889.

Winter, William. *Shadows of the Stage*. Second Series. New York, 1894.

————. *The Wallet of Time*. 2 vols. New York, 1913.

Wilt, Napier. *File of Theatrical Performances in Chicago, 1837–1967*. (Unpublished.)

III. RACHEL AND RISTORI

Anon. *Ein Brief über Signora Ristori als "Myrrha" auf der Berliner Bühne*. Berlin, 1856.

Anon. *Rachel et la Comédie Française*. Brussels, 1842.

Agate, James E. *Rachel*. New York, 1928.

Arna, J. and Briquet, P. *Rachel et son temps*. Paris, 1939.

B., D. *Lettres sur la Ristori*. Paris, 1856.

Barréra, Mme. de. *Memoirs of Rachel*. New York, 1858.

Barthou, J. L. *Rachel*. Paris, 1926. (A book on Rachel by a former Prime Minister of France.)

Beauvallet, Léon. *Rachel and the New World*. ed. and transl. by Colin Clair. London, 1967. (A new translation of Beauvallet's memoirs of Rachel's American tour. It includes Rachel's contract with her brother Raphael.)

Brontë, Charlotte. *Villette*. London, 1857. (Novel.)

Cabanes, P. "Ungedruckte Erinnerungen an Rachel," *Deutsche Revue*. vol. 27, no. 2. (1902.)

Chambrun, Adolphe de Pineton, Marquis de. *Quelques réflexions sur l'art dramatique: Mlle. Rachel, ses succès, ses défauts*. Paris, 1853.

Chevalley, Sylvie. *Rachel en Amérique*. Paris, 1957. (A well prepared new evaluation of the supposedly "disastrous journey.")

Coquatrix, Émile. *Rachel à Rouen*. Rouen, 1840. (Poem.)

Cost, March. *I, Rachel: a Biographical Novel*. New York, 1957.

———. *Rachel, an Interpretation*. London, 1947.

Cremiéux, Adolphe. *Autographes*. Paris, 1885.

Curti, P. A. *Adelaide Ristori*. Milan, 1855.

Dino, Dorothée de Courlande, Duchesse de. *Memoirs*. 2 vols. New York, 1910.

Doazan, Gabriel Eloi (pseud. "Urbanus"). *Lettres sur le théâtre français en 1839 et 1840*. Paris, 1841.

Dumas, Alexandre (*père*). *Memoires*. Brussels, 1852.

———. *Souvenirs dramatiques*. Paris, 1928.

Eustis, A. A., Jr. "Rachel's Racine: Classical or Romantic?" *Modern Language Quarterly*. vol. 10. (1949.)

Falk, Bernard. *Rachel the Immortal*. New York, 1935. (A long book in a rather overblown style.)

Faucigny Lucinge, Alix, Princesse de. *Rachel et son temps*. Paris, 1910.

Fellows, O. "Rachel and America, a reappraisal," *Romanic Review*. vol. 30, no. 4. (Dec., 1939.)

Field, Kate. *Adelaide Ristori, a Biography*. New York, 1867. (The campaign biography for Ristori's first American tour.)

Fiorentino, Pier Angelo. *Comédies et comédiens*. Paris, 1866.

Fleischmann, H. *Rachel Intime*. Paris, 1910.

Gribble, Francis H. *Rachel: her Stage Life and her Real Life*. New York, 1911.

Hawkins, Raymond L. *Rachel and Arsène Houssaye*. Cambridge, Mass., 1933.

Heylli, Georges d'. *Rachel d'après sa correspondance*. Paris, 1882.

————. *Rachel et la Ristori*. Paris, 1902.

Hingston, E. Peron. *Adelaide Ristori: the Siddons of Modern Italy*. London, 1856.

Houssaye, Arsène. *La Comédienne*. Paris, 1884. (Novel.)

Janin, Clément. "Rachel et Jules Janin," *Revue de France*. vol. 16, no. 3. (1936.)

Janin, Jules Gabriel. *Correspondance*. Paris, 1877.

————. *Critique dramatique*. Paris, 1877.

————. *Rachel et la tragédie*. Paris, 1859.

Judith, Jule Bernat ("Mlle. Judith"). *My autobiography*. New York, 1913.

Kennard, Mrs. N. H. *Rachel*. Boston, 1886.

Klein, Arthur. *A Study of Rachel Elizabeth Félix*. Ann Arbor, Michigan, 1948. (Unpublished Ph.D. Dissertation, University of Michigan. Contains the memoirs by Jean Chéry of Rachel's American tour.)

Lamartine, Alphonse. *Correspondance*. 6 vols. Paris, 1875.

————. *Portraits et salons romantiques*. Paris, 1927.

Lamothe-Langon, Etienne Léon. *Rachel*. Paris, 1838.

Laplane, Gabriel, ed. *Rachel: lettres inédites*. Paris, 1947.

Launay, Robert. *Figures juives*. Paris, 1921.

Lee, A. van. *Remarques générales sur le jeu de Mlle. Rachel*. Amsterdam, 1847.

Legouvé, Ernest. *M. Samson et ses élèves*. Paris, 1875.

————. *Soixante ans de souvenirs*. 2 vols. Paris, 1887.

Louvet, A. *Mademoiselle Rachel . . . étude sur l'art dramatique*. Paris, 1892.

Lucas-Dubreton, J. *Rachel*. Paris, 1936. (The most enlightening anecdotal biography.)

Maurice, Charles. *La Vérité-Rachel*. Paris, 1850. (The most scurrilous work on her.)

Mirécourt, Eugène de. *Rachel*. Paris, 1869. vol. 75 of *Histoire Contemporaine*.

Morley, Henry. *The Journal of a London Playgoer, 1851–1866*. London, 1891. (Very good on Ristori's performances.)

Musset, Alfred de. "Un souper chez Mlle. Rachel," *Oeuvres Posthumes*. Paris, 1867.

Ornano, Philippe Antoine. *La vie passionante du Comte Walewski*. Paris, 1953.

Pailleron, Marie Louise. *François Buloz et ses amis*. Paris, 1920.

Piéchaud, Martial. *La vie privée de Rachel*. Paris, 1954.

Heylli, Georges d'. "Les quatre-vingt ans d'une tragédienne. Rachel et la Ristori," *La Revue*. series 3. vol. 11. (Jan. 15, 1902.)

Posener, S. *Adolphe Crémieux*. 2 vols. Paris, 1933–1934.

Richardson, Joanna. *Rachel*. London, 1956. (A very readable modern biography.)

Ristori, Adelaide, *Memoirs and Artistic Studies*. New York, 1907. (With a biographical memoir by L. D. Ventura.)

———. *Studies and Memoirs*. London, 1888. (Both this and the preceding item are translations of the original Italian *Ricordi e studi artistici*, Turin, 1857, but this earlier version is in less distressing English.)

Sainte-Beuve, Charles-Augustin. *Chroniques Parisiennes*. Paris, 1876.

Salvini, Tommaso. *Discours en commémoration d'Adelaide Ristori*. Paris, 1907.

Samson, Joseph Isidore. *Epître à Mlle. Rachel*. Paris, 1839.

———. *Mémoires*. Paris, 1882.

Samson, Mme. J. I. *Rachel et Samson*. Paris, 1898. (The memoirs of Samson's widow.)

Schneider, Louis. *Aus meinem Leben*. 3 vols. Berlin, 1879.

Séchan, Charles. *Souvenirs d'un homme de théâtre, 1831–1855*. Paris, 1883.

Stone, Samuel. "Rachel and Soumet's Jeanne d'Arc," *Publications of the Modern Language Association*. vol. 47. (1932.)

Tampier, L. C. Camille. *Dernières heures de Rachel*. Paris, 1858.

Thomson, Valentine. *La vie sentimentale de Rachel*. Paris, 1910.

Trapadoux, Marc. *Mme. A. Ristori*. Paris, 1861.

Veber, P. *Samson*, Paris, 1925.

Véron, L. *Mémoires d'un bourgeois de Paris*. 6 vols. Paris, 1854. (Much of vol. 4 is devoted to Rachel.)

IV. BERNHARDT AND DUSE

Agate, James E. *Alarums and Excursions.* London, 1922.

————. *The Contemporary Theatre.* London, 1924–1925. (The volumes for 1923-1924.)

Agate, May. *Madame Sarah.* London, 1945.

Antoine, André. *Mes souvenirs.* Paris, 1928.

Antongini, Tom. *D'Annunzio.* London, 1938.

Archer, William. *The Theatrical "World" for 1893.* London, 1893. (Annual volumes until 1897.)

Arthur, Sir George C. A. *Sarah Bernhardt.* London, 1923.

Bab, Julius. *Kränze dem Mimen.* Emsdetten, 1954.

Bahr, Hermann. *Essays.* Linz, 1962.

————. *Wiener Theater (1892–1898).* Berlin ,1899.

Barbey d'Aurevilly, J. *Le théâtre contemporain.* 6 vols. Paris, 1892. (For the years 1866 to 1883.)

Baring, Maurice. "Eleonora Duse," *The Fortnightly Review.* New Series, vol. 115. (June 2, 1924.)

————. *Sarah Bernhardt.* New York, 1934.

Bäumer, Gertrud. *Eleonora Duse.* Tübingen, 1963.

Beerbohm, Max. *Around Theatres.* New York, 1930.

Bérendt, Rachel. *Sarah Bernhardt, en mi recuerdo.* Buenos Aires, 1945.

Bernhardt, Lysiane Sarah. *Sarah Bernhardt, ma grandmère.* Paris, 1945.

Bernhardt, Sarah. *The Art of the Theatre.* London, 1924.

————. *Dans les nuages: impressions d'une chaise.* Manuscript in the Harvard Theatre Collection.

————. *Memories of my Life.* New York, 1907.

Berton, Thérèse. *See* Woon, Basil, below.

Binet-Valmer, Gustave. *Sarah Bernhardt.* Paris, 1936.

Boglione, Giuseppe. *L'arte della Duse.* Rome, 1960.

Bordeux, Jeanne. *Eleonora Duse: The Story of her Life.* London, 1924.

Brandes, Georg. *Erinnerungen.* Munich, 1907.

Brémont, Louis. *Le théâtre et la vie.* Paris, 1930.

Brereton, Austin. *Sarah Bernhardt.* Sydney, 1891.

Bron, Ludovic. *Sarah Bernhardt, la pensée française.* Paris, 1925.

Campbell, Mrs. Patrick. "First Lady of Her Time," *Stage*. (January, 1937.)

Castelot, André. *Sarah Bernhardt*. Paris, 1961.

Churchill, Winston. "Sarah Bernhardt," *Blackwood's Magazine*. vol. 213. (May, 1923.)

Colombier, Marie. *Life and Memories of Sarah Barnum*. London, 1883.

———. *Sarah Barnum: Memoirs of a Parisian Actress*. New York, 1884. (This and the item preceding it are translations of *Les mémoires de Sarah Barnum*. Paris, 1883.)

Craig, Edward Gordon. "On Signora Eleonora Duse," *Life and Letters Today*. London. vol. 6. (June-Dec., 1928.)

———. "To Mme. Eleonora Duse," *Mask*. Florence. vol. 1. (1901.)

Daudet, Alphonse. *Pages inédites de critique dramatique*. Paris, 1923. (Covers the years 1874–1880.)

[Duse, Eleonora.] "Lettere inedite di Eleonora Duse agli amici russi," *Il Dramma*. anno 41, nova seria. no. 342. (March, 1965.)

[———.] *Eleonora Duse e la guerra*. ed. by Carlo Vittorio Riva and Maria Pierazzi. Turin, 1927. (Mainly letters by Duse.)

Faguet, Emile. *Propos de théâtre*. Second, third and fourth series. Paris, 1905–1907. (From the *Journal des Débats*.)

[Gaillet, Eugène.] *Sarah Barnum's Reply: the Life of Marie Colombier, by one of her ****. transl. by F. C. Valentine. New York, 1884. (A translation of *La vie de Marie Pigeonnier*. Paris, 1884.)

Geller, Gyula Gaston. *Sarah Bernhardt, Divine Eccentric*. New York, 1931.

Gilder, Rosamond. "La Nostalgilder: some Letters of Eleonora Duse," *Theatre Arts Monthly*. vol. 10. (June, 1926.)

Grein, James T. *Dramatic Criticism*. London, 1899–1904.

———. *The New World of the Theatre*. London, 1924.

Gros, Johannes. *Alexandre Dumas et Marie Duplessis*. Paris, 1923.

Hädelmayr, Roman. *Grande Amatrice*. Graz, 1948.

Harden, Maximilian. *I Meet my Contemporaries*. Transl. by William O. Lawton. New York, 1925.

Harding, Bertita. *Age Cannot Wither*. Philadelphia, 1947. (A fulsome account of the Duse-D'Annunzio relationship.)

Hermant, Abel. *Essais de Critique*. Paris, 1912.

Hommage des poètes à Sarah Bernhardt à l'occasion de sa nomination dans l'Ordre de la Légion d'Honneur. Paris, 1914.

Hofmannsthal, Hugo von. *Gesammelte Werke. Prosa*. vol. 1. Frankfurt, 1950.

Howells, William Dean. *Literature and Life*. New York, 1902. (Includes an essay on Bernhardt as Hamlet.)

Huneker, James Gibbons. *Iconoclasts*. New York, 1905.

Huret, Jules. *Sarah Bernhardt*. London, 1899.

James, Henry. *Parisian Sketches: Letters to the New York Tribune, 1875-1876*. New York, 1957.

Jochamowitz, A. *Sarah Bernhardt en Lima*. Lima, 1943.

Lanco, Yvonne. *Sarah Bernhardt: souvenirs*. Paris, 1961.

Leblanc, Georgette. *Mes conversations avec Eleonora Duse*. Paris, 1926.

Le Gallienne, Eva. *The Mystic in the Theatre: Eleonora Duse*. New York, 1966.

————. "Sarah Bernhardt and Eleonora Duse," *Stage*. (January, 1937.)

Lemaître, Jules. *Les contemporains*. Paris, 1889. (From the *Journal des Débats*.)

————. *Impressions du théâtre*. 11 vols. Paris, 1888-1898.

Lhombeaud, Roger. *Arthur Symons*. London, 1963.

Lugné-Poe, Amélien François. "Avec Eléonora Duse," *Les Oeuvres Libres*, no. 137. (Nov., 1932.)

————. *Sous les étoiles*. Paris, 1933.

Lyonnet, Henry. *La Dame aux Camélias de Dumas*. Paris, 1930.

Mamoulian, R. "Bernhardt vs. Duse," *Theatre Arts*. vol. 41, no. 9. (Sept., 1957.)

Mapes, Victor. *Duse and the French*. New York, 1898. (The fullest account of her encounter with Bernhardt in Paris, 1897.)

Montesquiou-Fézensac, Robert Comte de. *Les pas effacés*. 3 vols. Paris, 1923.

Noble, Iris. *Great Lady of the Theatre*. New York, 1960.

Norman, Gertrude. "Interview with Eleonora Duse," *Theatre Magazine*. vol. 6, no. 62. (April, 1906.)

Pirandello, Luigi. "The Art of Duse," *Theatre Arts*. vol. 38, no. 12. (Dec., 1954.)

Pronier, Ernest. *Sarah Bernhardt*. Geneva, 1942. (The only biography that brings modern methods of research to bear on the facts of her life.)

Raynaud, Ernest. "Le scandale de Sarah Bernhardt et la Duse," *Mercure de France*. vol. 190. (Sept., 1926.)

Reed, Isaac George. *"Too Thin": or, Skeleton Sarah*. New York, 1880.

Renard, Jules. *Journal*. ed. and transl. by Louise Bogan and Elizabeth Roget. New York, 1964.

Renner, A. L. *Sarah Bernhardt, Artist and Woman*. New York, 1896.

Resnevic-Signorelli, Olga. *Eleonora Duse*. Berlin, 1942(?).

Révész, Andrés. *La vida patética de Eleonora Duse*. Barcelona, 1947.

Rheinhardt, E. A. *The Life of Eleonora Duse*. London, 1930.

Rhem, Walter. "Rilke und die Duse," *Begegnungen und Probleme*. Bern, 1957.

Rhodes, Anthony. *The Poet as Superman: a Life of Gabriele d'Annunzio*. London, 1959.

Richardson, Joanna. *Sarah Bernhardt*. London, 1959.

Rilke, Rainer Maria. *Gesammelte Briefe*. Leipzig 1939. vol. 3.

Rolland, Romain. "Gabriele d'Annunzio et la Duse," *Les Oeuvres Libres*. vol. 246. (1947.)

Rostand, Maurice. *Sarah Bernhardt*. Paris, 1950.

Row, Arthur William. *Sarah the Divine*. New York, 1957.

Rueff, Suze. *I Knew Sarah Bernhardt*. London, 1951. (In contrast to others, she really knew her.)

Salten, Felix. *Geister der Zeit*. Vienna, 1924.

Sarcey, Francisque. *Quarante ans de théâtre*. 8 vols. Paris, 1900–1902.

Schneider, Edouard. *Eléonora Duse, souvenirs, notes et documents*. Paris, 1925.

Scott, Clement. *The Drama of Yesterday and Today*. 2 vols. London, 1899.

———. *Some Notable 'Hamlets' of the Present Time*. London, 1905.

Shaw, George Bernard. *Collected Works*. New York, 1930. vols. 23-25, "Our Theatres in the Nineties." (Criticism from the *Saturday Review*, Jan., 1895 to May, 1898.)

Skinner, Cornelia Otis. *Madame Sarah*. Boston, 1967. (An enjoyable, imaginative biography.)

Segantini, Bianca, and Francesco von Mendelssohn. *Eleonora Duse: Bildnisse und Worte*. Berlin, 1926.

Sheean, Vincent. "When Duse Tapped on Boito's Window; the Chronicle of a Love Affair," *High Fidelity*. vol. 9, no. 10. (Oct., 1959.)

Symons, Arthur. *Eleonora Duse*. London, 1926.

————. "Impressions of Sarah Bernhardt," *London Mercury*. vol. 8. (Oct., 1923.)

Teasdale, Sara. *Sonnets to Duse*. Boston, 1907.

Vergani, Leonardo, ed. *Eleonora Duse*. Milan, 1958.

Verneuil, Louis. *The Fabulous Life of Sarah Bernhardt*. transl. by Ernest Boyd. New York, 1942.

Walkley, Ernest Bingham. *Drama and Life*. London, 1907.

————. *Playhouse Impressions*. London, 1893.

Wechsberg, Joseph. *Red Plush and Black Velvet*. Boston, 1961.

Winwar, Frances. *Wingless Victory*. New York, 1957. (An interesting and well prepared account of Duse and d'Annunzio.)

Woon, Basil. *The Real Sarah Bernhardt*. New York, 1924. (Thérèse Berton's memoirs, which are more unreal than anything else.)

Young, Stark. "Sense about Duse," *Theatre Arts Monthly*. vol. 23. (April, 1939.)

Yorska, Lottie. *Une actrice française aux Etats-Unis*. Paris, 1920.

INDEX

346 INDEX

A Note About the Author

Henry Knepler was born in Vienna, Austria in 1922, the son of Hugo and Hedwig Knepler. His father was the head of one of the oldest and largest concert managements in Europe; at times he also produced plays and knew Bernhardt and Duse well.

Henry Knepler left Austria after the German occupation in 1938, and continued his education in England and later in Canada, where he received B.A. and M.A. degrees from Queen's University, Kingston, Ontario. He then came to the United States to study for a Ph.D. at the University of Chicago. Before receiving it in 1950, he began to teach English at Illinois Institute of Technology, where he now serves as Professor of English and Chairman of the Department of Language, Literature and Philosophy.

Professor Knepler's interest in drama and theater has led to journal articles, four years of service as director of drama at IIT, and work in film and television. He produced some thirty television programs in the first year of operation of the Chicago Educational Television Station WTTW. As an amateur actor, he has performed in three languages: English, French and German.

At present Henry Knepler lives with his wife and three daughters in Chicago.